Curriculum

Construction and Critique

Master Classes in Education Series
Series Editors: John Head, School of Education,
Kings College, University of London and
Ruth Merttens, School of Education, University of
North London

Curriculum
Construction and Critique

Alistair Ross

London and New York

First published 2000
by Falmer Press
11 New Fetter Lane, London EC4P 4EE

Simultaneously published in the USA and Canada
by Falmer Press
Garland Inc., 19 Union Square West, New York, NY 10003

Falmer Press is an imprint of the Taylor & Francis Group

Typeset in Garamond by Taylor & Francis Books Ltd
Printed and bound in Great Britain by TJ International Ltd,
Padstow, Cornwall

British Library Cataloguing in Publication Data
A catalogue record for this book is available from the British Library

Library of Congress Cataloguing in Publication Data
Ross, Alistair, 1946–
    Curriculum : construction and critique / Alistair Ross.
    (Master classes in education series)
    Includes bibliographical references and index.
    1. Education–Curricula–Social aspects–Great Britain.
    2. Curriculum planning–Social aspects–Great Britain.   I. Title.
    II. Series.
    LB1564.G7R66   1999
    375'.001'0941–dc21   99–36823

ISBN   0–750–70797–6 (hbk)
ISBN   0–750–70621–X(pbk)

Contents

Contents

Illustrations

Illustrations

Series Editors' Preface

It has become a feature of our times that an initial qualification is no longer seen to be adequate for lifelong work within a profession and programmes of professional development are needed. Nowhere is the need more clear than with respect to education, where changes in the national schooling and assessment system, combined with changes in the social and economic context, have transformed our professional lives.

The series, *Master Classes in Education*, is intended to address the needs of professional development, essentially at the level of taught masters degree. Although aimed primarily at teachers and lecturers, it is envisaged that the books will appeal to a wider readership, including those involved in professional educational management, health promotion and youth work. For some, the texts will serve to update their knowledge. For others, they may facilitate career reorientation by introducing, in an accessible form, new areas of expertise or knowledge.

The books are overtly pedagogical, providing a clear track through the topic by means of which it is possible to gain a sound grasp of the whole field. Each book familiarizes the reader with the vocabulary and the terms of discussion, and provides a concise overview of recent research and current debates in the area. While it is obviously not possible to deal with every aspect in depth, a professional who has read the book should be able to feel confident that they have covered the major areas of content, and discussed the different issues at stake. The books are also intended to convey a sense of the future direction of the subject and its points of growth or change.

In each subject area the reader is introduced to different perspectives and to a variety of readings of the subject under consideration. Some of the readings may conflict, others may be compatible but distant. Different perspectives may well give rise to different lexicons and different bibliographies, and the reader is always alerted to these differences. The variety of frameworks within which each topic can be construed is then a further source of reflective analysis.

The authors in this series have been carefully selected. Each person is an experienced professional who has worked in that area of education as a practitioner and also addressed the subject as a researcher and theoretician. Drawing upon both pragmatic and theoretical aspects of their experience, they are able to take a reflective view while preserving a sense of what occurs, and what is possible, at the level of practice.

Curriculum: Construction and Critique

The notion of curriculum seems obvious – 'what is taught' as opposed to 'how you teach it'. However, a few minutes in a classroom shows that there is no easy and obvious distinction between the two. Is it possible to separate what we teach from how we teach it? If 'problem-solving' is an item on a curriculum list, this precludes certain types of didactic teaching. If 'tables facts' have to be taught and will be assessed, discovery learning may go out of the window. What guarantees a particular subject a place in the curriculum? What makes a curriculum subject a 'subject' at all? How are its boundaries sustained and a necessary homogeneity assured? And then there are the political questions, with a small and a large 'p'. Who decides what is included in the curriculum and what is not? One stage further back, who should decide? Is the curriculum decided on the basis of utility, pragmatics, or educational theory?

Questions surrounding the curriculum touch on fundamental issues for education. When the chips are down, do we believe that education is a 'drawing out' or a 'putting in'? Are we educating to produce good citizens, creative innovators, competent operators, contented members of society, or none of the above?

When faced with such a complex array of questions and issues, what can we expect in a book on curriculum? Alistair Ross has started with the assumption that the least the reader has a right to expect is that the ground of the argumentation should be laid out in a clear and unambiguous fashion. This enables the reader to appreciate the parameters of the various debates, the ways in which particular arguments are positioned and polarized, and the political alignments that emerge for historical as well as pragmatic reasons. Professor Ross provides a clear overview of curriculum debate. Starting from an historical perspective, he charts specific lines of argument through their various transformations, and their adaptation under different guises in new political circumstances. However, his view is not only that of the interested historian. There is a political dimension to this book, which allows the reader to engage with both the theoretical ideas and the practical positionings that are constantly present in the politics of curriculum construction and critique. The chapter on curriculum and reproduction in particular, should be required reading for every person working, or with an interest, in education; the ideas and debates discussed are central to the endeavour of the educational process at all levels.

Discussing curriculum, we as readers may look for a comprehensive and clear coverage of the complex issues involved, and this is certainly provided in the pages following this preface. However, there is a much harder and more important criterion by which Professor Ross also succeeds, and that is the hallmark of fairness. The classicist, S.J. Tester, when reviewing Coppleston's *History of Philosophy*, wrote that histories tend to be interesting in inverse proportion to their accuracy! Certainly, it is rare to find an account of a theoretical construct as central and important as curriculum that displays an unswerving faithfulness to the various thinkers and writers who have played a part in the articulation of this concept at the various stages in its development. If such an account exists, it is likely to be only a little less lengthy (and dull) than the proverbial *Encyclopaedia Britannica*. But in his book, Ross has succeeded in presenting us with a fascinating yet objective (in the post-postmodern sense of the word) narration of the argumentation around the construction of the curriculum.

The book starts with an extended metaphor – that of the curriculum as garden. It finishes with another metaphor – that of 'Englishness' as Roast Beef. The book is written in a style that draws heavily on metaphor and simile in order to elaborate and exemplify a series of abstract and difficult concepts. Thus is the reader provided with the opportunity to 'surround' some of the more theoretical ideas, coming at them from different sides and in a variety of contexts, until they appear as familiar and comfortable as gardens and roast beef. It is only when we reach the end of the book that we are, like innocent back-packers who have traversed a high mountain pass, aware of the difficulties and dangers in the terrain that we have negotiated and the distance we have travelled.

Can a book on a subject as contentious and disputed as curriculum, provide definitive answers? Not if its author is to remain both honourable and faithful to his task. But it can and should provide readers with a clear outline of the history, the parameters, and the political constraints within which these arguments continue to be waged. It should explain and elaborate the theories underlying some of the argumentation. And finally, it should allow the reader to emerge with a series of questions which are peculiarly his/her own; questions which arise not simply from the debates but rather from the reader's particular engagement with those debates. As series editors, we are happy to recommend *Curriculum: Construction and Critique* as just such a book.

John Head and Ruth Merttens
Series Editors

Acknowledgments

Acknowledgments are always invidious: too many friends and colleagues have helped me form my ideas through discussion, comment and debate for me to able to list them, or even to be sure of which ideas they contributed, and who suggested what.

However, I would particularly like to thank Alan Blyth, who first encouraged me to think about the curriculum; my colleagues on the Faculty Research Committee at the University of North London, who helped me find the time to start work on this book; friends who have commented on sections and drafts – Greg Condry, Merryn Hutchings, Ian Menter, Ruth Merttens, Cass Mitchell-Riddle; my research students and students on my MA courses who have discussed some of these ideas with me; my series editors, John Head and Ruth Merttens, for patience well beyond the call of duty; and above all my family, Maggie, Susanna and David, for support, encouragement and critical comment – and the space to write the book.

The help, encouragement, support and the ideas were theirs: the outcome, errors and omissions are my responsibility alone.

1 Curriculum Gardening

In late 1959 the Central Advisory Committee for Education (England) (chaired by Sir Geoffrey Crowther) reported on the education of 15–18-year-olds. It highlighted the extra- ordinary wastage of talent – largely of working-class origin – caused when children opted to leave school at the age of 15. In March 1960, the House of Commons debated the Crowther Report. The Minister of Education, Sir David Eccles, used the opportunity of the debate to announce a change in government policy towards the curriculum. Up to this time the Ministry had almost exclusively been concerned with the resourcing of education: with teacher supply and remuneration, with school building plans, and with the organization of different types of schools. But in future, Eccles announced, he would also take an interest in what was being taught in the schools: he would 'try to make the Ministry's voice heard rather more often and positively and no doubt more controversially'. He would open up 'the secret garden of the curriculum'.

In selecting this phrase he intended more than to simply draw attention to the covert way in which discussion on the content of education – inasmuch as such discussion existed at all – was almost exclusively confined to professional educators. It had been regarded as their prerogative: an area in which parents, politicians and society at large were not expected to have an opinion. He later suggested that he had in mind a 'commando-type unit' for the curriculum (Kogan, 1978, p. 63). But the metaphor of the curriculum-as-garden is perhaps helpful in beginning an analysis of the school curriculum and the ways in which it is, and is not, changing. This metaphor is not new: Alexander has traced back organic and botanical metaphors as 'an abiding characteristic of the language of primary education' (Alexander, 1988, p. 153).

Gardens are strange institutions. Certain plants are designated weeds, and regarded as intruders: hoed and weeded out, but often showing remarkable tenacity in springing up again. Other plants, often close cousins of the weeds, are highly prized, and nurtured and tended to full growth, even though they may show every disinclination to take effective root, or require particular and difficult-to-achieve conditions if they are to thrive. There may be an analogy here with the different subjects of the curriculum, and with the non-subjects. But perhaps more interesting is the concept of the garden as a whole, its design and purpose, rather than the individual component plants.

What is a garden for? It is perhaps the English tradition of utilitarianism that allows such a question to be asked, but there is certainly no shortage of answers. Gardens may be variously justified: as extensions of nature into the built environment;

as inculcating useful habits amongst gardeners (enabling them to feed their families; or exercise their flabby bodies; or to relax in and recuperate); they may express formal embodiments of the shapes and geometries of the world, as in the baroque garden; or they may be regarded as there because they're there, representing a tradition of English particularism (whether suburban mixture, or country cottage) whose purpose is to distinguish our habitat from that, say, of the French – who have no such preoccupation with the garden, and are thus quite rightly different from us.

Who are gardens for? Do they exist for the benefit of the plants themselves? Some gardens undoubtedly do serve this purposes: Kew Gardens preserves particular varieties, herbaria preserve gene stocks for someone's (or some plant's) posterity. Other gardens exist for the sake of society: public parks that afford recreation, of the body or the spirit. Many gardens exist for the sake of the gardener; while others are maintained for those who own the garden, but who do not labour in it. Market gardens exist for the consumers of their products, while also providing a living for those who work in them, and a profit for those who own them.

Each of these justifications for the garden can also be mirrored in arguments for particular forms of curriculum design, and these purposes provide us with a fresh set of analogies to consider the curriculum. In some cases, the curriculum can be seen to preserve subjects – such as Latin, for example – that many would argue serve no utility and have an uncertain value, against the belief of some others that the future will be ill-served if such a species becomes extinct. More common is the notion that the curriculum exists at the behest of society, and is there to serve society's needs – though determining the extent of the diverse needs of a fragmented society is highly problematic. There are a few teachers who behave as though the curriculum existed for their sakes, and who wish to relock the gate. The State often argues that, as the owner of the educational system, it must be the sole arbiter of its purposes. Social marketeers often hold that schooling and the curriculum must be exposed to the forces of natural selection, where variations will flourish or perish as consumers make their individual choices.

This book explores various arguments for different kinds of curricula. It attempts to summarize and analyse competing models and patterns of what schools and other educational institutions provide. These models have in common the fact that they are all – like gardens – constructed by people: they are social constructions open to criticism and analysis. Gardens classify territory: land is defined with different kinds of frames or boundaries – hedges, pathways, arbours, borders, ditches – each area having its own purpose and system of cultivation – herbs, vegetables, varieties of flowers, grassy areas, and so on. In precisely the same way, Basil Bernstein (1975) has described the classification and framing of the educational knowledge that constitutes the school curriculum: classification is 'the *relationship* between contents ... where classification is strong, contents are well insulated from each other by strong boundaries [while] where classification is weak ... the boundaries between contents are weak or blurred' (p. 49). The garden as a whole is bounded by a framing fence: to Bernstein, the framing of educational knowledge is the 'strength of the boundary between what may be transmitted and what may not be transmitted in the pedagogic relationship' (p. 50).

Four major forms of curriculum will be analysed, each predicated on a different set of assumptions about the purposes and functions of education. Each of these forms is mirrored by a particular philosophy of garden design in a way that is more than simply metaphor or analogy: the different ideas about the form and purposes of gardens are part of the same cultural movements that expressed different ideas about the structures and objectives of the school curriculum.

The Baroque Curriculum

Early gardens were walled and private places. The first known picture of a garden is an Egyptian papyrus, dating back to about 1400 BC: it shows the symmetrical garden of Nebamun, bounded by a rectangular stone or brick wall. Other classical references to gardens describe them as balanced, trimmed and within walled enclosures (for example, in *The Odyssey*, the gardens of Alconous and of Laertes). This tradition is carried through to the medieval garden, typically geometrically arranged, with square beds, hemmed in by rectilinear hedges (or pergolas, trellises or arbours), each planted with a particular crop of herbs, flowers, fruit or vegetables.

Walled gardens are reflected in the walls of academia, even today: in our older universities, miscreant students may still be 'gated', or kept within the high walls that surround the College. And university activities that take place beyond the undergraduate/postgraduate spectrum are significantly called 'extramural studies': beyond the walls.

This form of garden perhaps reached its peak in the baroque and rococo gardens of continental western Europe in the seventeenth and eighteenth centuries. The key features of this form of garden are its enclosure within a strong frame, defining what is within and without the garden, and ideas of balance, regularity and symmetry, so that the forms of plants themselves are trimmed and shaped into idealized and often classical forms. Each bed or area has its own specialist function, with its own traditions and forms of cultivation. This is the curriculum of clearly demarcated subjects, classified by both content knowledge and by the discourse forms appropriate and specific to each discipline. Such strongly framed curricula have what Bernstein distinguishes as a 'strong collection code' (1975, p. 50).

As in the baroque garden, where selected species are not only specific to particular areas, but must be cultivated in certain ways and trained into special shapes, in such an academic curriculum (Goodson, 1988) the 'strong framing' allows the learner 'little control over the selection, organization and pacing of transmission' (Bernstein, 1975, p. 179). In Sir Francis Carew's massively-walled garden at Beddington Manor fruit trees had their natural cycle repressed, so that when Sir Francis entertained Elizabeth I he was able to lead her 'to a cherry-tree, whose fruit he had of purpose kept from ripening at least one month after all cherries had taken their farewell of England: he had done this by putting on a canvas cover and keeping it damp' (Platt, 1608, quoted in Thacker, 1979).[1] Another example is the formal gardens designed by Nicolas de Pigage at Schwetzingen, which were being established in the 1750s when Voltaire stayed there as guest of the Elector Carl Theodore while he wrote *Candide*. The balanced formality of these gardens is reflected in the idea of a curriculum in which distinctly bounded subjects, limited in number, are 'balanced' against each other, and in which each retains and preserves its unique processes and form of knowledge. Such curricula are considered in Chapter 7 of this book.

The Naturally Landscaped Curriculum

There was a perhaps inevitable revolt against such a style of garden as unnatural. The formality and artifice of the baroque was rejected in favour of the landscape garden, as expressed by the character Theocles in Shaftesbury's *The Moralists* (1709) when he speaks of:

> The *Genius* of the Place ... I shall no longer resist the Passion growing in me for Things of a *natural* kind; where neither *Art*, nor the *Conceit* or *Caprice* of Man has spoiled their *genuine Order*, by breaking in on that *primitive State*. Even the rude *Rocks*, the mossy *Caverns*, the irregular unwrought *Grotto's*, and broken *Falls* of Waters, with all the horrid Graces of the *Wilderness* itself, as representing NATURE more, will be the more engaging, and appear with a Magnificence beyond the formal Mockery of Princely Gardens.

This was echoed in Joseph Addison's articles in *The Spectator* in 1712: his objections to topiary and the mathematical figures of the formal garden, in which 'we see the marks of the Scissars upon every Plant and Bush' (25 June 1712); his delight in his own irregular garden, 'a confusion of Litchin and Parterres, Orchard and Flower Garden ... a natural Wilderness' (6 September 1712).

The landscape garden was made possible by the invention of the ha-ha, 'a technological advance in the craft of gardening which is quite exceptional' (Thacker, 1979, p. 181). Instead of the boundary fence, a raised enclosing barrier, the ha-ha is a dry ditch, a sunken barrier, which creates an illusion that the garden and the surrounding countryside are a unity. In curriculum terms, this creates the impression of 'a weak boundary between what may and what may not be transmitted' (Bernstein, 1975, p. 50). Such a curriculum claims not to be governed by the artifice of subjects, but by the nature of the learner. Subjects are portrayed as artificial, dividing forms of knowledge with contrived distinctions of process, knowledge and procedures.

The natural garden and the natural curriculum are directly linked in the person of Jean-Jacques Rousseau. In *La Nouvelle Héloïse* (1761) he attacks the formality of French gardens (such as those at Versailles) and extols 'Julie's garden', which appears to grow spontaneously, without fixed lines, and is bounded by concealing thick trees and bushes. Nature, uncontaminated by society and social forms, is equivalent to virtue; society is corrupt, and civilization a harmful constraint. This theme is replicated in his writings on education: in *Emile* (rep. 1964) he propounds a system for education based on the child's unfolding nature, rather than on the requirements of a pre-established adult-centred cultural system. For example, Emile's understanding of mathematics and his language skills are developed by the artful and well-informed teacher, who exploits the situations of everyday life to find meaningful contexts for learning. Although a devastating attack on educational traditions – a 'romantic iconoclast attitude towards the values and rules of traditional culture' (Skilbeck, 1976) – the regime that Rousseau proposes is in fact highly structured, orderly and disciplined. The apparent freedom of the learner is conditioned by the constant surveillance of the teacher, which makes this difficult to reconcile with 'natural' learning.

The learner-centred curriculum, the subject of Chapter 9, fails to recognize that in any society, even one of two people, there can no longer be a 'natural' state or 'natural learning', and that the idea of society as a virtuous state of nature is chimerical. The same is true of the landscape garden: far from being natural, it is constrained, in its own way, by the prejudices and beliefs of its designer, and the ha-ha only gives the *illusion* of unity with the countryside; it is in functional terms as substantial a border as the wall or hedge. The 'seamless robe' of knowledge necessarily retains some notion of boundary and subject division, simply by virtue of being knowledge, because the making of knowledge is a social process that involves categorization and labelling. This generalization in itself is an act of boundary-making.

The artificiality of such 'naturalistic' settings is evident in the methodology of the most well-known landscape gardener, 'Capability' Brown. After working at Stowe, one of the first landscaped gardens, he set up in 1751 as a freelance garden designer. When asked to give an opinion on the possibilities of landscaping a property, he was supposed to have invariably replied that, were he given the task, the land in question had 'capabilities' which he might be able to mould and make distinctive. Thacker's analysis is that his best work was 'the development of the latent capabilities of a site, the *natural potential* of a scene ... the inspired detection, analysis and encouragement of the *genius loci*, the "spirit of the place"' (1979, p. 209). Making decisions about what is 'natural', and then constructing this vision, is pure artifice, however aesthetically pleasing it may appear. In just the same way, a curriculum formulated on notions of natural personal growth and development may be perceived as rewarding (to teacher and to learner), learner-centred and empowering, but is as much socially constructed as the subject-centred, traditional academic curriculum.

Capability Brown's name also has resonances with current ideas of a 'capability curriculum', but this latter is in reality part of a quite different curricular tradition, that of utilitarianism, analysed in Chapter 5. There is also, of course, a parallel tradition of utility in gardening design, which I here describe as digging for victory.

The Dig-for-Victory Curriculum

The baroque garden and the landscape garden are both large-scale, owned by and designed for the rich (who do not themselves, however, provide the labour for maintaining the garden, other than in the symbolic play of Marie Antoinette in the Petit Trianon). Most gardens are much smaller, and are today owned, designed and cultivated by individual families. They are often seen in utilitarian terms, sometimes providing food, sometimes a pleasing place in which to relax, sometimes a way of indulging in recreational manual labour.

The curriculum of educational institutions can also be interpreted and designed to meet very similar functions. The idea that the curriculum must in some way be useful, and in particular that the learning that takes place in schools must in some way prepare children for their future roles in work and in society is not new. Jamieson and Lightfoot (1982) point to the continuing debate on the relationship between schooling and industry dating back to the 1851 Great Exhibition. The comparative economic decline of the United Kingdom, over the past twenty years in particular (and over the past 150 years more generally), has been analysed as a consequence of inappropriate schooling, that prefers 'academic' non-industrial, or even anti-industrial, values over the acquisition of 'useful' skills. Wiener's now classic thesis in *English Culture and the Decline of the Industrial Spirit 1850–1980* (1981) had a very significant impact on the shaping of the UK curriculum in the 1980s (Lawton, 1994; Ross, 1995b). It was argued that there was a skills deficit in the workforce, and that this led to relative incompetence in production. The existence of this skills deficit was attributed to an inappropriately focused, weakly directed and poorly delivered school (and post-school) curriculum.

This view of the curriculum, explored in more detail in Chapter 8, requires the structure and content of education to be directly relevant to the needs of (adult) society, and in particular to the needs of employers. There is continuous and increasing emphasis on international comparisons and league tables, in terms of percentages of young people obtaining training qualifications, in terms of ability in various forms of mathematics and of attainment of scientific knowledge, which are then related to levels of industrial output and national income. The crisis that has been generated has generated a response, particularly since James Callaghan's speech at Ruskin College in 1976, which has analogies with the crisis in food and raw materials shortages of 1939. A large proportion of the nation's food had been imported up to that date, and this supply was then threatened by Axis naval attacks on supply convoys. The response was to divert attention to controlling consumption and to increasing domestic supply. 'Dig for Victory' was the slogan that led to domestic gardens being turned over to vegetables on a large scale, absorbing effort and resources into what was a relatively inefficient and small-scale contribution to food stocks (and increasing demand from households for seeds and gardening equipment, which caused a shortage) (Calder, 1969, p. 496).

The idea that gardens must have a useful purpose has been further extended as the leisure time of the population has increased. Gardens now become both a place in which people can relax, and a place in which they can take useful exercise. This is mirrored by the proliferation of recreational adult education classes through the 1960s to 1980s: courses in leisure pursuits, fitness classes, and the like. Gardens have also become part of consumerism, and are now places in which consumption can be conspicuously displayed, but this aspect of gardening has unfortunately not been mirrored in the staffing, equipping and general resourcing of the nation's schools.

The utilitarian view of education has wider implications than pure instrumentalism. It is reflected in behavioural models of learning, which lead to movements to pre-specify learning 'objectives', and thus to rate some objectives as more useful than others. Through refinement in cultivation and training techniques, it becomes more possible to predict the effects of both gardening and teaching. We know better when plants will bloom or fruit, how large they will grow, and can thus determine the future desired appearance in a way not possible before.

The Cottage Curriculum

Most of our gardens will not exactly fit any of the above models. The typical contemporary English garden is often a higgledy-piggledy mix, with a semi-formalized lawn and herb beds intermingled with vegetables, flowers and fruit. Such gardens are largely the way that they are now because this is the way they were thirty, fifty or a hundred years ago. The suburban garden largely attempts to reproduce this 'heritage' view of the garden, with a rather more evidently planned mixture of the formal (lawns, patios, pergolas), the landscape (ponds, waterfalls, irregular shapes and even garden gnomes) and the utilitarian (the vegetable bed, potting shed and compost heap). Challenges to such garden designs are almost pointless. They are a mixture of styles that is not simply traditional, but ossified in form and function to the point that the reasons for their existence are simply because they have always been like this: change them, and they no longer fall within the category of 'garden'.

The contemporary curriculum is very much like this: a preservation of cultural forms achieved through time-honoured processes, resistant to challenge or criticism. But these forms of curriculum, just as much as the baroque curriculum, the landscape curriculum and the utilitarian curriculum, are socially constructed, the result of competing claims to truth, of bargaining and negotiation. Very often this arbitration is unseen, even by those engaged in it. Sheltering behind notions of common-sense, tradition, ideas of 'natural' learning, possessive individualism, instrumentalism and the norm, the curriculum appears to evolve and to emerge – like Topsy, 'it just growed'. But this appearance of a natural process at work, akin to natural selection, is deeply misleading. This book will analyse purposes, forms and constructions of the curriculum within the social context.

The discussion will focus on the nature and purposes of the curriculum. But teachers are more than simply busy people: they have a class to teach at nine tomorrow morning, and will necessarily have to *deliver* some sort of curriculum. A curriculum must be taught, just as a garden must be dug. Voltaire's protagonist, Candide, spends most of the novel in pursuit of the meaning and purpose of life: in the end – in the final words of the book – he dismisses all of that which has gone before as mere metaphysical speculation: *Cela est bien dit, répondit Candide, mais il faut cultiver notre jardin* ('"That is well said," replied Candide, "but we must cultivate our garden"') (Voltaire, 1758). Both the gardeners at Schwetzingen and teachers must, like Candide, get on with the business of living. Nevertheless, it is important that teachers analyse and justify what they cultivate, and the ways and directions in which they plan, prune and train their charges. In one sense it matters less whether gardens are secret or open to unlimited public access, than that it is recognized that they do not just grow of their own accord; they are designed and nurtured to achieve some desired effect. The nature of that design is too important to be left to habit – or to the politicians.

Note

1   A personal footnote: Beddington Manor was used as part of the Grammar School at which I began my secondary education in 1957, along with Chris Woodhead, who is now responsible as head of OFSTED for the enforcement in England and Wales of the current baroque curriculum. The curriculum that we endured together over the following seven years reflected the ordered beds of Carew's gardens and the training of plants into particular paths and forms. There was intense competition by the teachers of different disciplines for the allegiance of the pupils to specialize in 'their' subjects.

2 What is the Curriculum?

Everyone believes that they know what other people should learn. Though they might not be able to express the precise detail, they could certainly advance the categories, whether in terms of bodies of knowledge, skills, or by an appeal to a higher or 'more educated' authority. The fact that defining the curriculum, like much of education, is seen by many to be part of 'common sense' does not make it any easier to engage in debate about purposes and priorities.

This chapter will explore the hegemonic relationship exerted by culture through the curriculum, relating this particularly to the ways in which a curriculum might be assessed. Global manifestations of curriculum form will be described, which suggest that an international curriculum form is emerging that is perhaps related to the near-ubiquity of a liberal educational culture: but the particular curricular history of the United Kingdom (which will be analysed in Chapters 3 to 5) suggests that there are at least some local resistances to the global form, deriving from particular and diverse ideologies.

A curriculum is a definition of what is to be learned. The origins of the word are from the Latin curriculum, a racing chariot, from which is derived a racetrack, or a course to be run, and from this, a course of study. The term is often confined to formal definitions of what is to be taught in specific institutions – perhaps even as narrow as the notion of a National Curriculum that confines its coverage to the prescribed content of learning during the years of compulsory education. But even within compulsory education, it is also possible to refer to the 'hidden' curriculum: that which is not overtly stated, and which may be unintentionally passed on through the processes of education. Beyond this, curriculum exists in much wider domains, and it can – and perhaps should – include any socially constructed or prescribed activities, selected in some way from the culture of that society, that result in the transformation of the individual. It is possible, for example, to refer to a curriculum for parenting, in that in contemporary society there are a range of activities that, formally and otherwise, construct individuals as parents. These include formal learning activities (prenatal classes, parenting classes), structured open learning (magazines and books on bringing up babies and children), informal learning (from relatives and neighbours), and responses to pressures from producers (to behave in a particular manner, conform to a particular image and (in particular) to consume particular goods or services), all of which together constitute a curriculum for parenting. Though such a curriculum appears to be purely voluntary and informal, it is in fact governed not only by the socially accepted view of what constitutes 'good parenting', but through a series of laws such as the Children Act and Education Acts requiring parents to ensure the education of their children, and influenced by strictures from politicians and others about what they see as appropriate parental behaviour.

Perhaps the best brief definition of curriculum was that offered by HM Inspectorate (HMI) in 1985 as a contribution to the then current debate on curriculum aims:

> A school's curriculum consists of all those activities designed or encouraged within its organisational framework to promote the intellectual, personal, social and physical development of its pupils. It includes not only the formal programme of lessons, but also the 'informal' programme of so-called extracurricular activities as well as all those features which produce the school's 'ethos', such as the quality of relationships, the concern for equality of opportunity, the values exemplified in the way the schools sets about its task and the way in which it is organised and managed. Teaching and learning styles strongly influence the curriculum and in practice they cannot be separated from it. Since pupils learn from all these things, it needs to be ensured that all are consistent in supporting the school's intentions.
>
> (DES, 1985a, para. 11)

This is a very broad conceptualization, but one that properly emphasizes that anything that schools do that affects pupils' learning, whether through deliberate planning and organization, unwitting encouragement, or hidden and unrealized assumptions, can all be properly seen as elements of the school's whole curriculum.

While most of this book will be concerned primarily with the overt curriculum, within formal educational institutions, it is important to bear in mind that this is one end of a spectrum of activities, and that, even within such institutions, many of the processes of teaching and learning take place outside the prescribed content. It has been argued that many of the aspects of schooling that are outside the material of lessons are more important than that material itself: uniforms and uniformity, time-keeping, subservience and obedience, the acceptance of orders and of roles imposed by others, social stratification and hierarchies – all of these, it has been held, are calculated to induce those behaviours and attitudes in adult life that are necessary to serve the needs of (capitalist) employers for a docile and tractable workforce (for example, Bowles and Gintis, 1976). Conversely, it has also been observed that the pupils' own counter-cultures – which are often created and transmitted within the boundaries of the schooling system – can sometimes be more powerful mechanisms for learning than any outcomes that were intended by the system's formal controllers, whether this was to produce complaisant workers or to transmit formal knowledge (Willis, 1977). Chapter 6 will explore further some of these arguments.

Curriculum and the Reproduction of Culture

One of the key issues in the analysis of curriculum, which will be a running theme through this book, is how a selection is made from a society's culture of the material that is to be included in the curriculum – what is chosen, by what processes, by whom, with what intent and with what result. Basil Bernstein suggested that 'how a society selects, classifies, distributes, transmits and evaluates the educational knowledge that it considers to be public reflects both the distribution of power and the principles of social control' (1971a, p. 47), from which list the selection, classification and evaluation of particular knowledge are central to the definition of a curriculum. This is not a simple or deterministic model of social and cultural reproduction of the dominant ideology. There are many detailed studies of the growth of particular disciplines within the curriculum that suggest the processes are considerably more complex (e.g. Goodson, 1984a; Whitty, 1985; Layton, 1972).

There are two particular issues of cultural reproduction that are of note at this stage.

First, society is no longer – if it ever was – possessed of an unmistakable and clear culture: we are now increasingly aware of a range of multiple cultural identities, each with its own necessary cultural impedimenta, from which individuals make their own selection. The individual constructs and projects a particular range of identities, utilizing an appropriate set of discourses. These cultural repertoires arise from constructions of ethnicity, gender, class, age-sets, sexual orientation and the like, and are often mutually exclusive. While individuals can adapt to their immediate chosen context and discourse – displaying different cultural traits, using specific language, selecting particular and specific identities – this can appear much more problematic when we are asked to do it on the scale of selecting a set of cultural attributes for conscious transmission, through the curriculum. The plurality of our society means that children come from a range of cultural backgrounds: they may come from different ethnic origins, have (or have parents of) different faiths, different attitudes, beliefs and experiences concerning gender and sexual orientation, come from homes with widely varied experiences of the nature of work, have different expectations of the efficacy of political systems. To make a selection for transmission through the school curriculum will necessarily be contentious, and the greater the scope of a curriculum definition – for example, at national level – the greater the degree of contention. There is a necessary tension between the narrowest of possible curricula and the widest. The narrowest would probably be a curriculum that was directly and exclusively selected from the culture of the parents or guardians of the child, in which the cultural reproduction of schooling directly mimicked the biological reproduction of the genes: few would argue for such a ghettoized curriculum, even if it were possible to deliver. But a national curriculum requires someone, somehow, to rule that certain cultural artefacts (selected, by very definition, from particular cultures) should be elevated to be passed on to all children, and that other cultural manifestations be excluded from formal education, even though they will probably be the principal cultural determinants of many children in the system. This leads to the second potential problem with simple cultural reproduction theory.

The very analysis articulated by Bernstein in the early 1970s has, in itself, altered the nature and processes of curriculum description. As with many aspects of the social sciences, the description and broadcasting of a social rule means that it becomes possible consciously to manipulate the situation that the rule purports to describe, and, at least to an extent, the generalization that the rule represents is no longer valid.

Once a policy-maker grasps that the act of defining the curriculum is a conscious selection of which culture shall be transmitted to the next generation, then it becomes possible to reverse the process: to decide what form of culture (or society) will be desirable in future, and to ensure that it is this which is included in the curriculum. For example, if a group of curriculum-makers feel that individuals should be more enterprising and responsible for their own social and economic progress, then they can ensure that the curriculum includes themes that emphasize individual initiative, that prioritize individual duties and obligations over social and communal rights, and that put a high value on entrepreneurial activities in schools (Ross, 1995b). If curriculum-makers are concerned that their society is losing its sense of identity, then they can manipulate the curriculum so that – in the words of Nick Tate, Chief Executive of the Schools Curriculum and Assessment Authority for England and Wales – its key function becomes

> the explicit reinforcement of a common culture. … Pupils first and foremost should be introduced to the history of the part of the world where they live, its literary heritage and main religious traditions … the culture and traditions of Britain should be at the core. Seen in this light, the central role of British history, Christianity and the English literary heritage are axiomatic.
>
> (Tate, 1994)

If, as Tate goes on to argue, 'a national curriculum … plays a key part in helping society maintain its identity', then it is possible for those who have views about what that social identity should be to set out to construct a curriculum that does not just reproduce the existing diversities, dichotomies and contradictions in society, but produces the new order that they seek. This discussion on the role of the curriculum in creating a national (or other) identity will be returned to in the final chapter of this book.

The curriculum can be construed in this way as a way of constructing both individuals *and* society. The individual and society are created, by the processes of the curriculum, as related parts: society as composed of a set of individuals; individuals as existing through a set of social references; and society and individuals in contradistinction to each other. The curriculum is, therefore, a social construction, as individuals and societies decide what constitutes the processes and contents of the construction. The inevitable tension lies in the differences between what an individual learner (or their parent or guardian) might want from a curriculum and what a much wider social grouping might want – or indeed, what a narrower and more powerful group, such as a curriculum authority, might want.

Curriculum and Assessment

One of Bernstein's key processes was the evaluation of educational knowledge. The mechanisms for assessing the curriculum often reveal as much about the motivations and ideologies of the educationally powerful as they do about the efficacy of the learning that has taken place. Decisions about what to assess, about why the assessment is to take place, and about how to conduct assessment are usually framed within the language of maintaining and improving standards, but this very often masks ways in which power is selectively transmitted to the next generation. Whatever the reasons for which assessment is carried out, however, it is clear that any kind of assessment has very far-reaching consequences for the nature of the curriculum, and consequently assessment is invariably seen as an aspect of curriculum design, rather than an independent variable. The dangers of this have long been apparent: the Spens Report (Board of Education, 1938) quoted a Board Circular (1034 of March 1918) that set out as 'a cardinal principle that the examination should follow the curriculum and not determine it': Spens also noted 'in practice, this principle has been reversed'. However much it is argued that assessment should be curriculum-driven, it seems almost inevitable that, even at the most straightforward level, it is inevitable that 'teaching for the test' will happen – that the curriculum is assessment-driven (Gipps and Stobart, 1993).

If an educational system is designed to be selective – to act as a filter – then assessment systems must be devised that only allow the necessary number or proportion of people to pass through to the next stage. Much of the educational system in Britain, and employers generally, demand that assessment (and thus the curriculum) be designed to select those students who are 'fitted' for further and more advanced study, or for particular employment needs. Such assessment systems must be norm-referenced; that is, the qualification level is related to the group taking the test. The old eleven plus examination system is an example of this: since there were, in a given area, only a fixed number of grammar school places, only that number could be awarded a pass. In a 'good' year, children would need to achieve a higher mark than would be necessary in a 'poor' year. Moreover, since girls as a group consistently outscored boys, and since it was held that an approximately equal number of each sex should receive grammar school education, the pass mark for girls was generally fixed at a higher level than the pass mark for boys. Other examinations also act as filters, though they are designed not to be norm-referenced: GCSE examinations filter students into sixth-form and FE college study; A levels filter students into degree-level study – even though the correlation between A-level results and degree classifications is only 0.4. University education, in principle 'available to all those who are qualified by ability and attainment' (UK, 1964), is in practice limited to those with the best ability to demonstrate their ability and attainment, because the number of places for study are limited.

The effect on the curriculum is to value processes and content that are amenable to grading. This can mean that a curriculum is, at least in part, determined by its ability to filter: knowledge and skills (traditionally knowledge in particular) that are relatively inaccessible are given a more important place, because they will make it easier to construct filters that achieve the desired result. The use that was made of the study of classical languages is an example of this: irrespective of the merits of learning Latin and Greek, proficiency in one or both of these languages was used as a way of filtering applicants to University and to careers beyond this. A classical education, to degree level, was an important requirement for recruitment to the administrative level of the colonial civil service, for example. It was argued that a successful mastery of the discipline of such education provided an assurance of the calibre of the individual to deal with the exigencies of the job, and indeed, the correspondence and reports of such colonial officers are littered with evidence of their education, from Latin epigrams to historical parallels between the Roman and the British Empires. It could equally have been argued that a scientific education provided a similar level of ability for abstract thought (if that was what was required for the task), and that chemical and physical metaphors and analogies would have been as effective in analysing the behaviour of the local population. Indeed, mathematics and science (and, very recently, technology) have supplanted the classics in the pole position as subjects necessary for today's filtering mechanisms. Mathematical knowledge and ability have been accorded the status of high-level knowledge, suitable as a means of sorting out the elite from the non-elite. It can be argued that we have given this status to these subjects, not because of their intrinsic interest or usefulness, but because it is possible quickly and efficiently to grade people in their ability to perform, and to make appropriate categories in consequence. In view of the great difficulties that were encountered through the nineteenth century in recognizing science as a subject to be included anywhere within the school curriculum, the present reification of scientific knowledge as an essential element of the well-educated person is ironic.

Of course, it can be argued that mathematical and scientific knowledge is useful, in particular in contemporary society with its dependence on technology, and that this is why such forms of knowledge have now, rightly, acquired such high status. This leads to the second broad set of purposes of an educational system: to provide the necessary skills that will be useful to individuals, both in their immediate and future roles in society. This in turn requires an assessment system that can certify that a particular competence or level of knowledge has been reached: a criterion-referenced assessment. Such a system allows for the vagaries of a 'good' or a 'bad' year of students: all those who reach the standard will be awarded the grade, and only those students. It would be theoretically possible for all students to meet the required grade, or all to fail, in any given period. The argument for such testing is not simply that it is fairer and unambiguous: such assessment is related solely to the ability of the student to demonstrate that they can do or know something, irrespective of any other person's competence at the same task. The driving test or a swimming test are both simple examples of criterion-referenced tests. Once a description of the abilities necessary to be 'able to drive' or 'able to swim' have been determined, then one has only to meet these criteria to pass. There is no reason why virtually everyone should be able to eventually learn to drive, or be able to swim. In terms of utility for employment and adult life, the advantages of such assessment are that one can, in theory, determine the skills and knowledge needed for a particular task, and then demonstrate competency at the necessary level. But it could be argued that an employer (or an educational institution recruiting) would find this system unhelpful, in that they find it easier to select on the basis of a norm-referenced system: they will take those judged best at a particular attribute, not those sufficiently able to perform the task successfully or take the educational course with advantage.

The effect of criterion-referenced assessment on the curriculum is to place special emphasis on measurable competencies. In practice, the setting of strict criteria may be too difficult, and the device of 'grade descriptors' (or 'level descriptors') is often used: an account of the standards expected of students reaching each grade. GSCE examinations were reorganized along these lines in the late 1980s, and have been followed by criterion-referenced National Vocational Qualifications (NVQs). These latter establish levels of abilities, and have marked a shift in the curriculum away from the idea of knowledge to one of competency: content becomes less important than standards of achievement, curriculum is defined in terms of desired outputs, rather than of inputs and processes, and competence itself is related to the whole work role. In these curriculum descriptions knowledge is usually closely linked with understanding, rather than being identified in its own right: this can be seen perhaps as lowering the status of knowledge. Given that many sociologists of knowledge (from Berger and Luckman, 1966, onwards) have argued that knowledge consists simply of perceptions of reality, heavily filtered through cultural constraints, and thus that all knowledge is relative, this process may be seen as an opening up, or freeing of the curriculum from particular elite cultural forms. But competencies are themselves constructs, and can only be assessed through observation, so that one set of cultural filters may merely be replaced by another (Wolf, 1995).

A third set of assessment purposes may be seen in what Gipps and Stobart (1993) distinguished as the managerial functions of assessment. While a professional assessment may be concerned with providing teachers with useful diagnostic material, with screening to detect special needs, or providing material that helps in record-keeping, managerial assessment is designed to produce data that will allow the comparison of teachers', schools' and local education authorities' performances. Assessments that produce direct comparisons over a wide range of the population are rarely sufficiently finely tuned to produce diagnostic feedback, or to provide more than the most crude ranking for the individual child, but do allow league tables to be constructed that – if everything else were equal – allow the direct comparison of the 'standards' or 'effectiveness' of different schools and LEAs. What effect will such assessment have on the curriculum? The introduction of this kind of assessment occurred in 1862 in England and Wales, when the revised code made teachers' salaries dependent on the results their pupils achieved, which resulted in an extraordinary narrowing of the curriculum to focus very largely on the tested elements.

The reasons why assessment is carried out thus have a very powerful effect on the content of the curriculum, and are very much associated with what are seen as the overall purposes of education, whether these are to limit the group who will have access to power in the future, or to ensure that individuals are educated towards particular levels of competence, or to enable individuals to gain access to as wide a range of knowledge and abilities as they are able to do.

Global Trends in School Curricula

The diversity of the ideologies that seek to create curricula might be expected to result in a great diversity of curricular patterns around the world. It would not be surprising to find some societies with wholly utilitarian curricula, geared closely to the local means of production, and other societies which valued and taught particular cultural forms to a stratified elite.

An important study of world-wide trends in the curriculum suggests that this may not be so. John Meyer's team at Stanford University has looked at the curricular categories used in primary education in over seventy countries since the 1920s. Instead of diversity, they discovered 'an extraordinary homogeneity across the extraordinarily variable countries of the world' (Meyer et al., 1992, p. 6). Comparing nationally-provided accounts of curricular provision, it was perhaps not surprising that local influences on the curriculum appeared to be unimportant, as mass education overrode local cultural content: what was unexpected was the degree to which national pressures were also apparently unimportant, and that the broad similarities between curricula greatly outweighed the differences.

Meyer's team took official data from a variety of government and international sources, and from these analysed descriptions of the curriculum into broad categories, looking both at the lists of subjects taught and the percentage of total instruction time given to each subject. In some countries, they were able to trace accounts back into the earlier part of the nineteenth century; in other cases, they were looking at the educational systems of nations that have only achieved statehood since the 1960s. Admittedly the data is limited and superficial: it is not possible to discover what a particular curricular category might mean in any given country. There could be significant variations in the syllabus, in teaching materials, in pedagogy or in assessment; the implementation may differ from country to country, and it is possible that the category may in practice mean very different things for different children, when differentiated, for example, by class, or gender or ethnic grouping. But having allowed for all these caveats, their data still suggested that 'the labels, at least, of mass curricula are so closely tied to great and standardised versions of social and educational progress, they tend to be patterned in quite consistent ways around the world' (p. 166).

The world curriculum that they describe has changed through the period of their analysis, and local national variations have been ironed out as a pattern of international conformity has prevailed. The professionalized or 'framed' curriculum generally now consists of

- One or more *national languages* (no longer classical languages): the reality of the nation state is that local languages and dialects are relatively downgraded in the teaching of a nation-wide language. What variation that there is in language policy tends to be on matters such as which languages are to be regarded as national or official; how much use might be made of local languages or mother-tongue teaching in the early part of the elementary school; the methods and emphases used in language teaching; and whether and how to legitimize local languages. Very few systems now include at their core the study of classical texts or sacred moral texts (Cha, 1991).
- *Mathematics* is now found universally in educational systems: it has become 'a critically important element in the rationalistic modern world' (Meyer et al., 1992, p. 12). In some states in the nineteenth century, mathematics had been seen as either a speciality for an elite group, or as particularly necessary for those entering trade or commerce: now mathematics is seen as a requirement for everyone, and controversy in mathematics education is confined to matters of technique or emphasis (Kamens and Benavot, 1991).
- *Science* has also become canonical: as Meyer et al. observe, 'all future little citizens are to learn that the world is empirical and lawful, governed by natural forces which can be scrutinised through rigorous investigations' (1992, p. 12). Science was introduced as a compulsory subject significantly later than the date at which

mathematics became mandatory in different countries, as is seen in *Figure 2.1* (see also Kamens and Benavot, 1991). The process began, it seems, in the primary curricula of European countries, and then spread around the world.

*   The fourth curricular area that is found in all of the survey nations was some form of *social science*. This core area was generally taught either under the combined social studies rubric, or divided into separate subjects, such as history, geography and civics. The social world, like science, seems to be presented as having 'factual evidence and law-like properties' (Meyer et al., 1992, p. 12), taught not just to an elite group but to all future citizens. Wong (1991, 1992) has shown that the variations in social science teaching are greater than those in language, mathematics and science, and concern issues of categorization and organization as social studies gradually supplanted the separate subjects of history and geography (though this may be a trend that has recently been put into reverse) (Ross, 1996).
*   Aesthetic education (in art and music) and physical education are not quite so ubiquitous as the four areas described above, but are still found in over 95 per cent of all national curricula.

Table 2.1 summarizes both the proportion of countries including various categories in their curricula, and the percentage of time given to each: Meyer et al. conclude that in

Figure 2.1   Dates at which mathematics and science were first made compulsory in the school curriculum, shown as a percentage of countries

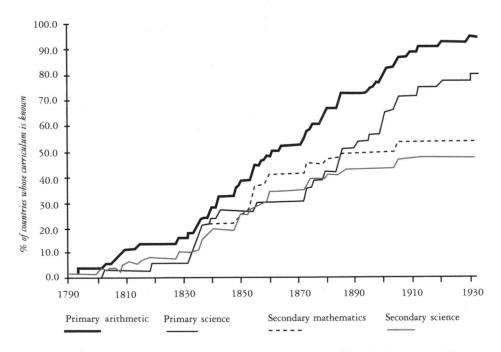

Source: Derived from Kamens and Benavot, 1992 (in Meyer et al., 1992), Table 8.1, pp. 105–6.

subject area after subject area ... controversy is limited – matters of outline are settled, and national society is rooted in modern culture through universal socialisation schemes. True conservative protest, which might object to the whole system as an intrusion on the natural properties of society and communal life is dead ... radical protest ... focus more on styles of instruction ... than on content categories.

(1992, p. 13)

The data are not watertight – the categorizations may well conceal major variations in intention and in practice, and the sources used may well have put strains on responding government departments to make their practice 'fit' the requirements of the various surveys that were conducted. But the general conclusion is that there is what Ivor Goodson has described as an 'aggrandising world rhetoric' that has shaped the curricula of most countries (preface to Meyer et al., 1992, p. x).

This does not, however, mean that analysis of the curriculum is inevitably confined within curricular category boundaries. Questions of cultural transmission and utilitarianism, of child-centred or subject-centred emphases are still valid. General world conceptions of curricula are not, it will be suggested, as hegemonic as Meyer's team seems to suggest, and more local forces still have a pervasive influence on the forms and purpose of the curriculum. Such local forces are particularly to be found in the shaping of the United Kingdom's school curriculum, especially in the curriculum in England and Wales, where, it will be suggested, there is a relative impermeability to international trends and forces in education. The next chapter will therefore survey some of the major changes in the English and Welsh curriculum, identifying the variety of forces at work, and the interests that they might represent. It may well be that very similar interests are to be found in the creation of the curricula of other nations.

Table 2.1 Subjects and percentage of time given to them, 1970–86

Subject	% of time given	% of countries	N
Language: (all)	34	100	73
national, local	25	92	75
official, foreign	8	61	74
Mathematics	18	100	82
Natural sciences	8	100	78
Social sciences	8	100	76
History, Geography, Civics	3	53	76
Social studies	5	61	76
Aesthetic education	10	99	76
Religious or moral education	5	75	76
Physical education	7	96	76
Health/hygiene education	1	42	76
Vocational or practical education	5	68	75

Source: Derived from Benavot et al., 1992 (in Meyer et al., 1992), Tables 4.1 and 4.2, pp. 47, 49.

3 Conflict in the Curriculum: Growth and Diversity, 1860–1976

Changes in the curriculum offered in England and Wales, and to a degree in Scotland, illustrate the various controversies that surround the construction of curricula. The shifting ambiguities of control and responsibility that have marked the governance of education show an almost cyclical quality in the way that the same debate and issues are returned to again and again, in only superficially different guises.

Codification and Control: 1860–1926

The elementary schools of the late nineteenth century were required, almost from their inception, to teach to a centrally designed curriculum. The Newcastle Commission of 1861 sought to establish value for money from state-supported schools through

> a searching examination by a competent authority of every child in every school to which grants are to be paid with the view of ascertaining whether these indispensable elements of knowledge are thoroughly acquired, and to make the prospects and position of the teacher dependent, to a considerable extent, upon the results of this examination. The examination will exercise a powerful influence over the efficiency of the schools.
>
> (quoted in Maclure, 1986, p. 73)

This was codified the following year: a school would receive a grant of 8 shillings (40p) for each pupil who attended 200 sessions in a year, but from this would be deducted 2s 8d, or one third of the total, for each of the three tests (in arithmetic, reading and writing) that was failed. Payment by results meant that the state directly controlled the work of teachers, prescribing a narrow curriculum of the 'indispensable elements of knowledge'. Matthew Arnold, one of the inspectors to whom this task was given, observed how teachers could teach to the test and was critical:

> In the game of mechanical contrivances the teacher will in the end beat us, and ... by ingenious preparation get the children through the Revised Code examination ... without their really knowing any one of these matters.
>
> (Matthew Arnold, *General Report 1867*, quoted in Maclure, 1986, pp. 81–2)

He acknowledged that the system was popular, but argued:

> the question is not whether this ... suits ordinary public opinion and school managers [but] ... whether it suits the interests of schools and their instruction. ... I feel sure that our present system of grants does harm to schools and their instruction.
>
> (ibid.)

The curriculum for older pupils was considered in 1868 by the Taunton Commission, which reported a revealing set of accounts of what parents of different social classes expected in terms of curriculum reform (*Table 3.1*). This displays a wide range of attitudes towards the purposes of education, and the curriculum that would be necessary to accomplish this, ranging from claims for the teaching of the habitual forms of knowledge, through curricula intended to cater for those striving for an assurance of social position for their children through the education they received, curricula to meet the needs of impatient utilitarians, curricula that demanded 'intellectual discipline', to curricula designed to meet basic needs of society. The categories Taunton employed were essentially class-based: the Commission was apparently impressed by the Prussian system, and proposed three forms of secondary schooling, segregated from each other and leading to different ends. First grade schools would be for the sons (*sic*) of the aristocracy and landed gentry, second grade schools for the sons of businessmen and manufacturers, and third grade schools for the sons of artisans and tradesmen: each grade would have the appropriate matching curriculum, as indicated in the table: 'it is obvious that these distinctions correspond roughly ... to the gradations of society' (Schools Inquiry Commission, 1868, pp. 15–16).

The key position of classical languages was very much at the heart of the curriculum debate for these older pupils: they were advocated (at least in part) for the mental discipline that they supposedly inculcated. The pressures for expanding the secondary school curriculum to include the natural sciences were growing, and were the subject of the Devonshire Commission of 1872–5. But the principal arguments put forward for the addition of science were neither the utilitarian needs of the parents drawn from the industrial and commercial sectors cited in the Taunton Report, nor the requirement to have a wider scientific knowledge-base in the population, but were instead very similar to arguments that had hitherto been used as justification for the classics, that science would provide an intellectual training:

> the true teaching of Science consists, not merely in imparting the facts of Science, but in habituating the pupil to observe ... to reason ... and to check ... by further observation and experiment. And it may be doubted whether ... any other educational study offers the same advantages for developing and training the mental faculties.
>
> (Devonshire Commission (Sixth Report), 1875, quoted in Maclure, 1986, p. 108)

For the next quarter century there was discussion about the perceived economic stagnation of Britain, and the links that there might be to the educational system (Banks, 1955;

Table 3.1 Views of the curriculum given by parents to the Taunton Commission, 1868

Stage	Parental class	View of an appropriate curriculum	
Education to age 18	'men of considerable incomes independent of their own exertions, professional men and men in business whose profits put them on the same level'	'no wish to displace the classics from … the forefront of English education, but … a strong desire to add other subjects … modern languages and natural science [and] to cultivate mathematics more carefully than at present'	
	'professional men, the poorer gentry, having received a cultivated education themselves, are anxious that their sons should not fall below them'	'would be glad to secure something more than classics and mathematics. But they value these highly for their own sake, and perhaps even more for the value at present assigned to them in English society'	
Education to age 16	'parents who could keep children at school 2 more years, but intend them for employment'	'would no doubt accept Latin as an important part in Education, partly because it is in some cases of real practical use … partly because of its social value, partly … to facilitate a more through knowledge of modern languages, and partly … as a mental discipline'	' disposed barely to tolerate Latin, if they will even do that'. Evidence given showed 'a greater desire for less instruction in classics, and more thorough teaching in modern subjects … mathematics, modern languages, chemistry and the rudiments of physical science are essential'
	'parents who require their boys at 16 to find their own living'	'would … consent to give a high place to Latin … on condition it did not exclude a very thorough knowledge of important modern subjects, and they would hardly give Greek any place at all'	
Education to age 14	'smaller tenant farmers, the small tradesman, the superior artisans'	'very good reading, very good writing, very good arithmetic …. [If] more than that … merely [because] they wish to learn whatever their betters learn'	

Source: Taunton Commission, cited in Maclure, 1986, pp. 92–5

Wiener, 1981). The better performance of other states – particularly Germany and the USA – was ascribed to what was seen as the way in which their educational systems were linked to technological needs and scientific understanding: the case was made for a new kind of technological secondary education, rather than a purely vocational or an academic post-elementary curriculum. The 1902 Education Act took what Wiener was to call 'the wrong path' (p. 81), as 'the genteel pattern of the later-Victorian public school was fixed (one level lower) on the new state grammar schools', with their decidedly traditional academic, anti-vocational and anti-technological curriculum.

By 1904 the curriculum for post-elementary school education was almost entirely described in subject-terms: the Regulations for Secondary Schools of that year (Board of Education, 1904) include a prescriptive list of subjects and minimum teaching times per week that filled some 90 per cent of the available time (though this time element was relaxed three years later). See *Table 3.2*.

By way of contrast, however, the curriculum categorization for elementary schools had by this stage become less prescriptive as the effects of the Revised Code wore off, following its abolition in 1895. The New Code of 1904 presented a much more liberalized set of purposes for primary schools: 'to form and strengthen the character and develop the intelligence of children, and … assist both girls and boys, according to their different needs, to fit themselves, practically as well as intellectually, for the work of life.

As well as a list of what might now be called 'areas of experience' (rather than subjects): habits of observation and clear reasoning … [to] gain … some of the facts and laws of nature; an interest in the ideals and achievement of mankind; familiarity with the literature and history of their own country; power over language as an instrument of thought and expression; a taste for good reading and thoughtful study; natural activities of hand and eye by suitable forms of practical work and manual instruction;

Table 3.2 *Regulations for the secondary school curriculum, 1904*

Subject	*Number of hours per week*
English language and literature	4.5
at least one language other than English*	3.5 if one, 6 if two
Geography	4.5
History	4.5
Mathematics } Science }	7.5 together, at least 3 for science
Drawing	
Manual work	
Physical exercises	
Housewifery (in girls' schools)	

* *Normally Latin would be the second language, if offered: special reasons had to be advanced if Latin was not to be taught if two languages were offered.*

appropriate physical exercises; some of the simpler laws of health, the Code also proposed a set of moral virtues to be encouraged:

> to implant in children ... the sense of discipline ... habits of industry, self control and courageous perseverance in the face of difficulties ... to revere what is noble, to be ready for self-sacrifice, and to strive their utmost after purity and truth, ... a strong respect for duty, and consideration and respect for others.

The suggestion that such elementary education was simply preparatory to selection for secondary schooling was specifically rebuffed: such an objective was 'important though subsidiary'. The tenor of instruction was, as described in the *Handbook of Suggestions for the Consideration of Teachers* (Board of Education, 1905), quite child-centred in its pedagogic basis:

> the teacher must know the child and must sympathise with them ... the mind of the teacher should touch the mind of the child ... to take them into partnership for the acquisition of knowledge. Every fact ... should be exhibited not in isolation but in relation to the past experience of the child; every lesson must be a renewal and an increase in that connected store of experience which becomes knowledge.
>
> (Board of Education, 1905, p. 14)

Elementary schools thus provided an education for the masses that was complete in itself, and this left secondary schools with an academic or subject-based curriculum orientated at least in part towards the universities. H.H. Asquith, Prime Minister in 1916, established a Reconstruction Committee that was intended to investigate the role of subjects in the post-war secondary school: subcommittees investigated the neglect of science, the role of modern languages, and the position of English. A series of Prime Minister's Reports followed, of which perhaps the most significant was the Newbolt Report (1921), which made English central to the curriculum, arguing that 'every teacher is a teacher of English'. The secondary curriculum was confirmed in its role of preparing pupils for examinations in academic subjects by the establishment in 1917 of the Secondary Schools Examination Council, which was to implement the School Certificate by coordinating the various university examining boards which administered it. The Certificate was designed to be taken by pupils at the age of 16 after four years of study: passes in at least five subjects had to be obtained in order to be awarded a Certificate. It was significant that the Certificate brought with it exemption from matriculation to University: the curriculum that was examined after secondary schooling was, first, confined to the minority who could afford to stay in full-time education to the age of 16, and, second, was specially designed to prepare students for University entry. The Higher Certificate was available for those who had successfully completed a two-year 16–18 course in two to four subjects (Aldrich, 1988).

Diverse Approaches and the Individual Child: 1926–64

From these unpromising beginnings, a sense of unified purpose across the whole school curriculum was developed in the three reports of the Hadow Committee (Board of Education, 1926, 1931, 1933). Hadow identified in secondary education

> two opposing schools of modern educational thought. ... One attaches primary importance to the individual pupils and their interests; the other emphasises the claims of society as a whole, and seeks to equip the pupils for service as workmen and citizens in its organisation. When either tendency is carried too far the result is unsatisfactory ... [the] educational system must combine these two ideas in the single conception of social individuality.
>
> (Board of Education, 1926, p. 101)

The nursery and infant school advocated by Hadow was explicitly not concerned with 'uniform standards of attainment. Its business is to see children ... grow in body and mind at their natural rate, neither faster nor slower' (Board of Education, 1933, p. 145). In primary schools (7 to 11), he urged the confinement of the curriculum to things that have immediate potential value to children: 'the curriculum is to be thought of in terms of activity and experience rather than of knowledge to be acquired and facts to be stored. ... [and thus] attain control and orderly management of his energies, impulses and emotions ... [and] discover the idea of duty' (Board of Education, 1931, p. 93). Secondary education for all was to be attained through the creation of new Modern Schools, to supplement the existing selective (and academic) Grammar Schools: here the curriculum was to be subject-based but also planned as a three or four year whole, with subjects 'much the same as those in Grammar Schools [with] more time devoted to handwork and similar pursuits'; and, in the 13–15 phase

> the treatment of the subjects ... should be practical in the broadest sense and brought directly into relation with the facts of everyday life. The courses of instruction, though not merely vocational or utilitarian, should be used to connect the school work with the interests arising from the social and industrial environment of the pupils.
>
> (Board of Education, 1926, p. 173)

Hadow's proposal was revisited by a Board of Education Consultative Committee established in 1938 with special reference to Grammar Schools and Technical High Schools (the Spens Report). This drew on psychological evidence that suggested that it was possible to sort children at an early age into groups with different aptitudes, and to provide a curriculum particularly suited for the group. The idea of classifying children by their 'ability to benefit' from a particular form of education grew initially from the need to ration the scholarships providing free grammar school education, established by the 1902 Act. Testing at the end of the elementary phase, it was claimed, could predict future performance in the grammar school. Drawing on the work of Cyril Burt, the report argued that 'intellectual development ... appears to progress as though it were governed by a single central factor ... "general intelligence", which ... can be measured approximately by means of intelligence tests ... [which make it] possible at a very early age to predict with some degree of accuracy the ulti- mate level of a child's intellectual power' (Board of Education, 1938, p. 124). From this process, it was possible – even desirable – to differentiate children by type, with academic, technical and 'modern' curricula to match.

While such sociobiological casuistry later came in for much criticism (see for example Kamin, 1977), it seemed to advocate a form of curriculum moulded to the needs of the individual child, and to match some of the elements of a child-centred, 'naturalistic' curriculum. It also happened to broadly match the reproduction of the existing social order and the predicted needs of broad categories of the labour market. Torrance (1981) points out that this was not a conspiracy, but a demonstration of how educators made partial use of a new discipline, psychology, to underline existing prac- tices and prevailing opinions.

Nevertheless, the Spens Report was critical of the over-academic nature of the Grammar School curriculum, which it noted was in thrall to the School Certificate examination: 'the examination is now the dominant factor in determining the curriculum for the majority of the pupils below the age of 16'. It went on

> in several important aspects the influence of the examination and the process of preparation for it are inimical to the healthy growth in mind and body of a large number of children who pass through Grammar School. ... We desire to leave as much freedom as possible to schools in the selection of studies and in their content.
>
> (Board of Education, 1938, p. 124)

A little later, the Norwood Report laid out these curricula in greater detail, for

> the pupil who is interested in learning for its own sake ... the pupil whose inter- ests and abilities lie more markedly in the field of applied science or applied art ... and [those who] deal more easily with concrete things than ideas.

But it also advocated

> freedom to schools to devise curricula suited to their pupils and to local needs. ... Examinations should be a sub-ordinate part of the school economy ... [and] the examination is best conducted by the teachers themselves as being those who should know their pupils' work.
>
> (Board of Education, 1938, p. 124)

The expansion that was planned post-war was, however, not to be vocationally or tech- nologically driven. Barnett (1986) has argued that the activities of the Board of Education during the war showed 'an overriding humanist bias in favour of bringing 'liberal education' to the British masses' (p. 278). The White Paper of 1943, precursor of the 1944 Act, is quoted in support: 'the reforms [proposed are] to secure for children a happier childhood and a better start in life: to ensure a fuller measure of education and opportunity for young people, and to provide means for all of developing the various talents with which they are endowed and so enriching for the inheritance of the country whose citizens they are. ... In the youth of the nation we have our greatest national asset. Even on the basis of mere expediency, we cannot afford not to develop this asset to the greatest advantage' (United Kingdom, 1943). Barnet notes that although the White Paper calls for better educated industrial and commercial workers, 'such sentiments did *not* inspire the White Paper's fundamental approach to the whole question of national education' (Barnett, 1986, p. 278, emphasis in original).

The 1944 Education Act, which finally brought about both the primary/secondary distinction at the age of 11 as had been recommended by Hadow, Spens and Norwood, and gave Local Education Authorities (LEAs) the duty of creating secondary education as Grammar, Technical and Modern Schools, was almost completely silent on the curriculum. Perhaps, as Tomlinson (1993) has detected, there was the sense that the recent experience of totalitarian regimes abroad had convinced most people that the State should not be involved in determining what went on in classrooms. The principal activities of the LEAs over most of the next thirty years were in providing the resources for non-University education: providing buildings, maintaining them, training teachers and employing them, and the organization of the different phases of education. The Ministry of Education was also, through the 1950s, unconcerned with the curriculum. George Tomlinson, Minister of Education in 1947, is reputed to have summed up the position as the 'Minister knows nowt about curriculum' (quoted in Kirk, 1986).

But there were three major pressures on the curriculum in the two decades following the 1944 Act, the significance of which was not fully discerned until the following period.

First, there was an enormous growth in the amount and organization of knowledge, particularly scientific and technological knowledge. Manifest originally at the level of higher education, this subsequently impacted on the 16–18 curriculum (as Universities demanded a greater knowledge and understanding of each subject from the students that they recruited). The General Certificate in Education was introduced to replace the School Certificate in 1951: 'A' (advanced) levels, taken normally at age 18, became the necessary matriculation for university entry, while the 'O' (ordinary) level became the 16-year-old leaving examination. The O level subjects were individually certificated – it was no longer necessary to pass in five subjects – and began the process of increasing the number of secondary subjects available. A levels further developed the idea of academic specialisation in the 16–18 curriculum.

Second, the understanding of the processes and the consequences of teaching and learning were changing. Sociological examination of education began to reveal the differential impact of selective secondary education. There were three forms of inequality evident. The first was in different geographical regions where there were greater or lesser proportions of Grammar School places available (Yates and Pidgeon, 1957; Vernon, 1957). The second was on the level of specific coaching offered in preparation for the tests, which it was known could dramatically influence the scores (Watts, Pidgeon and Yates, 1952). Lastly, there was a clear correlation between social class and score (Simon, 1953). Vernon's edited collection, the result of a British

Psychological Society working party, refuted the idea of an innate and fixed intelligence. The minimum school leaving age, although raised to 15 by the 1944 Education Act, still left most children at Secondary Modern schools without any qualification when they left school. Because social class had became closely identified with secondary school selection at 11, the majority of children from a middle-class background were assured of an opportunity to secure qualifications, while most children of working-class background were unable to achieve any kind of leaving qualification when they completed full-time schooling. Added to such class-based analyses of the types and outcomes of secondary education in the 1950s and early 1960s were analyses of curriculum and achievement in secondary education attached to gender differences and to ethnic origin, in the late 1960s and 1970s.

Third, society itself was changing, and perhaps fragmenting. The unexpected affluence of the 1950s and the growth in consumerism brought with it aspirations and demands for a range of social goods and services, including educational qualifications and access to post-compulsory education. Though it is an illusion that British society was ever homogeneous, there was from the early 1950s a more plural society. With this recognition of social, cultural, linguistic and ethnic diversity some people came to realize that traditional curricular forms of knowledge tended to value only a particular category or sub-set of knowledge, and that there were possibly other kinds of curricular knowledge that were also of value. Much of the cultural cannon enshrined in the traditional or given curriculum reflected a relatively narrow culture. Added to this, the rapid technological and economic developments of the post-war period were creating vast new areas of knowledge and understanding, with matching demands for skills and capabilities in the population – not merely demands for particular technological specialists, but also for a broader level of understanding and ability in the population as a whole, in literacy and in numeracy as much as in science and technology.

A seminal event leading to the recognition that the educational curriculum was falling behind the social, scientific and technological requirements of the times was the launching of the first Sputnik spacecraft in 1957. The realization that the USSR was so technologically advanced sent shock waves through both the American and British administrations (Kennedy, 1988). A series of changes in the educational system was one of the results (Dean, 1992): an increased emphasis on science in schools, concerns about the status of technology in higher education (the Colleges of Advanced Technology were designated soon after this), and the expansion of Russian language degrees are but three direct examples.

The problem of qualifications for secondary modern pupils was approached by the Secondary School Examination Council in 1958. A Committee chaired by Robert Beloe recommended the establishment of the Certificate of Secondary Education in its report in 1960 (Ministry of Education, 1960). While the GCE O level (in the hands of the University examining boards) catered for the most academically able 20 per cent, the CSE would cater for the next 20 per cent of the ability range. They would have to take at least four subjects: but a further 20 per cent of the ability range could attempt individual subjects. The significance for the school curriculum lay in two factors: first, the examinations were explicitly not to replicate GCE O level examinations, but were to be specially designed to meet the needs and interests of the pupils; and second, the examinations were to be largely in the hands of the teachers and schools using them, thus echoing aspects of both Spens and Norwood.

A more fundamental re-appraisal of the curriculum followed: Tomlinson (1993) suggests that 'the first sign of central reassertion of control came in 1962' when in March Sir David Eccles, Minister of Education, established the Curriculum Study Group (CSG). Consisting of some HMI, some Ministry administrators, and 'appropriate experts from outside' (Professor Jack Wrigley claims that he was the only 'expert' so appointed (Wrigley, 1983)), the Group appears only to have been established after internal dissent from some HMI. The announcement of its formation by the Permanent Secretary in a circular letter – 'the Ministry and the Inspectorate have a useful contribution to make to thinking about the educational process', which might result in the Group 'placing before our partners in the educational service a range of possible solutions to future problems' (quoted in Jennings, 1985, p. 16) – led to a furore of criticism, notably from the LEAs and the teacher unions. Although at the time denying any intention to interfere in teachers' prerogatives over the curriculum, Eccles was later to admit that he had been envisaging 'a commando-type unit' to advance and enliven curriculum debate (Kogan, 1978, p. 63). The head of the unit was Derek Morrell, a civil servant who had earlier in his career aroused LEA antagonisms. He first of all formed a strategic alliance with the senior HMI on the group, Robert Morris. Next, he decided that any consideration of the curriculum must include deliberation on the significance of assessment, and in particular the position of the Secondary Schools Examinations Committee (SSEC). The Beloe recommendation of the CSE had been accepted by Eccles, who asked the SSEC to establish the arrangements for the examination. The Committee's experience and traditions lay wholly in the grammar schools and Universities: it 'was notably short on people who knew what a secondary modern school was like' (Jennings, 1985, p. 17), and new members with such a background were added (including Arnold Jennings, a secondary school headteacher). But the CSE Standing Committee of SSEC, established in 1962, still had a majority of those with little real knowledge of such schools, and it was becoming increasingly clear that the SSEC itself would need to have its terms of reference and membership reviewed.

Derek Morrell used the position at SSEC to advantage. Wrigley, the only outsider on the CSG, and later Director of Studies at the Schools Council, subsequently described 'the imagination of a remarkable civil servant ... [whose] aim was to plan for a national initiative in curriculum innovation without incurring the risk of central control of the curriculum by his fellow administrators' (Wrigley, 1983, p. 43). According to Jennings, Morrell produced a paper with 'four brilliant ideas':

1   to remove the Curriculum Study Group from the Ministry of Education, and reconstitute it as an independent body responsible to both LEAs and the Ministry, but controlled by neither;
2   to widen the SSEC membership to make it fully representative;
3   to merge the SSEC with the CSG into a single body, with responsibility for both examinations and curriculum;

4   but to unequivocally direct that the curriculum should be determined first, that assessment would be subservient, and that teachers would have a majority on the new body.

A new Minister for Education, Sir Edward Boyle, set up a committee of enquiry (The Lockwood Committee), which recommended the establishment of the Schools Council for the Curriculum and Examinations, that would give 'new cooperative machinery in the fields of the schools' curricula and examinations' (Ministry of Education, 1964). Thirty-four of the sixty-six members of the Governing Council were to be representatives of the teacher associations. The Council began work on 1 October 1964, under the chairmanship of Sir John Maud, and with Morrell and Morris as joint permanent secretaries.

The Polarization of Innovation and Tradition: 1960–76

The Schools Council was from its inception a large, committee-driven institution. It inherited subject-based committees from its SSEC predecessor, and this alone inhibited the possibility of a clear consideration of the curriculum as a whole. Instead, it took on an almost deliberately piecemeal approach, funding a vast array of projects: some major initiatives in, for example, mathematics, reading and the humanities; and other small-scale local projects. A series of Working Papers considered areas of debate. Possible initiatives were debated and examined, and project teams commissioned, either in University Departments of Education or in Local Authorities (often in both) to develop materials for pupils and guidance for teachers. Some of these projects were related to traditional curriculum areas in the secondary school, such as the Schools Council History Project, which developed new criteria and activities for the exploration of the subject (using evidence-based approaches, for example, and developing skills of historical empathy), and opening up new areas of content that challenged the established themes (for example the history of medicine). Other projects challenged the traditional subject boundaries that were becoming petrified: the Humanities Curriculum Project (Schools Council/Nuffield, 1972; Stenhouse, 1975), for example, sought to bring together aspects of established subjects of history, English, geography and (less established) the social sciences in a radical new teaching approach, designed in part in preparation for the raising of the school-leaving age to 16. The need for a curriculum for this age range, signposted by Crowther (CACE, 1959), was also tackled in subject specific terms by projects such as Geography for the Young School Leaver. Many projects tried – with varying degrees of success – to accommodate the social changes of the 1960s and 1970s: for example, deliberately addressing gendered stereotypes, or taking on the changing multi-cultural and multi-lingual nature of British society. (This was not always easy ground: the Humanities Curriculum Project ran into serious difficulties over its materials on race and racism, for example.) Other curriculum projects tackled specific skills, for example the Breakthrough to Literacy project for 5- to 8-year-olds.

Projects were proposed and agreed by the Council, and then usually developed by a specially recruited team, generally (like most of the Schools Council staff) on secondment. The team would be based in a University or a College Department of

Education, or in a Local Authority; and would develop materials with schools in selected LEAs: the development and writing programmes were generally very close to classroom practice. A very high proportion of projects were materials-based: that is, they developed materials for classroom use by pupils, and sometimes teacher materials. When a project had material ready for publication and dissemination, commercial publishers were invited to tender for the right to produce and sell the materials.

During the early years of the Council, before its reconstitution in the latter part of the 1970s, there was no attempt to describe an overarching view of the curriculum (though Schools Council, 1975a, was a specific overview for the 13–16 age range). The view was taken, embedded in the Schools Council's constitution, and in the Lockwood Report, that 'each school should have the fullest possible measure of responsibility for its own work, with its own curriculum and teaching methods based on the needs of its own pupils and evolved by its own staff.' The role of the Council was 'to assist all who have individual or joint responsibilities for ... the schools' curricula and examinations to co-ordinate their actions in harmony with this principle' (Ministry of Education, 1964, p. 9). The schools would make selections from the growing *à la carte* menu that the Schools Council projects began to make available to supplement the traditional diet. Diversity was the order of the day.

In part the Council's agenda for curriculum innovation was taken from the great group of educational reports that came from the Central Advisory Council for Education in the 1959–67 period. The Crowther Report, *15 to 18* (CACE, 1959) set out the curricular concerns for secondary modern schools (particularly those associated with the raising of the school leaving age), for sixth formers, and for those in further education that it claimed were needed to meet the twin aims of 'the right of every boy and girl to be educated' and 'the need of the community to provide an adequate supply of brains and skill to sustain its economic activity'. It advocated school-based examinations for secondary modern schools (the Beloe Committee's (Ministry of Education, 1960) development of this led directly to the establishment of the Schools Council, as has been noted above), a broader curriculum for those taking A levels, with courses to make the science specialists more literate and the arts specialists more numerate, and an alternative non-academic curriculum for the further education colleges. The Newsom Report, *Half our Future*, (CACE, 1963), examined the curriculum of 13–16-year-olds of average or less than average ability. It recommended schools provide a broader choice of courses in years 10 and 11, with pupils not rigidly streamed. The year 11 programme in particular should be outgoing, developing links with further education, the youth service and the youth employment service: work experience courses might be useful, it suggested. The Schools Council response was to commission a wide range of projects for the young school leaver (Schools Council, 1975a). The Plowden Report, *Children and their Primary Schools* (CACE, 1967), strongly supported child-centred approaches to learning and to the curriculum, and to integrated learning. It also suggested that Middle Schools (for years 4–7 or years 5–8) be introduced. It was suggested that such schools might need a greater degree of curriculum coordination than that found in primary schools: the Schools Council's response was to call a conference to consider ideas for the middle school curriculum (Schools Council, 1969), and then to develop a variety of integrated curriculum projects for the primary age range, and to plan ideas and materials for the middle school curriculum (Schools Council, 1975b; also Blyth et al., 1976, for a specific curriculum development project; Blyth et al., 1987).

Projects were disseminated in a variety of ways: Local Education Authorities were encouraged to establish Teachers' Centres, where in-service courses could be organized. The Schools Council encouraged LEAs to support them, as suitable mechanisms both for the development of curriculum development, and for the dissemination and support of completed programmes. The James Report, *The Report of the Committee of Inquiry into Teacher Education and Training* (DES, 1972), further supported Teachers' Centres as part of its 'third cycle' of in-service training for teachers. The approach for both development and dissemination was intended to be through developmental formative evaluation: eschewing large-scale curriculum development models, the Schools Council usually sought regular early feedback and iterative development processes for its curriculum programmes (Wrigley, 1983). The problem of ensuring participation in changing the curriculum was, it was assumed, addressed by teachers having such a controlling role within the governance of the Council, and it was not sufficiently recognized that it did not follow from having a simple majority on the Council that teachers across the country would feel sufficiently involved. Consequently dissemination was not addressed sufficiently early in the Schools Council's period of activities.

As the LEAs established a far greater influence over the curriculum in their schools in the later part of the 1970s, the problems of disseminating the Schools Council innovations became more apparent. The larger local authorities generated their own materials and projects, more specific to the needs of their teachers, usually designed and piloted by their own schools, disseminated and supported through their own Teachers' Centres – 'far more effectively than had been, or ever could be established at national level', commented Eric Briault, the Inner London Education Authority's Chief Education Officer (Briault, 1985). The ILEA had established its own publishing and television production facilities to develop curriculum materials for its schools, and by the late 1970s these were including specific guidance for teachers on aspects of the curriculum, and not just classroom materials. As LEAs became more and more involved in both in-service training and curriculum leadership, the paradox of the Schools Council became more apparent. Wrigley, the Council's Director of Studies, recalled Briault making this plain at a Schools Council meeting. Speaking for the LEAs on the Council, he said 'something like this: "we can see the need for local curriculum development but we cannot see why local money should be provided for a national organisation such as the Schools Council to plan local work back in the Local Education Authority itself"' (Wrigley, 1983).

The Schools Council's work on examinations was considerably slower. The CSE was introduced in 1965, and in 1967 the Council began discussions about the introduction of a single examination system at 16+, bringing together the CSE and the GCE 'O' level examinations. It was twenty more years before the General Certificate in Secondary Education (GCSE) was introduced to do this. Advances in reforming the 18+ examination system were even less successful. The lack of change in both sets of examinations had an inhibitory effect on curriculum developments.

The curriculum innovations of the Schools Council, and of bodies such as the Nuffield Foundation, attracted some critics. Initially, these criticisms were of the level of impact that the innovations had on school and classroom practice. Various studies indicated that teachers' perception and knowledge of the range of Schools Council's projects were limited. Figures on the dissemination and take-up of materials-based projects showed that, with few exceptions, most projects were only reaching a minority of the target teachers, and in some cases, only a very small minority (Steadman et al., 1978, 1980; Whitehead, 1980). Such criticism, however, was of the efficiency of the Council's curriculum development policies, not of their character.

From the mid-1970s, these various curriculum innovations, and the changes in teaching styles and methods that became associated with them, began to also attract criticisms of their purpose and content. A series of 'Black Papers on Education' were published erratically from 1969 (Cox and Dyson, 1969, 1970). The educational changes brought about by the incoming Labour government that had attracted the criticisms of the right were initially those concerning the *structure* of educational provision. The curriculum innovations brought about by the Schools Council (and by bodies such as the Nuffield Foundation) were rather different: it was remarkable that most of them were ignored by the right for a long period of time. With the exception of occasional critiques of 'new maths' and, less often, of the teaching of reading, the attacks on educational innovations were confined to other matters.

For example, the first 'Black Paper' (Cox and Dyson, 1969) made virtually no criticism of the curriculum in schools, apart from a few remarks about 'free play methods' in primary schools, and 'taking to an extreme' 'discovery methods'. The two papers on primary education presented calls for concentration on literacy and greater planning and teacher-directed work, but had virtually no references to curriculum content (Johnson, 1969; Browne, 1969). The principal critiques of the 'Plowden philosophy' of the primary curriculum had been academic, rather than political (for example Peters, 1969). The main thrusts of the Black Paper articles were concerned with the introduction of comprehensive education, student involvement in the management of Higher Education institutions, and the expansion of Higher Education. The two side-swipes at the curriculum were the exception: Kingsley Amis attacked courses in the 'non-subjects' of sociology and social psychology (Amis, 1969, p. 10), and Robert Conquest attacked University degrees in sociology 'as the bastion of ... barbarism' (Conquest, 1969, pp. 17–18). But the significance of these is that the preponderance of complaint was not about the curriculum innovations that were being introduced, but about other issues. The second Black Paper (Cox and Dyson, 1970) was very similar: the curriculum criticism was confined to modern mathematics and to the teaching of reading in primary education (Crawford, 1970; Froome, 1970).

Boyson was one of the first to express a concern over the direction of curriculum changes brought about by the innovations of the 1960s and 1970s. In 1975 he claimed there had been a 'breakdown in the "understood" curriculum' in schools, and described 'compulsory education [as] a farce unless all schools follow the same basic syllabus as preparation for society' (Boyson, 1975a). He argued that if schools were to be made more accountable, then there needed to be 'either a nationally enforced curriculum or parental choice or a combination of both' (Boyson, 1975b, p. 141), presently identifying the distinction that was to emerge between the neo-conservative and the neo-liberal wings of the new right.

James Callaghan became Prime Minister in 1976, and elected to make education one of the major issues of his premiership (Donoghue, 1987, p. 111). His speech at Ruskin College later in the year was a major commentary and critique of the curriculum. The speech, and the 'Great Debate' that followed will be analysed in the next chapter. Among other observations, he picked up criticisms of the Schools Council, which he had noted in his visits to schools soon after he became Premier (Callaghan, 1987, p. 409). He was concerned with 'new informal methods of teaching' (particularly when these are carried out by those without 'well-qualified hands'), though was rather more circumspect in his criticism of curricular diversity:

> I have been very impressed by ... the variety of courses that are offered ... there is little wrong with the range and diversity of our courses. But is there sufficient thoroughness and depth in those required in after life to make a living?
>
> (Callaghan, 1976)

His new Secretary of State for Education was Shirley Williams (who had taken over just five weeks before this speech), and one of her immediate responses was to ask for a review of the Schools Council and its role in curriculum change (Mann, 1985).

Three particular issues were to be addressed in this: the representation of lay groups within the Council – parents, and particularly employers (whose role, or lack of it, in education had been a major feature of the Ruskin speech); the continuation of the teacher majority on the Council; and the efficiency of the Council's activities. The restructuring of the Council that followed from this led to a elaborate structure that balanced the funders of the Council (still LEAs and DES), the teachers and the laity: from this, the Council reviewed its curriculum activities, limiting the traditional materials-based developmental projects in favour of five inter-related programmes: purpose and planning in schools; helping individual teachers' effectiveness; developing the curriculum for a changing world; helping individual pupils; and improving examinations. These programmes were barely under way when a new Government was elected, led by Margaret Thatcher, a former Secretary of State for Education (1970–4). (She had once visited the Schools Council – an unusual activity for a Secretary – and had seen an exhibition of materials. On reading about the Humanities Curriculum Project she commented, 'when I was a girl, I was taught to know the difference between right and wrong' (Plaskow, 1985, p. 13).) But by now the Schools Council was swept up in the curriculum turmoil that had been initiated by Callaghan's speech. Its influence was in rapid decline.

The changes that were about to begin were in one sense new: yet they were also a revisiting of a debate that had been initiated by Aristotle.

> In modern times there are opposing views about the tasks to be set [in education], for there are no generally accepted assumptions about what the young should learn, either for their virtue or for the best life; nor yet is it clear whether their education ought to be conducted with more concern for the intellect than for the character of the soul. ... It is by no means certain whether training should be directed at things useful in life, or at those most conducive to virtue, or at exceptional accomplishments.
>
> (*The Politics*, Book VIII, Chapter ii (1337a33))

4   Turmoil in the Curriculum: 1976–1986

Callaghan's speech at Ruskin College marked the beginning of a series of discussions about the purposes of education and the nature of the curriculum. Initially an issue largely confined to politicians, professional teachers, HMI and the Department of Education and Science, it spread in the late 1970s to a wider public. Determined to distinguish his premiership, Callaghan had selected the education system as the focus for a 'big idea': education was at this time, a most unusual area for a Prime Minister to become involved with.

Three actions cleared the ground for Callaghan's initiative. First, he was able to approve the appointment of a new Permanent Secretary at the DES in June 1976. Sir James Hamilton displaced Sir William Pile. Hamilton, a relatively young civil servant, was transferred from the Department of Trade and Industry and brought with him an awareness of industrialists' criticisms of the education system (see, for example, Weinstock, 1976) – and a determination to further involve the Department in the curriculum: 'I believe that the so-called secret garden of the curriculum in which HMI already walks by professional right cannot be allowed to remain so secret after all' (Hamilton, 1976).

Callaghan had inherited Fred Mulley as Secretary of State for Education from Harold Wilson's administration. Callaghan's second action was to plan to replace Mulley with Shirley Williams, a younger politician perceived to be on a rising political trajectory. Following visits to schools made soon after he became Prime Minister, Callaghan challenged Mulley on aspects of both the primary and the secondary curriculum (Callaghan, 1987, p. 409: meeting of 21 May 1976 with Mulley). Found wanting in application and in dynamism, Mulley was asked to resign in September.

Third, Callaghan directly commissioned the DES to prepare an internal document on the shortcomings of the education service, which would give the background for his speech and the rationale to open a 'Great Debate' on education and schools. This became known, from the colour of its cover, as 'The Yellow Book' (DES, 1976a).

The Great Debate: The 'Yellow Book' and *Education in Schools*

School Education in England: Problems and Initiatives (DES, 1976a) was widely leaked to the media following Callaghan's speech, in justification of his strictures. It was critical of schools, LEAs and particularly of the Schools Council, which it described as mediocre and unwilling to suggest firm proposals for the curriculum; the report urged the establishment of a core curriculum and of 'generally accepted principles for the composition of the secondary curriculum for all pupils'. On the other hand, it was totally uncritical of the role of the DES, and identified HM Inspectorate as 'the most powerful single agency to influence what goes on in schools, both in kind and standard', and recommended its role be developed. (The DES was criticized elsewhere, however: the *10th Report of the House of Commons Expenditure Committee* (House of Commons, 1976) noted that the DES officials considered that the allocation of resources was the same as planning the educational system, while the OECD had reported that they found that the DES had no central policy for education (OECD, 1975).)

The Ruskin Speech asserted that the curriculum and purposes of schools were to be scrutinized and debated by a wide variety of interest groups, and that the balance between personal development and preparation for working life needed to be scrutinized and addressed through a common curriculum:

> no one [has] exclusive rights in this field. Public interest is strong and legitimate and will be satisfied. ... Parents, teachers, learned and professional bodies, representatives of higher education and both sides of industry, together with the government all have an important part to play in formulating and expressing the purpose of education.
>
> ... I am concerned ... to find complaints from industry that new recruits from the schools sometimes do not have the basic tools to do the job that is required ... to find that many of our best trained students ... have no desire to join industry. Their preferences are to stay in academic life or to find their way into the Civil Service. There seems to be a need for a more technological bias in science teaching that will lead towards practical applications in industry rather than towards academic studies. ... Is there not a case for a professional review of the mathematics needed by industry at different levels? To what extent are these deficiencies the result of insufficient coordination between schools and industry?
>
> ... It is not my intention to become enmeshed in such problems as whether there should be a basic curriculum with universal standards – though I am inclined to think that there should be ... [but that] where there is legitimate public concern it will be to the advantage of all if these concerns are aired and shortcomings righted or fears put to rest.
>
> ... The goals of our education ... are clear enough. They are to equip children to the best of their ability for a lively, constructive place in society, and also to fit them to do a job of work. Not one or the other, but both. For many years the accent was simply on fitting a so-called inferior group of children with just enough learning to earn their living in the factory ... there is now widespread recognition of the need to cater for a child's personality, to let it flower in the fullest possible way. The balance was wrong in the past. We have a responsibility now to see we do not get it wrong in the other direction. There is no virtue in producing socially well-adjusted members of society who are unemployed because they do not have the skills.
>
> (Callaghan, 1976)

The DES followed the speech with a document intended to open the debate, posed as a set of questions for the agenda for eight regional one-day conferences held in February and March 1997. The document was sharper than Callaghan had been in his speech: 'the curriculum has become overcrowded in response to constantly expanding demands, and arguably the attempt to meet social needs has been at the expense of the more strictly educational' (DES, 1976b, p. 3).

This quotation is a particularly obvious attempt to equate the 'academic' educational tradition described earlier with 'the strictly educational', at the expense of preparatory or developmental traditions. The Green Paper *Education in Schools* (DES, 1977a), which followed the conferences and sought to take further the 'Great Debate', drew attention to 'the background of strongly critical comment in the Press and elsewhere on education ... [that] the curriculum ... was overloaded with fringe subjects' (para. 1.2). In primary schools, 'less able and less experienced teachers' were applying freer child-centred methods uncritically and failing to recognize the need for careful planning and monitoring: in some classes 'the use of the child-centred approach has deteriorated into lack of order and application' (para. 2.2). Primary teachers needed to be clear about curriculum progression, to be precise about levels of achievement, 'to agree about what is to be learned', and to ensure that literacy and numeracy form 'the core of learning, the protected area of the curriculum ... no other curricular aims should deflect teachers from them' (para. 2.3). Secondary schools had equally had 'a good deal of curriculum experimental and diversity ... [but] not without attendant weaknesses'. Some teachers 'did not understand sufficiently clearly the nature of the changes on which they were embarking' (paras 2.9–2.11). Secondary schools needed to address the unease over the overcrowding of the curriculum, variations between different schools that penalized children who moved school or area, and the view that 'the curriculum ... is not sufficiently matched to life in a modern industrial society' (para. 2.14). It was proposed that the Department request LEAs to carry out a review on curriculum policies and practice within their schools, and report back on this 'as a preliminary to defining a new framework' (para. 10.5). As Salter and Tapper were later to observe, the DES was investing the Great Debate with the status of an ideological forum, in which the future of the curriculum was to be battled out (Salter and Tapper, 1981, p. 219).

The proposed interrogation of the LEAs on their knowledge of the curriculum being provided in their schools was formalized in DES Circular 14/77: LEAs were asked to report on how they exercised their duty to monitor the curriculum, and how they achieved balanced and broad curricula. The crucial question was A1: 'What procedures have the authority established to enable them to carry out their curricular responsibilities under Section 23 of the Education Act 1944?' (DES, 1977c). Further specific questions were asked about English, mathematics, modern languages, science and religious instruction 'because they have given rise to recent discussion and concern'. Particular details were requested on curriculum provision in 'preparation for Working Life': Authorities were asked about links between schools and local industries (including trade unions), about work experience and observation, about careers education, and 'finally, in view of the importance of understanding more about industry, they are asked to report on what steps are taken to encourage economic and political education in their schools' (para. F). Responses were collected by July 1978, but not published until the Conservative Government took office in the following year (DES, 1979a).

A Common Curriculum: *Curriculum 11–16*

Meanwhile HMI (perhaps provoked by the Yellow Book's comments on their role) had become considerably more assertive in commenting on curriculum provision, and in advocating particular curriculum practices. Sheila Browne, Senior Chief HMI, had already commissioned surveys to be undertaken by teams of Inspectors in 1975. The following year, just a month before Callaghan's speech, a major collaborative project was initiated between HMI and five LEAs to investigate the secondary school curriculum (*Curriculum 11–16*, DES 1977b, 1983a). There is some evidence to suggest that the DES officials' comments on the role of HMI in the Yellow Book pushed HMI into trying to seize the initiative in the curriculum debate – or at least to seize it away from the DES officials.

The first of the survey reports, *Primary Education in England* (made as a ten-year post-Plowden review) (DES, 1978), put great emphasis on the need for some specialist subject teachers in primary schools (paras 8.40–8.65), with numerous references to teachers having particular subject knowledge. They argued firmly for a broad curriculum, however: pupil's learning was best where the curriculum was broad, and a narrowing of the curriculum would not raise standards. But the delivery of such a broad curriculum, and particularly the teaching of science (often neglected, often badly taught), demanded some curriculum specialization. *Aspects of Secondary Education* (DES, 1979b) was a parallel report on secondary schools:

> the evidence of this survey is that many pupils are not well served by the curricular structures and organisation of their schools. Some are deprived ... of important areas of experience ... [others] are not readily enabled to relate what they learn in different subjects or to see applications in new contexts
>
> (DES, 1979b, para. 266)

Earlier, the report had likened the elements of the curriculum to building blocks 'with very few rules governing their selection and assembly': from this were constructed programmes for individual pupils that 'display marked disparities in the range and quality of experience' (para. 226). *Aspects of Secondary Education* was followed by similar reflections and analyses of the curriculum in first schools (DES, 1982a) and middle schools (DES, 1983b).

Curriculum 11–16 (DES, 1977b) bluntly made the case for a common curriculum for secondary schools 'for a substantial part of [pupils'] time, perhaps as much as two-thirds or three-quarters of the total time available'. It argued that the increased and accelerating pace of curriculum development had presented teachers with a confusing series of propositions about what the curriculum should contain: this might indicate vigour and development, but more probably was 'associated with an inadequate sense of direction and priorities, with too little coordination within and between schools, and with a reluctance to evaluate the curriculum offered as a whole' (p. 3). Teachers had been left to learn from their own mistakes, and any planning had been piecemeal: the country could not afford '– educationally as well as financially – the wasted effort, experiments embarked on and left unfinished or unexamined, unnecessary repetitions, and most of all, the apparent lack of agreement on fundamental objectives'. The paper spelled out what the authors felt these objectives should be: the curriculum should be concerned with

> introducing pupils during the period of compulsory schooling to certain essential 'areas of experience'. They are listed below in alphabetical order in order that no other order of importance may be inferred: in our view they are equally important.
>
> **Checklist**
> *Areas of experience*
> * The aesthetic and creative
> * The ethical
> * The linguistic
> * The mathematical
> * The physical
> * The scientific
> * The social and political
> * The spiritual
>
> (DES, 1977b, p. 6)

The paper went on to analyse the contribution of schooling to socialization, and to preparation for working life.

Meanwhile, the LEAs were responding to Circular 14/77 on the management of the curriculum in their schools. Before the results of the survey of curricular arrangements could be published, there was a general election that returned the Conservatives to office. This had no immediate impact on the policy of curriculum centralization. Mark Carlisle became the new Secretary of State – 'not a very effective Education Secretary [who] leaned to the left' (Thatcher, 1993, p. 151). Carlisle's commentary on the findings of the Circular 14/77 survey continued to follow the previous administration's lip-service to 'working with the LEA partners in the education service' – he did not intend to alter the existing statutory relationship, he said. He nevertheless admonished the LEAs, who, he claimed on the basis of their returns to the Circular, needed to be 'better informed about the curricular practices and aims of their schools' (DES, 1979a, p. 3, para. 6). The DES observed that two-thirds of the LEAs, in their response to question A1 (LEA procedures to carry out their statutory curricular responsibilities) had said that they delegated such matters to the governing bodies of the individual schools: the report quoted a 'typical reply' from one authority that it 'has not established and would not wish to see develop, a formal system of detailed control over the curriculum of individual schools' (p. 14, para. 1). This was not the correct answer. As Secretary of State, Carlisle proposed that he should therefore, as a priority for the education service, 'give a lead in the process of reaching a national consensus on a desirable framework for the curriculum' that met individual and social needs: such a framework 'could offer a significant step forward in the quest for improvement in the consistency and quality of school education across the country' (pp. 6–7, para. 13). Carlisle asked HMI to formulate a view of a possible curriculum, while the DES was to suggest the form a framework might take and the ground it should cover.

DES and HMI Tensions: *A Framework for the School Curriculum* and *A View of the Curriculum*

It was thus in January 1980 that the DES published *A Framework for the School Curriculum* (DES, 1980a): 'an openly centralist discussion document' (Lawton, 1989, p. 37); a 'mouse', presenting 'an impoverished view of the curriculum' (Tomlinson, 1993, p. 80). It was followed just a few days later by the HMI's *A View of the Curriculum* (DES, 1980b). The tensions between the two institutions were laid out clearly in these two papers (Gordon et al., 1991, p. 290).

A *Framework for the School Curriculum* marked the first attempts to prescribe nationally subjects and times of study for subjects, although it still offered what were by now ritual references to the need for different responses to local conditions. It was now proposed that each LEA should have a clear and known policy for the curriculum in its schools, and should continually monitor schools' performance in meeting this. It set out aims for the curriculum, which may usefully be compared with those in the Green Paper *Education in Schools* (DES, 1977a), from which it is obviously derived – and from which it significantly differs (*Table 4.1*).

The similar focus on the essential utility of educational aims in both lists is notable – 'to apply themselves to tasks', 'the knowledge and skills needed for employment' – as are the significant differences and omissions in the second list. Mathematics and language are linked, and to be used 'effectively' (out goes the 'imaginative' use of language); the knowledge and skills needed for employment are broadened from only the mathematical, scientific and technological. The references to disadvantage, and to 'a more just social order' are omitted (the reference to 'how the nations earns its living' and 'to esteem the essential role of industry and commerce', apparently missing here, is reformulated later in the 1980 document: see *Table 4.2*).

The prescription of certain subjects as core, and the allocation of proportions of school time that should be devoted to these, was perhaps more fundamental. The various justifications for privileging particular subjects as 'core' show a mixture of appeals to common-sense (subjects are 'essential in their own right') and utilitarianism, particularly shown by demonstrating how these subjects have practical and employment-related aspects. The approach – which was to be used repeatedly over the next eighteen years – was to describe an academic, subject-based curriculum as though it was a skills-based, utilitarian curriculum – often with references to a child-based curriculum ('vary according to age and ability').

The non-core area of the curriculum is described in the final section, 'Preparation for adult and working life', and, curiously, mathematics and language are both partly justified as core subjects on the grounds of their importance to these other curricular areas.

This bureaucratic approach to the curriculum was the civil service's response to the Great Debate, and reflects Sir James Hamilton's interests in policy control, efficiency

Table 4.1 Changes in the stated 'Aims of education' given in the 1977 Green Paper
Education in Schools *and the 1980 proposals in* A Framework for the School
Curriculum

Education in Schools (1977)	*A Framework for the Curriculum (1980)*
(i) to help children develop lively, enquiring minds; giving them the ability to question and argue rationally, and to apply themselves to tasks;	(i) to help pupils develop lively, enquiring minds, the ability to question and argue rationally and to apply themselves to tasks, and physical skills;
(vi) to provide a basis of mathematical, scientific and technical knowledge, enabling boys and girls to learn the essential skills needed in a fast changing world of work;	(ii) to help pupils acquire knowledge and skills relevant to adult life and employment in a fast-changing world;
(iv) to help children to use language effectively and imaginatively in reading, writing and speaking;	(iii) to help pupils use language and number effectively;
(v) to help children appreciate how the nation earns and maintains its standard of living and properly to esteem the essential role of industry and commerce in this process;	
(ii) to instil respect for moral values, for other people and for oneself, and tolerance of other races, religions, and ways of life;	(iv) to instil respect for religious and moral values, and tolerance of other races, religions, and ways of life;
(iii) to help children understand the world in which we live, and the interdependence of nations;	(iii) to help pupils understand the world in which they live, and the interdependence of individuals, groups and nations;
(vii) to teach children about human achievement and aspirations in the arts and sciences, in religion, and in the search for a more just social order;	(vi) to help pupils appreciate human achievements and aspirations.
(viii) to encourage and foster the development of children whose social or environmental disadvantages cripple their capacity to learn, if necessary by making additional resources available to them.	

Sources: DES, 1977a, p. 6, para. 1.19; DES, 1980a, p. 3, para. 9.

and value – as well as his own recollections of his education. Recruitment to the Administrative Class of the Civil Service in 1963–7 was 43 per cent from those who had attended public schools, and 27 per cent from other fee-paying schools or direct grant schools (quoted in the Public Schools Commission Report, UK, 1968). The professional response to the debate was exemplified by the HMI response *A View of the Curriculum* (DES, 1980b), which demonstrated the more regular and detailed involvement of HMI with the practice of state school education (many HMI, recruited from the teaching profession, would also have experiences as pupils and teachers of the curriculum of state schools, unlike most of the administrative class of the civil service).

Table 4.2 Subjects for the structure of the school curriculum given in A Framework for the School Curriculum, *1980*

Subject	Purposes/justification	Time allocation
English	essential in its own right	'must vary according to age and ability', but for all pupils at all stages should be not less than 10% of school time
	importance of language skills to other curriculum areas: a means of communication in all parts of the curriculum	
	opportunities should be taken, particularly at the secondary stage, to relate school work to the skills required in employment and adult life	
Mathematics	essential in its own right	'must vary according to age and ability', but for all pupils at all stages should be not less than 10% of school time
	importance of mathematical skills to other curriculum areas	
	at all stages mathematical skills and concepts should be related to a variety of practical examples and situations, and at later stages to their application in adult and working life	
Science	should form part of the experience of every pupil during the period of compulsory education should begin for all pupils in the primary school	during the later years of compulsory education [13–16] ... all pupils should normally devote at least 10% of their school time to science subjects or closely related work
	at the secondary stage, for pupils of all ability levels, it is important that attention should be paid to the industrial and practical applications of science and to links within the school curriculum between science, mathematics, and craft, design and technology	pupils should not normally devote more than 20% to science subjects
Modern languages	pupils should have the opportunity to become acquainted with another modern European language as part of their secondary education	a minimum of two, and preferably three years, amounting to about 10% of school time
		it is not normally desirable to devote more than 20% of school time
Religious education	it is right, as is customarily the case, for religious education to be linked with wider consideration of personal and social values.	

Continued:

Table 4.2 Continued:

Subject	Purposes/justification	Time allocation
Physical education	should normally be part of the curriculum for all pupils throughout the period of compulsory education	
Welsh	has a special position in Wales	
Preparation for adult and working life	the contribution 'to the preparation of young people for all aspects of adult life … requires many additions to the core subjects discussed above, such as CDT; the arts; history and geography; moral education, health education, preparation for parenthood and an adult role in family life; careers education and vocational guidance; and preparation for a participatory role in adult society'	the time given to these should vary according to local circumstances, ages and abilities of pupils – but should find a place in the education of all pupils at one stage or another
	'substantial attention should be given at the secondary stage to the relationship between school work and preparation for working life. Pupils need to acquire an understanding of the economic basis of society and how wealth is created'	

Source: DES, 1980a, paras 21–35.

In fact, *A View of the Curriculum* presented a variety of views of the curriculum, acknowledging what HMI saw as 'necessary tension' between the broad and common aims of education and individual abilities and characteristics. In a carefully argued introduction, the document is a coded attack by the Senior Chief Inspector, Sheila Browne, on the prescriptiveness and regimentation of James Hamilton's *A Framework for the School Curriculum*. Accepting that 'all pupils have to be prepared to meet the basic intellectual and social demands of adult life, and helped form an acceptable set of personal values', it argued persuasively that such a common policy 'cannot be a prescription for uniformity' (DES, 1981b, p. 2). The school curriculum must allow for individual differences – not just in age and stage of development, but also in terms of their ability to take advantage of opportunities, disadvantage, handicap, learning difficulties, diverse abilities and interests, and differentiated aspirations beyond school. With some scorn for the simple 'common-sense' subject divisions of the *Framework*, HMI reiterated the various lists of areas of experience that had been used in the Primary Survey (DES, 1978) and *Curriculum 11–16* (DES, 1977b), suggesting that they were more useful checklists of experience and understanding than subject titles: 'none of these formulations claims, or needs to claim, absolute authority. Other variants exist in the wide range of practical and academic writing published about the curriculum' (DES, 1981b, p. 3). In primary education, the document argued strongly for a broad curriculum: discussion should be less concerned with the range of work, and more about the extent to which parts of the curriculum were developed – more experimental and observational science, less French, for example (p. 11). The secondary curriculum discussions managed, without irony, but in pointed difference to the *Framework*, to critique 'the names of the lessons which appear on the timetable' as irrelevant to any serious discussion of the content of the curriculum. 'It is not possible to discern from [these] alone how far the seemingly common curriculum is qualitatively similar, either in different schools or for different pupils at the same school' (p. 13). Instead, a series of 'propositions' are made: these advance, through a series of axioms, a logic-based demolition of the subject-based simplifications of the *Framework*, advancing instead an 'entitlement' curriculum base on areas of experience.

Propositions 1 to 3 argued that 'there is a need for greater and much more explicit consensus on ... what secondary education is intended to do', and that 'the formal curriculum should offer all pupils opportunities to engage in a largely comparable range of learning' in which there would be 'comparable opportunities and qualities, locally and nationally, though not uniformity' (p. 14).

Propositions 4 to 6 formed the kernel of the argument: because there needs to be cohesion between education before and after 16, it was probable that 'an excessively instrumental view of the compulsory period of education runs the risk of actually reducing pupils' opportunities at a later stage, by requiring premature assumptions about their likely futures – for example, in highly specific occupational terms – and by narrowing the educational base on which their potential may be developed.' It was argued that what was needed was 'more coherence within the experience of individual pupils ... in current and traditional practice [pupils take] a number of discrete subjects, and any coherence has to be superimposed. ... Curricular polices which begin with a statement about the learning to be achieved ... have a better prospect of attaining coherence.' To achieve this, teachers of traditional subjects 'should identify explicitly the knowledge and skills each [subject] ... is expected to promote, and examine the combined significance' of all the subjects (p. 15).

From this, *Propositions 7 to 12* listed some of the essential knowledge and skills that could be inculcated through some of the subjects. There needed to be both a broader coverage of subjects up to 16, and 'a substantially larger compulsory element in the final two years'. Science was advocated not simply for its supposed instrumental characteristics in advancing technology and the national economy, but 'to familiarise all pupils ... with important concepts and knowledge which may both stimulate their minds and their imagination and equip them better for their future responsibilities as citizens ... [it will] also be helping to strengthen general powers of observation and reasoning'. All should take a modern language (not necessarily a *European* modern language) for 'intellectual stimulus and cultural benefit ... [as well as for its] increasing practical value'. All pupils should include the arts and applied crafts. A particularly strong argument was put forward for social and political education (almost certainly the work of the Staff Inspector for History, John Slater, who was both a leading advocate of political education and a strong ally of Chief Inspector Sheila Browne). This was linked to the

> particularly strong case for maintaining history in the final secondary years ... [the study of which would foster] an appreciation of the culture and traditions of this

country and of the rights and responsibilities in a democratic community … and a better understanding of the changing nature of our society both in its technological and multicultural aspects, and the increasing interdependence of nations.

This emphasis on practical skills for adult life (as opposed to skills for an adult life in employment) was strong: 'all pupils [need] opportunities for personal and social development … which will be contributed to by religious education, moral education, health education, community studies and community service.' Preparation for adult life would need to include 'careers education and guidance, preparation for working life, work experience, an introduction to the environmental, economic and political concerns likely to face any adult citizen' (pp. 16–17).

References to vocational education were scornfully relegated to the optional curriculum set out in *Propositions 13 and 14*. Subjects, justifying their position by reference to their ability to develop the areas of experience to which all were entitled, would need to differentiate levels of work, content and emphasis: 'there still needs to be room for differentiation and choice … the essential task is to explore [this] while keeping some parts of the subject accessible to all.' The 'optional' section of the curriculum would allow for new or additional subjects, and it was within this that 'some vocational interest can, where appropriate, be introduced either in the form of optional subjects – commerce, for example – or as an extension of compulsory subjects into studies involving more specific applications, for example technology' (pp. 18–19).

The professional response from the schools was broadly supportive of *A View of the Curriculum*, and almost universally dismissive of the prescriptive instrumentalism of *A Framework for the School Curriculum*.

The Response from the DES: *The School Curriculum*

The DES response was to produce what was, in effect, a capitulation to the critics: Lawton (1984, p. 10) claims that, unlike the *Framework*, the text of *The School Curriculum* (DES, 1981a) was discussed with HMI before publication. Although the DES re-presented their six-point list of educational aims (see *Table 4.1*), they backed down in four substantial areas. First, they emphasized the autonomy of schools in shaping the curriculum: 'neither the Government nor the local authorities should specify in detail what the schools should teach' (DES, 1981a, para. 10). Second, all references to specific periods of time for different subjects were removed: any suggested minima, the DES admitted, could be interpreted too rigidly, and individual LEAs should consult their teachers as to whether broad guidance was needed on minimum times in the locality (para. 43). Third, the HMI position on 'subjects' was broadly accepted: subject titles should be seen as 'a kind of shorthand, whose real educational meaning depends on the school's definition of what it expects children to learn and be able to do as a result of studies in the subject' (para. 19). Finally, virtually all of the economic/vocational instrumentalist justifications for specific subjects, and the curriculum as a whole, were left out. There were many references to the needs pupils would have as members of society, and how the curriculum must address this, but references to future working life and employment were relegated to a few paragraphs, late in the paper, within the context of 'Preparation for adult life'. (There was, though, a more rigorous assertion on this subject from the DES at the same time (DES, 1981b).) The general principles on which the curriculum should be constructed, the paper asserted, were that schools should analyse and publish their curriculum aims, within the context of an LEA policy that referred to skills or areas of experience for all pupils. This should be done in a way that reflected the 'fundamental values in our society', three of which were identified: the multicultural society, and the inherent diversity of values that followed from this; technological change, and the consequent need for adaptability and self-reliance; and the need for equal opportunities to be supported within the curriculum (para. 21).

The stress on multiculturalism, as an essential element for all pupils, is noteworthy. Many teachers and LEAs – particularly, but by no means exclusively, those in the inner-city areas where most of the ethnic minority population were living – had been advocating (and implementing) curricula that recognized and used such cultural diversity. These approaches had been generally ignored or derided by the Conservatives. However, the short-term civil rioting in areas such as Brixton in the summer of 1980 had led to a series of panic reactions by Government, and the beginnings of a recognition that the educational system might need to be required to respond to the greater cultural and social heterogeneity of the population: this reference in *The School Curriculum* almost certainly stemmed from this (see the Swann Report (DES, 1985i), also Arnot, 1985).

Despite the retreat from the *Framework* document, there were still many illogicalities and ambiguities in the new proposal. John White pointed to the curious mixture within the six recommended aims ('is this really the best that the minister and his mandarins can do?' (White, 1981, p. 11). The designation of certain areas as 'key' (English, mathematics, science, modern languages and religious education) was criticized as making it more likely that these would dominate the curriculum, at the expense of humanities, art and social subjects (White, 1981; Lawton, 1981). Political education, it was also noted (Crick and Porter, 1981) received only a mention (unlike the detailed approbation given in the HMI's *View of the Curriculum*), and there was no reference to the need for any study in the creative or aesthetic areas (Lawton, 1981). Dearden (1981) pointed out that the concept of a 'balanced curriculum' implied some prior commitment to something to be balanced – but whether it was areas of experience that were to balance, or forms of knowledge, or whatever, was not made at all clear.

The School Curriculum was followed by a DES Circular (6/81, DES, 1981c), which required LEAs to report on the progress that they were making in implementing their own curriculum plans and monitoring developments within their schools. Meanwhile, the Schools Council had also joined the debate over the nature of the curriculum. *The Practical Curriculum* (Schools Council, 1981) had been delayed in publication so that it followed the DES paper (Lawton, 1984, p. 10; Tomlinson, 1985, p. 127). This had been nearly two years in the writing – it 'required the line-by-line agreement of half-a-dozen different interests from teachers to CBI' (Tomlinson, ibid.) – and, despite its cogent advocacy of an entitlement curriculum based on areas of experience, was largely eclipsed by the evident intent of the government to dramatically curtail the activities of the Schools Council (Schools Council, 1983). Carr and Harnett see the Conservative Government's policy towards the Council as part of its programme of removing institutions that acted as centres for dissension and critique (1996, p. 162). One of Margaret Thatcher's antagonistic comments has been noted above: there was now to be a more sustained attack.

The Schools Curriculum Development Council, *Teaching Quality* and *Better Schools*

The new Secretary of State for Education and Science, Sir Keith Joseph, announced the appointment of Nancy Trenaman as a one-woman review of the functions and work of the Council in March 1981: his Minister of State, Sir Rhodes Boyson, commented that 'we must have some ritual blood-letting' (quoted in Mann, 1985, p. 190, as a comment to the Society of Education Officers in the summer of 1981). The DES had long been a critic of the Council (see Mann, 1985, pp. 182–9): the Yellow Book in 1976 had been censorious: the Council had 'performed moderately in commissioning development work in particular curricular areas ... [but] had scarcely begun to tackle the problems of the curriculum as a whole. ... The overall quality has ... been generally mediocre' (DES, 1976a). The DES now used the opportunity of the Trenaman review to attack the Council, which, it claimed 'required a competent, loyal and submissive staff ... but now there seemed to be a serious danger of disorder through lack of control' (evidence given by Walter Ulrich, DES Deputy Secretary, 30 July/3 August 1981, reported in *The Times*, 3 December, 1981). The Department recommended what amounted to the closure of the Council and the establishment of a new body (Jennings, 1985). The Report (Trenaman, 1981) was nevertheless broadly favourable to the Council: it recommended that it 'should continue with its present functions, and should not be made the subject of further external review for at least five years'. Sir Keith Joseph thought otherwise: he announced the Council was to be disbanded, and replaced with two bodies, one for examinations, the other for the curriculum (statement to House of Commons, 23 April 1982). Reasons for this were not advanced, though he claimed that he had evidence other than that seen by Trenaman (Mann, 1985, p. 190), and that experience since 1964 has cast doubt on the wisdom of having a single body covering curriculum and examinations (written Parliamentary answer, August 1982).

It took two years to complete the closure, and to establish the successor bodies. The Schools Curriculum Development Council (SCDC) was but a pale shadow of the Council, being firmly under the control and direction of the DES and the Secretary of State. The LEAs were given some token representation on the Council, the teachers none at all (at least, not through their associations). A small number of Schools Council projects were allowed to continue under the SCDC aegis, the most notable two being the Schools Council Industry Project set up at the time of the Ruskin speech (Jamieson and Lightfoot, 1982), and the Secondary Schools Science Review. The SCDC began its own new projects, but these tended to be initiated by the Secretary of State, rather than by the LEAs or HMI. For example, the Oracy Project can traced back to *A Framework for the School Curriculum*, where the list of priorities in English that was made by the Bullock Report (United Kingdom, 1975) was specifically supplemented by the Secretary of State's consideration 'that schools should pay particular attention to oral communication' (DES, 1980a, para. 22). Similarly Joseph's March 1985 initiative on economic awareness led, via an SCDC Consultative Conference, to a full project, Educating for Economic Awareness, which began work in 1987 (Ross, 1995b, p. 82).

Another of Carr and Harnett's 'institutions of dissension and critique' that the Government was to challenge was the teacher education institutions. The autonomy of the Universities in teacher education had long been compromised, in that admission numbers for initial teacher education courses in University Departments of Education were controlled by the DES in an attempt to plan teacher supply, and by the inspection of Teacher Education courses by HMI (unlike other University departments). The DES moved in 1983 to control the courses in much more detail, proposing new criteria for courses in initial teacher education, and requiring that prospective students must have or acquire a 'subject' of study relevant to the age that they would be teaching: it was argued that this would recognize 'teachers' needs for subject expertise if they are to have the confidence and ability to enthuse pupils and respond to their curiosity in their chosen subject fields' (DES, 1983c, para. 64). Teacher training was to be regulated by a new body, the Council for the Accreditation of Teacher Education (CATE), which would examine each course against the criteria. The HMI survey of middle schools (DES, 1983b) returned to the need to 'extend teachers' subject knowledge', which Rowland (1987, p. 90) argued 'may well be interpreted by teachers and others as recommending yet another means in the trend towards a more schematized approach to learning in which the focus is placed even more firmly on the subject matter than the child'. The qualifications about the use of the term 'subject' that had been made in the 1981 *School Curriculum* document appear to have been forgotten.

Joseph's appointment as Secretary of State for Education was unusual. He was a most trusted colleague of Margaret Thatcher, who had worked closely with him since her election as Conservative leader in 1975. He was frequently portrayed as some kind of guru to her, advising and supporting her on neo-liberal and monetarist policies. Predisposed to non-intervention, he claimed after he had left government that he would have preferred to leave all education to the market (Ball, 1990, p. 162).

A speech he had made in 1977 on the cycle of deprivation had included overtones of eugenic policies, and this had made it impossible for any prime minister to appoint him to any of the highest offices of state. He had become Secretary of State for Trade and Industry when the Conservatives were returned to power in 1979. This was historically an interventionist department, and, during Sir Keith's tenure, it made interventions into the curriculum arena of schools. The Industry Education Unit took a lively interest in developing science and technology in secondary schools, and financially supported the Schools Council Industry Project, and, occasionally, schools. The DTI also launched an innovative Computers in Schools programme in 1980, billed as a means of developing technological literacy in young people, but in reality no more than a means of supporting the UK micro-electronics industry.

In 1981 Joseph told Margaret Thatcher that he wanted to move from industry to education: 'with his belief that there was an anti-enterprise culture which had harmed Britain's economic performance over the years, it was natural that [he] should now wish to go to Education, where that culture had taken deep roots' (Thatcher, 1993, p. 151).

His intentions were to change that culture (Knight, 1990). On arriving at the DTI two years earlier, he had circulated his senior officials with copies of Adam Smith's *Wealth of Nations*: he now continued this policy at the DES by passing around copies of

Martin Wiener's *English Culture and the Decline of the Industrial Spirit, 1850–1980* (1981). Wiener attempted to explain Britain's industrial deterioration by the development of an anti-utilitarian, anti-change culture, which he claimed was entrenched in English middle-class attitudes. This desire to intervene to affect the fundamental attitudes of the educational establishment was at odds with his equally strong *laissez-faire* determination to let market forces prevail in education, with parental choice forcing up standards of excellence and driving out the mediocre. His resolution of this dilemma was to intervene to promote the virtues of allowing the market to prevail. Two strands stand out in this: the promotion of economic liberalism, to counter, as he saw it, generations of statist, centralist control of the economy and a prevailing culture of dependency; and second, a thrust towards making the educational system more vocational in orientation, merging the boundaries between education and training.

The first issue was to make pupils – and their teachers – aware of the processes of wealth creation. As was noted above, teacher education was in the process of being taken over by the DES, through the mechanism of the Council for the Accreditation of Teacher Education, which allowed the Secretary of State to approve every initial teacher education course as meeting specific criteria. These requirements were outlined in a White Paper, *Teaching Quality*. One of these was that all students should become aware of 'the ways in which pupils can be helped to acquire an understanding of the values of a free society and its economic and other foundations' (DES, 1983c).

Joseph began the process of influencing schools and teachers in post with a consultative letter to interested bodies, proposing that schools be asked to include economic awareness within the curriculum: this, he suggested, might include 'some understanding of such matters as the operation of supply and demand, price, quality, profit and loss, competition and monopoly; such aspects as the creation of the nation's private and public wealth, customer satisfaction, enterprise, management and productivity and taxation' (1985, quoted in SCDC/EEA, 1987).

A greater degree of vocationalism in the curriculum was introduced through the Technical and Vocational Initiative, introduced in 1983 by the Manpower Services Commission and funded by the Department of Employment. Direct grants totalling £46 million were made to volunteering LEAs to participate in the initial pilot project. The curriculum of 14–16-year-olds in the scheme was changed to include a far higher proportion of vocational and technical activities, run in collaboration with local employers. Before the pilot project was completed, the programme was extended to all schools, and the 1985–95 phase was estimated to cost £900 million – 'the largest single curriculum development project ever funded or attempted in Britain' (Tomlinson, 1993, p. 81). It has been claimed that David Young, the Secretary of State for Employment, announced the scheme in 1982 without consulting the DES, but it seems unlikely that Joseph, a political ally of Young's, was unaware of the proposal. The MSC initiative was based on a skills-deficit explanatory model of Britain's economic decline, while Joseph's economic education initiatives were premised on a culture lacking in enterprise, and an educational system isolated from industry, commerce and employers (Merson, 1992). There were now three Departments involved in attempting to direct the curriculum, a situation that was not resolved for more than a decade.

In the lead-up to the 1983 General Election, the Chancellor, Geoffrey Howe, established the Conservative Education Policy Group to contribute to the party's manifesto on education. Chaired by Lord Beloff, it recommended 'a more vocational slant to the curriculum', as well as a greater emphasis on moral and religious education. (Knight, 1990, p. 161; Lawton, 1994, p. 53). This instrumental approach, of making the curriculum responsive to industrial and commercial employers' needs, was very acceptable to Joseph, whose antecedents at the Department of Trade and Industry, and whose concern with what he saw as the emergence of a dependency culture in which many young people were simply unaware of how people earn their living, and how the nation created its wealth, have already been noted.

The DES document *The School Curriculum* (1981a) indicated that LEAs should have clear curriculum policies and ensure that they monitored how far their schools met these. Circular 6/81 (DES, 1981c) was a more explicit request for LEAs to carry this out, and to be prepared to report on progress. Two years later, Circular 8/83 (DES, 1983d) asked each LEA to provide a report on the progress that had been made, including a description of the roles of those in the education services in developing these. The DES found (DES, 1985h) that most authorities had drawn up statements following 'careful discussion and thought' and extensive consultations with both schools and governing bodies and parents. LEAs were addressing the questions of breadth and balance, and accepted that the curriculum needed to be relevant to what happens outside school. LEA staffing, particularly in the advisory services, was seen as being curriculum-led, and most schools were publishing their curriculum aims and beginning to evaluate how far they had been achieved (DES, 1985h, p. 12). The DES also identified five areas which it felt that LEAs needed to address further: how far teaching methods applied the curricular policies; primary–secondary school continuity; differentiation within the curriculum; policies for 'non-subject' elements in the curriculum; and the role of employers in curriculum development.

Following the re-election of the Conservatives in 1983, Joseph signalled that he wanted the discussion on curriculum objectives to be accelerated: there was a clear need, he argued, for parents and employers to reach a consensus with the educational establishment on a curriculum that was relevant (Lawton, 1994). It was necessary, he argued, 'to define the objectives of the main parts of the 5–16 curriculum so that everyone knows the level of attainment that should be achieved' (Joseph, 1984). A note by the DES, *The Organisation and Content of the 5–16 Curriculum* (DES, 1984b) extended (or amplified) the Secretary of State's requirements: any definition of curriculum objectives needed to be accompanied by descriptions of the contribution of each subject area or element; the content of the 5–16 curriculum as a whole (see *Table 4.3*); and objectives for attainment at the end of the primary phase and for age 16. The note emphasized that each subject, and the time given to it, needed to be justified by its particular contribution to the total knowledge, understanding, skills and competence that it was intended to foster – and to take into account the contribution made by other subjects. The process of defining this 'entails the removal of clutter, whether that takes the form of irrelevant or outdated material, or of unnecessary repetition' (para. 7). The suggested areas of curricular activity showed some match, in the primary phase at least, to the HMI 'areas of experience'.

This invitation to continue to discuss these aspects of the curriculum was also taken up, not least by HMI. (Two other specific contributions should also be mentioned. First, the DES had conducted its own review of science policy, in a consultative docu-

Table 4.3 The content of the 5–16 curriculum as a whole, as set out in The Organisation and Content of the 5–16 Curriculum, *1984*

Primary phase	*Secondary phase*
substantial competence in the use of language ... and in mathematics	English: 'no question that [this] should be compulsory for all pupils' Mathematics: 'no question that [this] should be compulsory for all pupils
introduction to science	all pupils should be introduced, under whatever guise, to each of [physics, chemistry and biology]
	foreign languages: some of the least able pupils should not do this; the majority should study one for 3 years; some should study one for 3 years and another for 2/3 years
worthwhile offerings which develop understanding in the areas of history, geography and RE	religious education during the five years, every pupil should study, on a worthwhile scale, history, geography, and, under whatever guise (which may be history or geography) the principles underlying a free society and some basic economic awareness. But choices will have to be made in years [10] and [11]
a range of aesthetic activities	aesthetic subjects ought to be on offer in due variety, but need not be taken concurrently ... in each of the five years each pupil should have at least either music or art or drama, and every pupil's five-year programme should contain all three
	the application of knowledge and skills ... notably mathematics and the sciences. Computers provide the opportunity to apply knowledge and skills in a wide range of subjects: 'the removal of "clutter", in the form of knowledge which is less than essential ... would make room for the practical application of what is learned'
opportunities for craft and practical work leading to some experience of design and technology and of solving problems	CDT – over five years, all pupils should this – 'to study and solve problems involving the use of materials, which entails some element of designing and making things'
	home economics for all pupils in the first three years [7–9]; then an option
	pre-vocational studies, specifically to assist young people prepare for the 'world of work' (such as TVEI)
physical and health education	physical education should be for all in years [7–9]: it might then be an option
introduction to computers	
some insights into the adult world, including how people earn their living	social, environmental education, health education – room is commonly found for these

Source: DES, 1984b, paras 8, 17–29.

ment (DES, 1982c) and in a *Statement of Policy* (DES, 1985g). Second, a major independent review of mathematics education, the Cockcroft Report (DES, 1982b) had
demonstrated the great diversities of mathematical understandings in school pupils
and the population at large: it maintained there was a seven-year difference in the
levels of conceptual understanding shown by the most and least able pupils at age 11.)
The HMI response, however, was the most substantial and comprehensive. The 'areas
of experience' approach, which HMI had begun with five local authorities in 1978
with *Curriculum 11–16* (DES, 1977b) was continued, and a fresh report on implementation and evaluation was published (DES, 1983a). A specific and extensive document
on history was published in 1985 (DES, 1985f). In 1984 they launched a new
curriculum series, *Curriculum Matters*, which over the next five years covered seventeen
different curriculum areas (see *Table 4.4*).

The series followed a fairly standard format, identifying the contribution each
subject or area made to different areas of experience, identifying skills, concepts,

Table 4.4 The Curriculum Matters *series by HM Inspectorate, 1984–9*

Year	Title
1984	*English from 5 to 16: Curriculum Matters 1*
1985	*The Curriculum from 5 to 16: Curriculum Matters 2*
	Mathematics from 5 to 16: Curriculum Matters 3
	Music from 5 to 16: Curriculum Matters 4
	Home Economics from 5 to 16: Curriculum Matters 5
1986	*English from 5 to 16: Curriculum Matters 1* (2nd edn incorporating responses)
	Health Education from 5 to 16: Curriculum Matters 6
	Geography from 5 to 16: Curriculum Matters 7
1987	*Mathematics from 5 to 16: Curriculum Matters 3* (2nd edn incorporating responses)
	Modern Languages to 16: Curriculum Matters 8
	Craft, Design and Technology from 5 to 16: Curriculum Matters 9
1988	*Careers Education and Guidance from 5 to 16: Curriculum Matters 10*
	History from 5 to 16: Curriculum Matters 11
	Classics from 5 to 16: Curriculum Matters 12
1989	*Environmental Education from 5 to 16: Curriculum Matters 13*
	Personal and Social Education from 5 to 16: Curriculum Matters 14
	Information Technology from 5 to 16: Curriculum Matters 15
	Physical Education from 5 to 16: Curriculum Matters 16
	Drama from 5 to 16: Curriculum Matters 17
	Other publications on the curriculum
1982	*Mathematics Counts: Report of the Committee of Inquiry into the Teaching of Mathematics in Schools* [Chair: Dr W. Cockcroft]
1985	*Science 5–16: A Statement of Policy* [DES publication, not HMI]
1985	*History in the Primary and Secondary Years: An HMI View*

attitudes and knowledge objectives, and exemplifying what pupils aged (usually) 11 and 16 might be expected to cover and understand. Perhaps the most significant volume in the series was the second, *The Curriculum from 5 to 16* (DES, 1985a). This – 'the best professional commentary on the school curriculum yet written' (Tomlinson, 1993, p. 83) – was largely the work of Colin Richards, newly recruited to HMI to coordinate the Inspectorate's curriculum policy (see also Richards, 1988). Drawing on both the 11–16 project and on primary school practice, it extended the 1977 HMI areas of experience to draw in elements of the DES/Joseph 1984 position. The curriculum was conceptualized as having two essential and complementary perspectives: areas of learning and experience and elements of learning – knowledge, concepts, skills and attitudes to be developed. It was argued that these perspectives could accommodate all the ways schools commonly used to organize teaching and learning. Cross-curricular issues (listed as environmental education, health education, information technology, political education, education in economic understanding), preparation for the world of work and careers education should also be accommodated in the framework.

The areas of learning and experience – the domains through which humanity has gained access to understanding the world – were analysed in some detail, and differed only slightly from the 1977 list (see *Table 4.5*). These were to be an analytic and planning tool: each would have to be sufficiently represented in each pupil's work, and would assist in the development of the elements of learning. The elements of learning were described in less detail (other than as a grouping of skills, to cover areas such as communication, observation, study, problem-solving, physical and practical, creative and imaginative, numerical, personal and social) (DES, 1985a, para. 100).

Curriculum Matters marked what was to be perhaps the last attempt to square the

Table 4.5 *Areas of experience in the curriculum, 1977 and 1984 compared*

1977	1984
aesthetic and creative	aesthetic and social
ethical	moral
linguistic	linguistic and literary
mathematical	mathematical
physical	physical
scientific	scientific
social and political	human and social
spiritual	spiritual
technological	

Source: DES, 1977b, p. 6; DES, 1985a, para. 33.

experience of the pedagogical approach to the curriculum with the arguments for relevance and technology-focused vocationalism of Joseph. Both the Secretary of State and HMI appeared at this moment to be in greater agreement than at any point since before the Great Debate, and both were united in their scepticism of a curriculum that was defined in terms of traditional academic subjects.

Many of the ideas contained in Joseph's 1984 North of England Education Conference speech were expanded in the following year's White Paper *Better Schools* (DES, 1985h). Partnership in achieving curriculum consensus was still the guiding objective: the paper held that there was now some broad agreement on objectives and content, and that this was an important and necessary step towards raising standards. The process was specifically acknowledged as a long-scale commitment to partnership with the LEAs: the government acknowledged 'the magnitude of the task it is setting itself and its partners. Objectives cannot be agreed for all time. Even initial agreement will take several years to accomplish' (1985h, para. 32). The curriculum itself was described very much in terms of the previous year's Note: the primary phase descriptions carefully avoid the names of specific subjects, and endorse 'appropriately varied teaching strategies and schemes of work' (para. 63). The tenor of the White Paper was that there was a planned consensus on curriculum development to be shared between schools, LEAs and government, and that this curriculum would be a balance (albeit a balance of tension) between the pedagogic concerns of the professionals (expressed largely through HMI and the LEAs) for a mixture of skills, knowledge, concepts and attitudes within areas of experience, and the vocational instrumentalism of the Government. This framework was openly conceded to be 'as yet incomplete: much remains to be done, at all levels within the education service, before the shared aim of broad agreement about the objectives of the school curriculum can be realised' (para. 87).

Shortly after the publication of *Better Schools* in March 1985, Joseph announced his intention to retire from ministerial office after the next election, which was due, at the latest, in 1988. The final two years of his time in office were overtaken and dominated by a long-running dispute with the teacher unions over pay and conditions. Working to rule and strikes in certain areas began in the summer of 1984, and these were extended in the next year: it was not until 1986 that the unions reached agreement with the LEAs, conceding the management control over conditions in return for fairly substantial increases in pay. Joseph had been an interventionist in driving out what he perceived as conservative professional cartels critical of his policies (the Schools Council), and in controlling the content and nature of teacher education (imposing CATE on the Universities and Polytechnics). He had ensured that his concerns about young people being unaware of the wealth creation process and of the 'economic realities' of life were to be addressed within the curriculum. He had also brought with him the concerns of the Department of Trade and Industry that schools were anti-industrial, and that there was a deep-rooted culture in the educational establishment that resented the instrumentalism of a vocationally orientated curriculum. But he had sought to incorporate the concerns of HMI and the LEAs, and to forge a partnership with them in defining curriculum objectives. The development of an agreed curriculum no longer seemed to be a point of contest.

The New Right and Curriculum Policy

The consensus and agreement were short-lived, however. To examine the reasons for this, it is necessary to examine the various ideologies and beliefs within the Conservative party at this time, and in particular the beliefs of what was known as the 'new right', the radical conservatism that identified itself with the policies of Margaret Thatcher. Joseph was an advocate of monetarism, and of minimal government intervention, in education as in everything else. In conversation with Stephen Ball he said,

> We have a bloody state system. I wish we hadn't got it. I wish we'd taken a different route in 1870. We got the ruddy state involved. I don't want it. I don't think we know how to do it. ... We've got compulsory education, which is a responsibility of hideous importance.
>
> (Ball, 1990, p. 62)

But he nevertheless took the responsibility of encouraging the development of a vocational orientation to the curriculum, and of encouraging the system to develop (capitalist) economic understanding for all, in the pursuit of wealth-creation. Within the new right movement, neo-conservatives such as Roger Scruton objected to this conception of curriculum relevance, as promoted in *Better Schools*, because, by reducing the role of traditional subjects, it threatened the reproduction of traditional high culture and the class structure enshrined within this (Scruton, 1991).

The divisions within the new right are important in understanding the changes of 1987. The following categories are not immutable, and individuals moved between them over time. But it is possible to see a number of competing curriculum ideologies at work in 1985 (drawing on Ball, 1990; also Chitty, 1988b; Coulby, 1989 and Whitty, 1988). At the risk of gross over-simplification, there seemed to be two distinct strands within the new right. There was a kaleidoscopic pattern of perhaps eight different philosophies, some of which were overlapping or in alliance with one another at various times. *Table 4.6* shows these schematically.

Table 4.6 Ideological groupings about the curriculum, c. 1985

Old right (A) elite/underclass socio-economic reproduction	Right (B) industrial training
New right: type 1 (C) neo-conservative – cultural restorationists	New right: type 2 (D) neo-liberal – market forces
Old left (E) training and class mobility reproduction	Left: type 1 (F) equal opportunities
New left (G) industrial trainer	Left: type 2 (H) learning-centred

Curriculum: Construction and Critique

Each group had a rather different understanding of the purposes of education, and, as a result, a different view of what curriculum was necessary to achieve them.

(A) Old right – elite/underclass socio-economic reproduction

Purposes of education

Education sorts pupils into a large underclass and an elite ruling class: the elite are given a suitable 'high culture' that distinguishes them from the rest, and are given suitable social and other skills to manage and rule, while the underclass have a compliant and accepting attitude inculcated through the schools.

Curriculum implications

High status knowledge through traditional subjects for the elite, taught in socially exclusive institutions; low status versions of knowledge for the *hoi polloi*. Examinations form the essential dividing mechanism.

Beliefs held by

Many traditional conservatives, and probably covertly by some senior civil servants (e.g. the author of the *Framework for the School Curriculum*, DES, 1981a).

(B) Right – industrial training

Purposes of education

Education is essentially a utilitarian activity, and should be linked to the needs of the nation to maintain and perpetuate itself. In the current situation of relative economic decline, this requires a break with traditional educational values.

Curriculum implications

A vocational direction, with a particular focus on technology and science, links with employers and entrepreneurs.

Beliefs held by

Keith Joseph, David Young (DTI).

(C) New right: type 1 – neo-conservative – cultural restorationists

Purposes of education

Education should reassert the traditional national values, and transmit the heritage of a golden age, when the nation was homogeneous and values were not contended. The national (English) heritage has been unnecessarily diluted by moral relativism and increasing social diversity/fragmentation.

Curriculum implications

Traditional academic subjects (i.e. the traditional Public/Grammar school subjects, with a traditional content that avoids contention and critical scrutiny, will restore the heritage and traditional ('Victorian') values.

Beliefs held by

Some reformist new-right conservatives, e.g. Roger Scruton, Margaret Thatcher; and also by pragmatist (or opportunist) conservatives such as Kenneth Baker.

(D) New right: type 2 – neo-liberal, market forces

Purposes of education

Education is a commodity: if it has a value, then the free market will determine what is provided, at what price, and who will purchase it. Freeing the organization of schools and the content of the curriculum will ensure that what societies, individuals, firms and families want will be provided most efficiently.

Curriculum implications

Subjects and courses should be left to meet the perceived needs of employers, parents, etc., take-up and payment for them will reveal their true worth.

Beliefs held by

Stuart Sexton, adviser to Keith Joseph at the DES, Adam Smith Institute, Dennis O'Keeffe.

(E) Old left – training and class mobility reproduction

Purposes of education

Education provides a ladder of opportunity, by which bright working-class children can aspire to move up the occupational and social ladder away from their origins.

Curriculum implications

A highly traditional curriculum, of grammar/public school subjects, with the same examination system, will best demonstrate the intellectual ability of successful working-class children and enable them to be compared directly with the children of higher social classes.

(F) Left: type 1 – equal opportunities

Purposes of education

Education is the means of redressing social inequality: wealth, class, gender and ethnic background should be immaterial in determining a child's chance of success. Private education and other forms of selection, streaming, etc. raise unwanted barriers.

Curriculum implications

The curriculum should be freed from particular cultural biases that privilege children from particular backgrounds: subjects and activities should therefore be pluralist, multicultural, free from stereotypical assumptions.

Beliefs held by

Shirley Williams, Neil Kinnock, Roy Hattersley, the ILEA.

(G) New left – industrial trainer

Purposes of education

Education has to be a utilitarian activity, and should be linked to the needs of the society to maintain and perpetuate itself, economically and socially. In the current situation of relative economic decline and social change, this requires new educational values.

Curriculum implications

A skills-based technical direction, with a particular focus on technology and science; but also a curriculum that is geared towards all of adult life, including leisure, democratic and social participation, etc.

(H) Left: type 2 – learning-centred

Purposes of education

Education is to develop the whole child/pupil in a variety of areas of experience, at a pace and in a direction that is governed by the learner's predisposition, and harnessed to their speed of learning.

Curriculum implications

A break from traditional subjects-as-bodies-of-knowledge: a greater emphasis on process, on learning by doing.

Beliefs held by

HMI, as shown in *Curriculum Matters 2: The Curriculum from 5 to 16*.

This schema uses a left–right axis, but it is of note that this axis is not necessarily the most significant. Both left and right include 'industrial trainers', and there are also, on both sides, traditionalists who want, perhaps for different reasons, to maintain a conventional subjects-based culture. There are also groups to be found on both sides arguing for greater freedom in the curriculum, as various forms of liberalization. The schema will be returned to in Chapter 9, when the various groups can be plotted within an analysis of different curricular philosophies.

Of importance in the current analysis are the beliefs and activities of the two new right groups. Both groups were dominated by highly opinionated individuals, who wrote extensively in pamphlets and booklets – often published by the growing number of privately endowed think tanks that were established in the 1980s. Later – much later – their efforts were seen by many Conservatives as insidious and destructive: one senior back-bencher was to denounce them as 'the lords of misrule' (Thornton, 1992, p. 173). Their writings were very largely self-referential, or referring only to each other's work; any commentary or criticism by others was denounced by them as the work of self-serving professionals – a 'discourse of derision' (Ball, 1990, p. 22). Their degree of influence on the formation of the National Curriculum was extraordinary.

For both groups the curriculum was an issue that arose in the early 1980s, as a necessary outcome of their earlier interests in the educational system. Chitty identified their activities and influence beginning in the mid-1970s, following the economic crises of 1973 and 1976 (Chitty, 1988b). Their concerns at that time were with structures and standards in education: the neo-liberals argued for greater choice and the creation of a market system that would provide the necessary discipline; the neo-conservatives saw dangers both to basic standards and to cultural and moral norms in educational emphases on equality, anti-racism, cultural pluralism and moral relativism. The neo-liberals were neutral on the effects of these issues, but neither group looked to the curriculum implications of their position until the mid-1980s, even though curriculum reform and definition had been by that time on the agenda of the DES and HMI for the best part of a decade.

The new right's relative silence on the curriculum is shown, for example, in the Social Affairs Unit's *The Pied Pipers of Education* (Anderson, 1981), in which the assembled ex Black-Paperites were primarily concerned with educational structures and the machinery of education: voucher systems, academic tenure, teacher education, and the like. At that time, it was only O'Keeffe who raised curricular issues for schools, in his discussion on truancy. He suggested that truancy could be analysed as a rational response to irrelevant curriculum subjects. He identified post-registration truancy, where school children selectively absent themselves from particular lessons, and suggested that children make curricular decisions (to attend lessons) either for reasons of investment in their future employment (for example, technical drawing) or for consumption arising from the intrinsic interest of the material (for example, O'Keeffe suggests, sociology) (1981, p. 33). What is significant is that O'Keeffe wrote from the neo-liberal wing (or faction) of the new right, not from the neo-conservative wing (Rawling, 1990).

The major neo-liberal challenge to the school curriculum was the publication of *The Wayward Curriculum* in 1986, edited by O'Keeffe. This combined O'Keeffe's own libertarian view, that the curriculum should be diverse and that parents should be able to exercise some genuine choice over which subjects were appropriate or useful for their children, with the academic elitism shown by a number of his contributors. O'Keeffe himself attempts to straddle both positions: he agrees with the neo-liberals that there should be a curricular choice, and that the discipline of such 'market forces' will determine the variety and quantities of the various subjects, but at the same time he is concerned that the current curriculum was no longer adequately transmitting 'the history and culture of society' (O'Keeffe, 1986, p. 12). Some of his contributors show the same confusion: Bantock argues first that the 'non-academic pupil' should have a curricular offering that 'takes his [*sic*] needs seriously', arguing that it is 'ideological confusion [that] all must follow the *same* curriculum [and], must take the *same* examination' (1986, pp. 20–1; emphasis as in original); and at the same time asserts that there is a core culture that must be enshrined in the curriculum of all. Other contributors were more decidedly neo-conservative, arguing, for example, that English teaching should explicitly develop first utilitarian skills, and then stress the cultural heritage that English is claimed to enshrine, eschewing notions of personal and social growth that many English teachers were alleged to have adopted – 'in some schools, English has become a rag-bag of social topics, a substitute sociology, even a form of therapy' (Barcan, 1986, p. 42).

The position of the neo-liberals was that they generally favoured exposing all elements of education to the disciplines of the market, thus offering a degree of choice to the 'consumer' (though with some lack of clarity as to whether 'the consumer' of education was the pupils, the parents, the employers, or some wider community). Most of them argued this case particularly for a range of structural aspects in the provision of educational services – for the abolition of the LEAs, for vouchers, for open enrolment, and so on. Some also argued for offering a wide range of curricular subjects, and some even extended the argument to suggest that school attendance be voluntary from a much younger age.

Regan's contribution to O'Keeffe's book argued differently: sociology and politics would be useful as *practical* subjects if their role was simply 'to equip pupils for citizenship of a democracy' (1986, p. 130), but in practice they had become both academicized and politicized. While Regan portrayed sociology as an essentially utilitarian subject (teaching practical life skills), O'Keeffe (1981) saw it as academic ('curricular consumption', see above): they agree that, suitably purged of left-wing theorists, it should be allowed to compete in the curricular market place. While these neo-liberal arguments were focused on secondary education, they were also applied to primary schools, where 'sociology' was seen to reside in social studies topic work. Hill (1986) makes this relationship specific in his analysis of urban studies in primary and secondary education in the Inner London Education Authority.

The Hillgate Group linked the neo-liberal critique of current sociology with the neo-conservative position, arguing that 'the new "soft" subjects have been nurtured by an inadequate and politically biased sociology, whose colonization of the school curriculum ... is cause for concern' (Hillgate Group, 1986, p. 5). The neo-conservative case derided sociology not because of the way it was taught, but because of its very existence. It grouped sociology together with other 'unsuitable or dubious newer subjects' (O'Keeffe, 1986, p. 12) – peace studies, urban studies, women's studies, anti-racist education and political education. From a completely different perspective, Whitty characterizes a rather similar list as 'radical curriculum initiatives' (Whitty, 1992, p. 96). The argument was not merely that these were potentially partisan, but that their presence cluttered up the curriculum to the detriment of the traditional subjects, and thus interfered with the transmission of standard cultural values (Jones, 1991). This was linked to the neo-conservative critique of egalitarian initiatives in education, particularly over multiculturalism (e.g. Flew, 1986). In terms of the primary school curriculum, project work, discovery methods, and learning through play filled the same role, squeezing out teaching of the core basic skills, and thus compromising standards. The objections of the neo-conservatives, such as Scruton, to the vocationalism and the concept of curriculum relevance that Joseph was advancing in *Better Schools* was that it potentially denied the role of the traditional subjects in reproducing traditional high culture, and (implicitly) the social class structure that this perpetuated.

David Marquand highlights this division of the new right, though outside the context of education. In 1988 he reported having had a conversation with 'a rather senior high Tory' whose analysis was that the liberal wing Conservative wets had been totally routed within the Cabinet:

> Everyone accepted the dry economic diagnosis, and everyone agreed with the dry economic cure. But, he went on, there is a very acute tension within the government even so ... between those who want to sell off every cathedral close to Tescos in the name of the free market, and those who want to preserve them in the name of being British, or at least being English: between those who believe in economic liberalism without qualification, and those who wish to erect barriers to market forces ... in the name of continuity, community and nation.
>
> (Marquand, 1988, p. 172)

Final Steps to the National Curriculum

Keith Joseph left office in May 1986, having been fatally weakened by the teachers' dispute. He was replaced by Kenneth Baker, who claimed in his autobiography that he was keen to be transferred to the education brief (Baker, 1993). While Joseph's political trajectory had been horizontal – he could rise no further, and was maintained on the plateau of middle-ranking Cabinet office – Baker was on an ascendant path. This was in itself unusual in an appointment as Secretary of State for Education and Science: as Lord Boyle, a previous incumbent, had remarked, the education portfolio tended in British politics to be a politician's graveyard (Kogan, 1978, pp. 117–18). Baker, initially seen as a Tory 'wet', had gradually worked his way up in Thatcher's governments, moving steadily rightwards and towards free-market monetarism, leading the privatization of British Telecom when at the DTI, and then moving to local government, where he led the abolition of the GLC. Lawton (1994, p. 57) claims that he had a long-standing interest in education – he had been chair of the Hansard Society, which promoted education about the workings of Parliament, and had been responsible for the Microcomputers in Schools initiative. Unlike Joseph, he appeared to be a committed centralist, unwilling to continue notions of partnership with the LEAs (his reform of municipal authorities showed his antipathy to alternative centres of power). His educational background and philosophy were very much in the traditional humanist mould: though he had worked in industry before entering Parliament, he saw himself as a champion of English verse, as a commentator on history; he was not a keen advocate of vocationalism or instrumental education.

He was also a political opportunist. The Thatcher administrations had been successively moving rightwards since 1979, as the various 'wets' and one-nation Tories with whom she had been obliged to balance her Cabinets were eased out of office (see Marquand, 1988, quoted above). Thatcher had resolved to make education one of the two keynote issues of the forthcoming election, and of her third administration's legislative programme (Thatcher, 1993, p. 589). Thatcher's brief for Baker was to radicalize educational provision in a way that would strike a balance between the neo-conservatives and the neo-liberals of the new right, rather than Joseph's balance between the industrial trainers and the views of the professional Inspectorate:

> I ... believed that too many teachers were less competent and more ideological than their predecessors. I distrusted the new 'child-centred' teaching techniques, the emphasis on imaginative engagement rather than learning facts, and the modern tendency to blur the lines of discrete subjects and incorporate them in wider, less definable entities like 'humanities'. And I knew ... that too many people left school without a basic knowledge of reading, writing and arithmetic.
>
> (Thatcher, 1993, p. 590)

Baker took this neo-conservative subject-based line on the curriculum, and tied it to the neo-liberal position of establishing a market place in education. A market depends upon consumers being able to make comparisons between different providers, and therefore being able to contrast the value offered by different schools. This would be achieved by league tables of performance, so that there would be some form of apparently objective assessment of what pupils had achieved, a yardstick for parental choice. To make comparative assessments, the schools would have to follow identical curricula, and therefore a National Curriculum was necessary:

> the scale of the problem could only be tackled by a coherent national programme, and time was not on our side. I knew what I wanted in the package, and I knew I would have to drive it through my Department ... and steer a major piece of legislation through Parliament and around all the obstacles which the vested education interest would throw in its way.
>
> (Baker, 1993, p. 164)

He saw as not least among these vested interests the civil servants of the DES and the Inspectorate: he claimed to detect

> a clear 1960s ethos and a very clear agenda which permeated virtually all the civil servants. It was rooted in 'progressive' orthodoxies, in egalitarianism and in the comprehensive schools system. ... Not only was the Department in league with the teacher unions, University Departments of Education, teacher training theories, and local authorities, it also acted as their protector against any threats which Ministers might pose. If the civil servants were the guardians of this culture, then Her Majesty's Inspectors of Education were its priesthood.
>
> (Baker, 1993, p. 168)

If this autobiographical account, written six years later, accurately reflects his ambitions and intentions at the time, then it is clear that Baker had set out to launch a major assault on those whom he saw as the traditional defenders of the curriculum – and that he had very little appreciation of the divisions and debates that had opened up over the previous decade.

5 The Imposed Curriculum: 1986–1998

In December 1986 Kenneth Baker, the newly appointed Secretary of State, announced in a television interview (ITV, *Weekend World*) that, if the Conservatives were returned for a third term in the election that was widely anticipated would be held in the first part of the following year, he would introduce a 'national core curriculum'. At the North of England Education Conference in the following month he drew comparisons between the English system and those in European countries (particularly in West Germany and France) (Baker, 1993, p. 165). They, he said, had 'tended to centralise and standardise. We have gone for confusion and variety. ... The school curriculum has been left to individual schools and teachers' (DES, 1987e). Later that month he said to the Society of Chief Education Officers,

> we should now move quickly to a national curriculum ... our school curriculum is not as good as it could be and needs to be ... we need to move nearer to the kind of arrangements which other European countries operate with success.
>
> (DES, 1987f)

The reasons given at this stage were comparative standards of achievement to European economic competitors. The link to the establishment of a market between schools was set in April, when – before any legislation – Baker appointed two working groups to advise on mathematics and science. (An English working group was not appointed at the same time, probably because the Kingman Committee – appointed by Baker in January 1987 to inquire into the teaching of the English Language – was still at work (DES, 1988e).) The working groups were required to set 'clear and challenging attainment targets ... for the key ages of seven, eleven and fourteen', from which they could set programmes of study containing 'the essential content, skills and processes to be taught in each subject' at each level (DES, 1987g).

The National Curriculum 5–16: A Consultation Document

The General Election was called in May 1987, and the Conservative Manifesto put the national core curriculum as first of its four major reforms:

It is vital to ensure that all pupils between the age of 5 to 16 study a basic range of subjects – including maths, English and science. In each of these basic subjects syllabuses will be published and attainment targets set so the progress of pupils can be assessed at around ages 7, 11 and 14, and in preparation for the GCSE at 16. Parents, teachers and pupils will then know how well each child is doing.

(Conservative Party, 1987)

The terms of reference of the working groups added the assessment elements of the National Curriculum, and the Manifesto made it clear that this assessment would allow national comparisons to be drawn between schools. But the defined subjects were, at this stage, still only three core elements. This was Thatcher's preference: 'I wanted the DES to concentrate on establishing a basic syllabus for English, mathematics and science with simple tests to show what pupils knew' (Thatcher, 1993, p. 593). Baker, however, wanted a broader – perhaps a more humanist – curriculum, that was 'broad and balanced', rather than narrowly concentrating on basic skills.

Their disagreement on this was set in the context of the Cabinet Sub-Committee on Education Reform, which set the main points of the Education Bill that would introduce the National Curriculum. Some of its workings are described by Lawson (1992). Thatcher, as Chair, would begin meetings 'putting forward various ideas' (some of which were derived from a briefing paper by one of Lawson's Treasury civil servants, which argued for the abolition of the LEAs, others of which came from the No. 10 Policy Group head, Brian Griffiths). After discussion,

Margaret would sum up and give Kenneth his marching orders. He would then return to the next meeting with a worked out proposal which bore little resemblance to what everyone else recalled as having been agreed at the previous meeting, and owed rather more to his officials at the DES. After receiving a metaphorical handbagging for his pains, he would come back with something that corresponded more closely to her ideas.

(Lawson, 1992, pp. 609–10)

But he prevailed on the breadth of the curriculum. The consultation document on the National Curriculum, published the month after the Conservatives were returned to office for the third time (DES, 1987h), proposed a curriculum based largely around ten foundation subjects, three of which were to be considered core subjects. Each would have programmes of study, with levels of attainment, and most would be assessed at the end of each key stage. The subjects selected were the simple traditional and unadorned subjects of the public and grammar school, and bear an uncanny resemblance to the 1904 *Regulations for Secondary Schools* (see *Table 5.1*): but while the 1904 regulations applied only to secondary schools, and the *Handbook of Suggestions for the Consideration of Teachers* published by the Board of Education in the following year specifically advocated a quite different approach for the elementary schools, the list of subjects published in 1987 was for all children from the age of 5 (except for modern foreign languages, which would start at 11). And, in shades of the 1980 *Framework for the School Curriculum* (DES, 1980a), indications of the proportions of time for different subjects were introduced again.

The *Consultation Document* (DES, 1987h) presents a detailed programme of activity for the following six or seven years. It begins by arguing that the 'agreement' reached to date on the aims of education had led to some, but insufficient, progress in establishing a good curriculum: what was now needed was to raise standards of attainment faster. While 'some' schools offered a good curriculum, 'many schools offer something far less good. The Government does not find this acceptable. Nor do parents and others in the community' (para. 7). A National Curriculum, with assessment, would,

Table 5.1 *Subjects in the* National Curriculum, *1988; subjects in the* Regulations for Secondary Schools, *1904: both with suggested time allocations*

1988 National Curriculum				1904 Regulations	
Primary	*Time*	*Secondary*	*Time*	*(Secondary)*	*Time*
Core subjects					
English		English	10%	English Language and Literature	13%
Mathematics	over 50%	Mathematics	10%	Mathematics	13%
Science		Combined Sciences	10–20%	Science	10%
Other foundation subjects					
		Modern Language	10%	Other language(s)	11–15%
Technology		Technology	10%		
History		History	10%	History	13%
Geography	less than 40%	Geography		Geography	13%
Art		Art	10%	Drawing	?5%
Music		Music			
Physical Education		Physical Education	5%	Physical Exercise	?5%
				Housewifery	?5%
				Manual work	?5%
Good practice: total up to 80–90%				Total: 90%	

it argued, raise standards by ensuring a broad and balanced range of subjects for all, and set clear objectives for achievement – under-expectation by teachers was 'a weakness far too frequently apparent' (para. 8). This populist approach seems to have been designed to alienate the profession. Besides raising standards, the National Curriculum would, it was claimed also help parents' job mobility, because they would be able to move areas without fear of discontinuity in their children's education; and it would mean that schools and teachers would be more accountable for the education that they offered: parents, LEAs and employers could all judge effectiveness of schools and their pupils' outcomes.

Each of the ten subjects would have a non-statutory subject working group to recommend programmes of work and attainment levels. The three core subjects were expected to take the majority of curriculum time in primary schools, and 30–40 per cent of the time in secondary schools. These and the foundation subjects 'commonly take up 80–90 per cent of the curriculum in schools where there is good practice' (para. 16): Religious education was already legally required as an addition to the foundation, and there were also other subjects or themes to be taught through subjects.

Attainment targets would be challenging at each level: the programmes of study would set out both the common content and the knowledge, skills and processes necessary to reach the targets. Assessment at 7, 11, 14 and 16 would be in all subjects, and though much of it 'would be done by teachers as an integral part of normal classroom work ... at the heart of the assessment process there will be national prescribed tests done by all pupils to supplement the individual teachers' assessments. Teachers will administer and mark these, but their marking – and their assessments overall – will be externally moderated' (para. 29). A special Task Group on Assessment and Testing was to be appointed to recommend a common strategy; it would report by December of 1987. National Records of Achievement would record each pupil's progress, and all assessment results would be made public, so that parents could compare their children's progress, teachers could decide on appropriate learning strategies, and parents, governing bodies, employers and the local community could assess a school's performance against other local schools: this would also help parents in selecting schools.

A National Curriculum Council (NCC) was to oversee the whole process: it was to replace the short-lived Schools Curriculum Development Committee. Members would be appointed in a personal, rather than a representative capacity, and would include professional educators. It would be funded wholly by the government, unlike the SCDC, which had been still co-funded with the LEAs. A Schools Examinations and Assessment Council (SEAC) would replace the Secondary Examinations Council.

The legislation necessary to implement the National Curriculum (and other changes, such as the local management of school budgets and the introduction of grant-maintained status, which added to the marketization strategy) was part of what Kenneth Baker called the Great Educational Reform Bill, which he proudly announced as the most significant legislation since the 1944 Act (and longer than that Act). Margaret Thatcher gave these reforms a major place in her speech to the Conservative Party Conference that October:

The most important task in this Parliament is to raise the quality of education. It's in the national interest. ... We want education to be part of the answer to Britain's problems, not part of the cause.

Too often, our children don't get the education they need – the education they deserve. And in the inner cities – where youngsters must have a decent education if they are to have a better future – that opportunity is all too often snatched from them by hard-left education authorities and extremist teachers.

Children who need to be able to count and multiply are learning anti-racist mathematics – whatever that may be.

Children who need to be able to express themselves in clear English are being taught political slogans.

Children who need to be taught to respect traditional moral values are being taught that they have an inalienable right to be gay.

Children who need encouragement – and so many children do – are being taught that our society offers them no future.

I believe that government must take the primary responsibility for setting standards for the education of our children. And that's why we are establishing a national curriculum for basic subjects.

It is vital that all children master essential skills: reading, writing, spelling, grammar, arithmetic; and that they understand basic science and technology.

(Margaret Thatcher, 1987, quoted in Moon et al., 1989, pp. 277–8)

As the Education Reform Bill passed through the legislative process, the mechanics of creating the National Curriculum moved forward. Some 10,000 responses to the National Curriculum consultation document (and a similar number concerning the other issues raised in the parallel consultations on issues such as the establishment of grant-maintained schools) were composed and submitted in the period from early July to mid-September 1997. Maclure suggests that many could not have been read (in Haviland, 1988): they were deposited in the library of the House of Commons (from which Haviland edited a collection of extracts (*Take Care, Mr Baker*, 1988).

Mathematics and English

The Working Group on Mathematics had very quickly run into difficulties. The rather polemical account by Duncan Graham (who became the Working Group's second chair, and then the chairman and chief executive of the NCC) needs to be treated with some caution (Graham, 1993, pp. 23–38). Members of the Group had been selected, he suggests, on the advice of HMI, and thus included professionals associated with curriculum innovation and change, which was not what Baker or Thatcher intended. Graham's analysis is that the membership represented an outdated style of educational enquiry: what was needed by Baker, he says, was a rapid, authoritative response that could be imposed on all schools. The first Chair, Roger Blin-Stoyle (also chair of the SCDC) found himself unable to keep the widely differing views of the Group together. On the one hand was Sig Prais, from the neo-right National Institute of Economic and Social Research, who claimed that he had been appointed personally by the Prime Minister to represent her views; on the other the professional mathematics educators, led by Hillary Shuard and Hugh Burkhardt. The *Interim Report* (DES, 1987i) of the Working Group did not meet with Baker's approval (or Thatcher's). Baker publicly castigated Blin-Stoyle for what he saw as shortcomings in the interim report:

> I regard it as essential to establish a clear structure of age related targets ... I want the group to tackle this as a matter of urgency. ... Your final report will need to recognise the risks as well as the opportunities which calculators in the classroom offer. ... I want the group to consider the balance between open-ended practical problem solving approaches and the more traditional pencil and paper practice of important skills and techniques.
>
> (DES, 1987i)

Prais made a note of dissent to the *Interim Report*; Blin-Stoyle resigned and was replaced by Graham.

The Task Group on Assessment and Testing (TGAT) made its first report in late December, which was published the following month (DES, 1988f), with three supplementary reports in March 1988 (DES, 1988g). Chaired by Paul Black, Professor of Science Education at King's College London, it took pains to reassure the teaching profession that the assessment procedures it proposed were firmly based in good curriculum practice. 'Promoting children's learning is a principal aim of schools. Assessment lies at the heart of this process' (1988f, para. 3). Assessment should inform teachers on the success of their teaching, and be used by them to form strategies for the next work to be tackled with the individual child. The group clarified the lexicon of assessment: for example, it distinguished between norm-referenced testing (where comparative judgments are made about a child's performance in relation to her or his peers) and criterion-referenced tests (which judge progress against set benchmarks). They advocated ten levels of achievement that would represent all the possible levels of attainment between the age of 5 and 16, so that the levels of competency were not related to specific years of education. Each subject working group, they recommended, should put forward a sequence of ten levels for each profile component within the subject. The forms of assessment were to be a mixture of teacher assessments, which were recommended as the major element, moderated by standardized assessment tasks (SATs), which were envisaged as normal classroom activities with built-in assignments, assessed by moderators external to the school. The four criteria that the task group emphasized throughout their report were the criterion-referencing of results, the formative nature of assessment, the moderation of results, and the link between assessment and progression. Had they been implemented, the effects of the recommendations on the curriculum could have been to subtly shift the emphasis on subject knowledge towards skills and abilities.

Baker welcomed the report warmly and quickly, and published it. Thatcher was unhappy:

Whether he [Baker] had read it properly I do not know; if he had it says much for his stamina. Certainly I had no opportunity to do so before agreeing to its publication, having simply been presented with this weighty, jargon-filled document in my overnight box for publication the following day. The fact that it was welcomed by the Labour Party, the National Union of Teachers and the *Times Educational Supplement* was enough to confirm for me that its approach was suspect. ... I minuted my concerns to Ken Baker but by now, of course, it had been published.

(Thatcher, 1993, p. 595)

This minute was leaked: she saw the proposal as 'enormously elaborate and complex', and thought that it placed too much emphasis on teachers making judgments for formative and diagnostic purposes, rather than for summative ends, and that it would be very costly and take several years to introduce (letter of PM's Private Secretary, 21 January 1988, published in *The Independent*, 10 March 1988, quoted in Lawton, 1989, p. 59): also, it 'was written in an impenetrable educationalist jargon' (Thatcher, 1993, p. 595). There was, however, no change at this stage: it took several years and the first trials of SATs before the TGAT proposals were diluted, when Kenneth Clarke (Secretary of State in 1992) described them as 'an elaborated nonsense' (Black, 1993).

The Kingman Report on a model of teaching English language for teacher training was submitted in March 1988, and published the following month (DES, 1988e). The report had been expected to endorse a return to the traditional teaching of Latinate grammar, but instead it called for children to be taught about language, rather than the 'old fashioned formal teaching of grammar [which] had a negligible, or, because it replaced some instruction and practice in composition, even a harmful, effect on the development of original writing' (1988e, para. 2.27). Thatcher dissented, and had to be persuaded to agree to its acceptance (Cox, 1991, p. 3). Baker was now able to appoint an English Working Group, to match the Mathematics and Science Groups (whose work was now near completion). He and his Minister of State, Angela Rumbold, selected Professor Brian Cox to chair the group: he was to comment 'I was well known as the Chief Editor of the Black Papers on Education, presumably traditional and right wing in their views on education. I presume neither Mr Baker nor Mrs Rumbold was aware that for over ten years I had been conducting a campaign to make creative writing a central feature of the English curriculum' (Cox, 1991, p. 4). He had, moreover, been a member of Kingman, and fully supported its approach. Cox was not consulted on the membership of the Group, but was astonished to find how progressive its members were. Despite the supposed care taken by Baker and Rumbold to select those of more conservative stance – all prospective members were interviewed and quizzed on their beliefs – the only 'traditionalist' was the author Roald Dahl (who attended only the first meeting, and whom Cox persuaded to resign). Cox's explanation was that Baker and Rumbold knew little about the debate on progressive education, and did not realize that the members would oppose Mrs Thatcher's predilection for grammar and rote-learning; 'they were amateurs, instinctively making judgements about the professional standing of the interviewees ... they did not realise that ... the language of educational discussion had changed radically since they were at school' (p. 6). The screening of potential members continued with the appointment of the other Working Groups, and was often as unsuccessful.

The final reports of the Working Groups on Science and Mathematics appeared at the end of June 1988. Prais had, much earlier, resigned (apparently to the annoyance of Margaret Thatcher, who wanted him arguing her points on the Group (Graham, 1993, p. 30). The Mathematics proposals were disliked by Thatcher; ' a small mountain ... a complicated array of "levels", "attainment targets" and "tasks" ', she was to write (Thatcher, 1993, p. 395). She was being briefed by her ex-appointee, Sig Prais. Detailed interviews with members of the Working Group, conducted and analysed by Stephen Ball (Ball, 1990) reveal the tensions within the Working Group, and the pressures that were being exercised by Graham, the DES officials and the Secretary of State on one side, and the professionals and the industrialists on the other (pp. 198–204). It is clear that some of the practical uses of mathematics in engineering, computer programming and industrial planning were left out of the National Curriculum because Baker and Graham neither recognized the mathematics nor understood its significance (Working Group member, quoted by Ball, p. 204; see also Brown, 1990, 1992). But the process of the Working Groups was now inexorably in progress, and the politicians were too busy steering the final stages of the Education Reform Bill through Parliament to become involved in the oversight of documents such as these. Duncan Graham, having delivered the final Mathematics Working Group report, was asked to be Chairman and Chief Executive of the National Curriculum Council (NCC). His account of this (Graham, 1993, pp. 8–9) suggests that there was from the first a deep antipathy from the DES Civil Servants to the idea of a quasi-autonomous Council with Executive powers (as opposed to an advisory role), and to his having the status and salary that the combined roles of chair and chief executive brought with them (Deputy Permanent Secretary level).

By September, Cox's English Group had prepared their report. This was on the Primary phase: unlike the other Working Groups, there was no interim and final report, because it was necessary to have the Primary schools proposals ready, alongside the already completed Mathematics and Science proposals, to start being taught in schools in September 1989. Baker was able to incorporate his comments in the foreword to the Primary English report: he asked that in the final report 'the programmes of study for writing should be strengthened to give greater emphasis to the place of grammatical structure and terminology within the matters, skills and processes otherwise covered' (DES, 1988h, p. iii). This was probably again a response dictated by Thatcher, or at least designed to acknowledge her concerns. Cox was anxious (Cox, 1991, p. 8) not to offend Baker, and be replaced: he carried on towards the final report. Graham claims that DES officials gave unattributable press briefings that Baker was most unhappy at the report's critique of the need for grammar (1993, p. 47).

By this stage the members of the NCC had been appointed: their role was to take the Working Party recommendations, with the Secretary of State's comments, and to arrange statutory consultations with interested parties. Having done this, the NCC would report back to the Secretary of State with a summary of the views expressed, the NCC recommendations on the proposals, and any other advice it wanted to offer. Following this, the Secretary of State would issue a draft Order (with any reasons why NCC advice had not been followed) for further consultation.

Graham therefore began the consultation process on the three final reports (science, mathematics and primary English). The English curriculum was a predictable centre of contention (see Ball, 1982; Barnes et al., 1987). What happened makes a fascinating case-study in the politics of curriculum construction: Cox and Graham give detailed and different accounts; Baker and Thatcher add additional perspectives. Graham decided that he should follow Baker, and add references to grammar (which Cox was to claim he did in seven different places, at none of which did he say what he meant by grammar). Graham's view was that Cox's recommendation that children needed to acquire 'knowledge about language' was the same as learning grammar, and he might as well use Baker's preferred terminology; to him, Cox's points were sophistry (Graham, 1993, p. 49). Cox's group retorted that they could not proceed with their secondary report if the primary foundations on which it was being based might be overturned (Cox, 1991, p. 10). The NCC and the Working Group were not allowed to meet – civil servants seem to have been the intermediaries – and this in itself caused difficulties. Baker and Graham backed down at this point: the Working Party then made major alterations to their secondary proposals, cutting out major sections of their draft programmes of study on knowledge about language. The primary proposals, with some emendation by the NCC, though considerably less than had at first been proposed, went ahead, and a limited number of 'grammatical' terms were introduced. Significantly, Baker did go beyond the NCC advice at one point, and insisted that primary-school children should learn some poetry by heart: 'direct ministerial interference in what should be taught in the national curriculum … the first indication that ministerial whim could be enshrined in law' (Graham, 1993 p. 51).

When Baker received the secondary phase report in June he was displeased. He and Angela Rumbold (who refused to meet and discuss the report with Cox) had wanted a short report, emphasizing grammar; Cox, anxious to carry the teaching profession with him, had been more prolix. At one stage it seemed the report might be edited, and only part printed: in the end, a compromise was reached by which chapters 15 to 17 (about the attainment targets, programmes of study, etc.) would be printed first, and on tinted paper, followed by the body of the report (an interesting example of the pervasiveness of post-structuralism, Cox later wryly observed).

Thatcher was still unhappy: she complained 'although there was acceptance of a place for Standard English, the traditional learning of grammar and learning by heart, which I considered vital for memory training, seemed to find no favour' (Thatcher, 1993, p. 595). She, too, intervened: one of the attainment targets for writing went through the following stages:

Working Party Report	Use Standard English, where appropriate
Margaret Thatcher's alteration	Use Standard English
Cox's compromise on version of the Report sent out for consultation	Use Standard English (except in contexts where non-standard forms are needed for literary purposes, e.g. in dialogue, in a story or a play-script)

(Cox, 1991, p. 12)

Disputes like this were endemic through the preparation of the various subjects within the National Curriculum. Though the Secretaries of State changed – John MacGregor (14 months) succeeded Baker (who lasted 38 months) in July 1989, Kenneth Clarke took over in November 1990 (17 months), John Patten in April 1992 (27 months), and finally Gillian Shephard in July 1994 (33 months) – the pattern of Ministers imposing their own beliefs persisted, often based on no more that folk memories of their own education (in very different schools, in different times), in the face of professional advice and extensive consultations. The influence of Ministers increased – as did that of their political advisers. The (Conservative) Chairman of the House of Commons Select Committee on Education spoke out in 1992 about the effects of these 'extreme right-wing think tanks' – 'lords of misrule' – on the curriculum:

> the ears of Ministers have been disproportionately influenced by extremists, whose pronouncements become ever wilder and further from the reality of the world of education which I recognise, in which I work and for which I care deeply. And who are they to foist upon the children of this country ideas which will only serve to take them backwards? What hard evidence have they to support their assertions? … Their insidious propaganda must be challenged. They seek to return to a world which, if it ever existed, cannot be recreated today. … [These people] are the spindle and loom of chaos, the offspring of bigoted minds and muddy understandings.
>
> (Thornton, 1992, p. 173)

The English dispute went on. After the National Curriculum documents were finally approved and distributed, an NCC project was established to produce materials for English in the National Curriculum (the LINC project). This very extensive project was suddenly stopped when its materials were on the point of distribution, and all the papers were (officially) withdrawn: they transgressed the new right's view of what constituted English (see Cox, 1992, 1995).

Meanwhile, almost unbelievably, HMI continued to produce its own inspection reports on the curriculum, almost as though they were oblivious of the debate (DES, 1988d, 1989f, 1989g, 1989h, 1989i; 1990a, 1990b, 1991a, 1991b).

History

The History Working Group's progress illustrates again the political impact of the restorationists (Heal, 1992). Baker appointed Commander Michael Saunders Watson as Chair: he was the owner of Rockingham Castle in Northamptonshire, and a former chairman of the Heritage Education Trust, whom Baker had met at a reception where the two men had found that they were both interested in history. 'He appeared to everybody to be a peculiarly Tory choice and looked to many as the first overt political appointment. Everybody feared the worst and characterised him as a right-wing amateur who would follow the party line' (Graham, 1993, p. 64). Baker's instructions to the Working Group required them to address a traditional national historical canon:

the programmes of study should have at the core the history of Britain, the record of its past, and in particular its political, constitutional and cultural heritage. ... They should take account of Britain's evolution and its changing role as a European, Commonwealth and world power ... they should also recognise and develop an awareness of the impact of classical civilisations.

(Baker to Working Group, in DES, 1989j)

The interim report, however, recommended that it would not be possible to include attainment targets based on facts: factual knowledge could be specified in the programmes of study. The members of the working group were here attempting to walk a tightrope between Baker's direction and the demands for a less Anglo-centric view – they argued that the attainment targets should specify understanding and skills, including the ability to empathize. At one point before the interim report was published, Baker apparently tried to persuade Saunders Watson to include facts in the attainment targets: he declined to do so (Graham, 1993, p. 65).

The interim report (DES, 1989j) was published just after Baker had been moved from the Department of Education and Science to become Chairman of the Conservative Party. While this was presented as a promotion, and Thatcher said at the time that his presentational flair was needed to prepare for the next general election, it should be remembered that Baker had fought Thatcher, and her advisers (such as Brian Griffiths), on the need for a broader based curriculum. He also had gained the reputation of not having a sufficient eye for detail, and to have let the professionals score too many points in the construction of the National Curriculum so far ('not even his greatest friends would describe him as either a profound political thinker or as a man with a mastery of detail' (Lawson, 1992, p. 606). His replacement by John MacGregor appeared to signify a return to relatively low profile (and perhaps more pliant) holders of the post.

Margaret Thatcher's view of the history proposals was unfavourable:

Though not a historian myself, I had a very clear – and I had naively imagined uncontroversial – idea of what history was. History is an account of what happened in the past. Learning history, therefore, requires knowledge of events. It is impossible to make sense of such events without absorbing sufficient factual information and without being able to place matters in a clear chronological framework – which means knowing dates. No amount of imaginative sympathy for historical characters or situations can be a substitute for the initially tedious but ultimately rewarding business of memorising.

(Thatcher, 1993, p. 595)

This passage indicates clearly the problems that arise when a curriculum is created out of the memories of an individual's own schooling. Thatcher's own study of history ended when she was 16, yet she professes a 'clear idea of what history is', and was prepared to try to logically derive from her recollections of her own schooling, more than forty years after the event, a sequence of necessary learning processes. In place of the debate of the previous forty years on the nature of history – Namier (1952), Carr

(1964), Elton (1967) and Tosh (1989) – she substitutes the nineteenth-century positivism of von Ranke: 'to show what actually happened' (Ranke, 1885, vii). It appears to be a near-perfect example of cultural reproduction, with its roots in *Hard Times* and the pedagogy of Gradgrind and Choakumchild.

MacGregor's response to the authors of the History *Interim Report* dutifully echoed Thatcher's views. 'I doubt whether [your] approach puts sufficient emphasis on the importance of acquiring such knowledge, and ensuring such knowledge can be assessed. It runs the risk that pupil's grasp of the substance of history will not be clearly established or assessed' (MacGregor, in DES, 1989j). He asked that the final report put greater emphasis on chronology, include 'essential knowledge' in the attainment targets, and increase the proportion of time spent on British history. Almost immediately, various neo-conservative groups emerged to 'defend' the teaching of 'traditional' history, attacking the concept of empathy, and reasserting the centrality of Britain within world history. The final report was submitted in February 1990, and not published by MacGregor until April (DES, 1990c). Unusually, the publication was not accompanied by any comment from the Secretary of State or direction to the NCC on the consultation process. Instead, MacGregor suggested that the importance of the subject was such that it required further public debate, and meanwhile he would conduct his own investigation into the Working Group's proposals. This report – nominally undertaken by the DES – was written by the NCC's history officer, Nick Tate (who was later to become Chief Executive to the successor body to the NCC). Tate rearranged some of the factual content, making the teaching of facts more prominent in the ways that they were described, but still not including them within the attainment targets. MacGregor was largely persuaded, but imposed his own rearrangement of the four proposed attainment targets, and their overall weightings (*Table 5.2*).

Table 5.2 *Changes in drafts of the National Curriculum for History*

	Working Group Proposals for Attainment Targets, April 1990 (DES, 1990c)		*MacGregor's Attainment Targets, July 1990 (Graham, 1993, p. 68)*	
1	Understanding history in its setting	25%	Knowledge and understanding of history	50%
2	Understanding points of view and interpretations of history	25%	Understanding points of view and interpretations of history	25%
3	Acquiring and evaluating historical information	25%	Acquiring and evaluating historical information	25%
4	Organizing and communicating the results of historical study	25%	(incorporated into 1–3)	

Source: DES, 1990c; Graham, 1993, p. 68.

The NCC's final report was prepared by December 1990 (NCC, 1990g), by which time John MacGregor had been replaced by a reluctant Kenneth Clarke. Margaret Thatcher had drafted him from the Department of Health, where he wished to remain to oversee the changes he had introduced to begin an internal market in the NHS. Thatcher was possibly unhappy with MacGregor's work at Education: some of the Conservative right wing sent out rumours that he had 'gone native', and was altogether too conciliatory to teachers' concerns on the developing curriculum. He had already had his junior ministers (Robert Jackson and Angela Rumbold, both with professional backgrounds in education, as a university lecturer and as a chair of an LEA respectively) replaced in June by Michael Fallon (a member of the 'no turning back' group and, according to Graham, 'the direct representative of the right wing' (Graham, 1993, p. 110), and Tim Eggar ('visibly prejudiced against the Council and what it was doing' (ibid.)), and had given a lack-lustre performance at the Conservative Party Conference. Thatcher saw MacGregor as unable to present educational policies well, and took the opportunity of the reshuffle occasioned by the resignation of Geoffrey Howe to bring in Clarke. When Thatcher was forced from office the following month, the new prime minister, John Major, confirmed Clarke in the Education post.

From the outset, Clarke did not appear to be in agreement with the activities of the NCC, according to Graham (p. 93). He made a significant number of changes to the proposals on the history curriculum. He decided, with minimal consultation with the Council, to remove the ten-subject curriculum for 14- to 16-year-olds (Key Stage 4), which he saw as over-prescriptive, inhibiting pupil choice and unworkable, and announced at the January 1991 North of England Education Conference that pupils would take either History or Geography (or possibly a mixture of two half-subjects) (DES, 1991c). When it was pointed out that this would have meant, under the proposals then current, that many 14- to 16-year-olds would not have covered *any* twentieth-century history, Clarke simply introduced a compulsory unit on the Second World War into the 11–14 programme of study. More significant was his antipathy to the history curriculum running up to the present. He wanted to proclaim that history came to a stop in 1945 (doubtless following Sellar and Yeatman's memorable Chapter LXII: 'America was thus clearly top nation, and History came to a .' (*1066 and All That*, 1930, p. 113)). Graham describes DES officials protesting at this and engaging in a Dutch auction, the result of which was included in the statutory order: the history curriculum was to end twenty years before the present, and this cut-off point was to move forward every five years (Graham, 1993, p. 70).

The Process of Revision

The assessment process had already begun to be weakened by MacGregor, when he downgraded the teacher assessment for 7-year-olds in favour of the Standard Assessment Task, following reported pressure from the Prime Minister in the summer of 1989 (Ball, 1990, p. 193). This was followed by Clarke's announcements in 1991 that attainment targets in mathematics and science would be reduced to simplify testing at 16, and that GCSE papers would be marked in all subjects with 5 per cent of the marks devoted to spelling. The SATs that were proposed by SEAC were condemned by Clarke as 'an elaborate nonsense': he urged them to introduce simple paper and pencil tests. Philip Halsey, the Chair of SEAC, resigned, to be replaced by Brian Griffiths, a former member of Margaret Thatcher's Central Policy Review team. Clarke's successor, John Patten, took the assault on the assessment processes even further, perhaps eager to demonstrate his credentials to the right wing of his party (Lawton, 1994, p. 80). Patten took his lead from John Major, who told the Conservative Party Conference in October 1992 'English examinations should be about literature, not soap opera' (Major, quoted in Chitty and Simon, 1993, p. 144). Patten attacked the examination boards:

> One [board] recently defended the use of a hamburger advertisement in a public exam by claiming that it provided just as important 'food for thought' as our great literary heritage.
> They'd give us Chaucer with chips.
> Milton with mayonnaise. ...
> I am determined to see that public confidence in those [GCSE] examinations in maintained, and that teachers, and above all pupils, are not let down.
> Of course, it is hard for parents to have much confidence in the exam boards when some of them include television programmes such as 'Neighbours' and even ''Allo, 'Allo' in their English syllabuses.
> Well, I have a message for those exam boards. 'Listen very carefully. I will say this only once. Get your act together!' The litany of educational let-down has gone on long enough.
> (Patten, to Conservative Party Conference, October 1992, quoted in Chitty and Simon, 1993, p. 147)

By this time, the National Curriculum was fully in place (Ribbin and Sherrat, 1997). Battles, similar to those fought over history, had been engaged in on the subjects of geography, art and music (for the last of these, for example, see Lawson, Plummeridge and Swanwick, 1993). Duncan Graham, unable to take further interference from Clarke, had resigned in July 1991, in the same week that Philip Halsey had resigned from SEAC. Graham was replaced by David Pascall, who had also been a member of Margaret Thatcher's Central Policy Review staff. 'Rarely have the fundamentals of curriculum construction been so palpably political in nature' (Hargreaves, 1994, p. 4). The NCC, though initially designed to be a standing body that would oversee, review and revise the curriculum (at Baker's suggestion, it had taken a 25-year-lease on its headquarters building in York), did not meet the needs of Clarke and his successor for a complaisant organization – and had, according to Graham, always been resented by the civil servants of the DES. Patten's Education White Paper, *Choice and Diversity* (DES, 1992b) announced (amongst much else) that the NCC and the SEAC would be wound up within a year, and the functions of the two bodies transferred to a new combined authority, the Schools Curriculum and Assessment Authority (SCAA). This would be London-based, and lose the quasi-independent position that had been enjoyed by the NCC.

The creation of distinct subjects in the National Curriculum did not necessarily mean that the relationship to areas of experience would be lost; nor were subjects *per se* necessarily incompatible with a society-related (or a work-related) curriculum as some kind of preparation for adult life. Lawton had much earlier pointed out that 'there is no reason why a curriculum based on disciplines should not be related to the children's own experience and interests. The fact that so much so-called academic teaching of subjects does tend to neglect children's everyday knowledge ... is a condemnation of traditional pedagogy or teaching method rather the disciplines themselves as a basis of the curriculum' (Lawton, 1975, p. 85). Lawton was responding to philosophers such as Hirst and Pring, who had suggested that the forms of knowledge that constituted the curriculum were beyond culture and history – Hirst in particular saw the curriculum in terms of the structure and organization of knowledge, which by his analysis was not culturally based, but in some way universal (Hirst, 1965; Pring, 1972). But disciplines are themselves socially created, and in flux. Each is a response to collective experiences and interests, both in terms of the content or subject matter and of the nature of enquiry within the discipline. However, if definition of the curriculum subject is left to those outside the discipline, and particular to those who seek to impose a particular ideology, then what may well be imposed is the folk-memory of the discipline, the particular interests and specific experiences of an earlier generations. This is what happened in the case of the National Curriculum.

> It is a curriculum which eschews relevance and the present, concentrating on the heritage and the canon based on temporal disengagement; a curriculum suspicious of the popular and the immediate, made up of echoes of past voices, the voices of a cultural and political elite; a curriculum which ignores the past of women and the working class and the colonised – a curriculum of the dead.
>
> (Ball, 1994, p. 46)

The Profession Strikes Back?

There were gaps where the professionals could try to re-assert their influence in the face of the political control that had been established. Two particular areas are focused on here: the first, an attempt – which failed – to wrest from the ten-subject formula the 'broad and balanced curriculum' which the Education Reform Act had promised; the second, an attack on the mechanics of the ten-subject curriculum, that stressed the unworkable overload of content and assessment, which succeeded to the extent of allowing a slimmer curriculum to be developed. Finally, the emphases of the 1997 Labour administration on the curriculum will be briefly examined, particularly in how they have re-established Thatcher's concerns to focus on 'the basics' at the expense of anything else, and the degree to which they prescribe the methods of classroom teaching and delivery.

The possibility of the 'whole curriculum' debate was present almost from the start in the National Curriculum. The 1987 consultative paper included a possible exception: 'some subjects or themes ... can be taught through other subjects ... for example, health education' (DES, 1987h, para. 18). The Schools Curriculum Development Committee (SCDC), at that time still responsible for curriculum development, had only three months earlier established Educating for Economic Awareness, and the project coordinator immediately responded by writing to LEAs and schools working on this, to suggest that economic awareness be included as one such 'cross-curricular theme' – the first time that this term was used (Pearce/EEA, 1987). In the period between the consultation document and the passing of the legislation, the possibility of including certain other curricular areas with some demi-official status was clarified. The Education Reform Act made it clear that the National Curriculum, with its ten subjects, was but a part of the 'broad and balanced' curriculum that the Act required. The National Curriculum subjects, together with Religious Education, formed the 'basic curriculum', defined and prescribed by law. But this in turn was but part of the 'whole curriculum', which schools were obliged to deliver. The NCC was to offer guidance to schools on what constituted the difference between the 'whole' and the 'basic' (Ross, 1993, explores this in more depth, see *Figure 5.1*).

The development of this whole curriculum was slow, and hampered by the DES officials who liaised with the NCC (Graham, 1993, pp. 19–21). After many delays, the Curriculum Guidance paper, *The Whole Curriculum* (NCC, 1990a), was published, in what Duncan Graham, the NCC's first chair was to describe as the 'Council's finest hour – it fought for the whole curriculum, and won' (Graham, 1993). Five cross-curricular themes were identified, and further guidance papers were issued on each: *Education for Economic and Industrial Understanding* (NCC, 1990b), *Health Education* (NCC, 1990c), *Careers Education and Guidance* (NCC, 1990d), *Environmental Education* (NCC, 1990e), and *Citizenship* (NCC, 1990f). It appears that Baker himself wanted to promote these themes (Baker, 1993, p. 189), but that the DES wanted the NCC to concentrate exclusively on the preparation of the ten foundation subjects (Graham, 1993, p. 20). Despite his declarations of triumph at ensuring the publication of *The Whole Curriculum*, Graham was also at times less sanguine about the objectives of the DES: 'what was really wanted was a narrow "basics" diet, minimally at risk of dilution' (Graham, 1993). Three cross-curricular dimensions (equal opportunities, multicultural perspectives and the European dimension) received less attention, as did the cross-curricular skills (communication, numeracy, problem solving, PSE and information technology). These did seem a signal, at least to some commentators, that a social dimension could exist within the framework of the 1988 Act, and that forms of the radical curriculum initiatives of the 1970s could persist (Whitty, 1992, p. 112; also Hall, 1992, Blyth, 1992).

MacGregor was Secretary of State when the various cross-curricular themes were published, and he endorsed them; but Clarke, taking over a few months later, was determined to streamline and simplify the National Curriculum proposals overall. The plans to develop a far-reaching whole curriculum document that would include the five cross-curricular themes and substantial sections on multicultural education, equal opportunities and the European dimension in the curriculum (Graham, 1993, pp. 21–2) were dropped.

The second area on which the profession sought to modify the National Curriculum was in the area of subject overload. The ten-subject model had brought nine ring-binders of documents to the desk of every primary teacher (modern foreign languages was not included), with supplementary volumes of good practice, guidance, examples of attainment targets, and much more. The average pupil would have been assessed against 700 attainment targets by the age of 16: and it was estimated that an infant

Figure 5.1   The relationship between the National Curriculum (core and foundation) and the whole curriculum

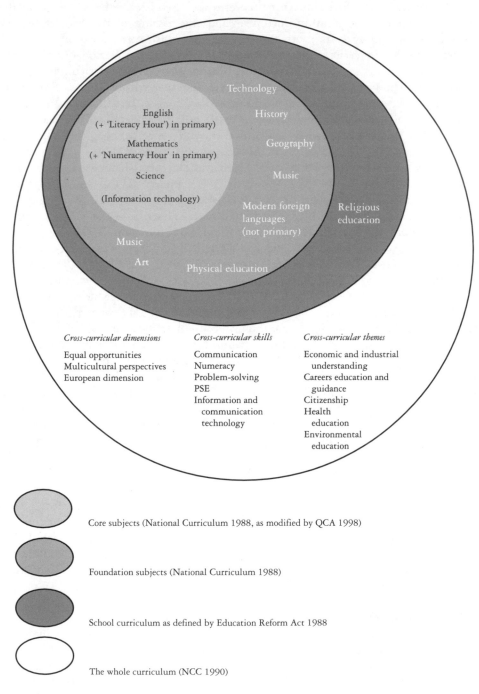

Source: Taken from Ross, 1993, p. 150.

teacher with 35 children in his or her class would need to make some 8,000 assessment judgments each year (NCC/SEAC, 1993a, 2.28). Mandatory testing through SATs had begun (for the core subjects) with 7-year-olds in 1991, after a trial year in 1990. The first trials for 14-year-olds were scheduled for 1992, with mandatory tests in 1993. Opposition to the nature of the tests crystallized first around the English tests, but rapidly spread to the other subjects, and to the primary schools: an effective teacher boycott was organized for 1993.

The Secretary of State, John Patten, had managed to alienate even more people than had Clarke and Baker. When the chair of the National Confederation of Parents Associations suggested that the proposed arrangements were unwieldy and would not help parents, she was dismissed by Patten as having 'Neanderthal views'; the President of the Independent Girls Schools Association was told that her views were ridiculous and full of outdated 1960s arguments when she protested that the tests for 14-year-olds concentrated on rote learning; the pre-emptory attack on the examination boards at the 1992 Party Conference has been quoted above; and Patten then managed to slander the Chief Education Officer of Birmingham. Patten's solution to the boycott of SATs was to enlist the aid of the chairman-designate of the new Schools Curriculum and Assessment Authority, Sir Ron Dearing. In April 1993 he was asked to conduct an urgent review, with an interim report by July, and final recommendations by December.

Dearing (NCC/SEAC, 1993a, 1993b) proposed a slimming down of the content of each of the ten subjects, and a virtual abandonment of the approach for the 14- to 16-year-olds so that they would be free to opt to study for vocational qualifications (General National Vocational Qualifications (GNVQs)) that were designed to have parity of esteem with GCSEs. Teacher Assessments were to be given equal standing with the SATs, but slimmed down SATs would be maintained in the core subjects. To allay teachers' fears of the misuse of league tables of results, he urged the rapid introduction of some form of 'added value' element in the reporting on SATs results for each school, so that proper consideration could be given to the effects of factors such as social disadvantage on the results. New Orders for the slimmed down curriculum would be ready, after all the necessary consultations, by March 1995, for the next academic year. Thereafter, he recommended sternly, there should be no more tinkering with the curriculum for the next five years: the teachers should be left to get on with the job, and no longer subject to changes in procedures from year to year.

Dearing calculated that the effect of his proposals would be to free significant proportions of the teaching week for the broader curriculum. There would still be certain elements in each subject which would be requirements, but other elements were to be specified as optional, that teachers could use, in the context of a broader curriculum, using their professional judgment. He claimed that 10–15 per cent of 5- to 7-year- olds' time would be freed in this way, 15–20 per cent of 8- to 11-year-olds' time, and 20–25 per cent of 12- to 14-year-olds' time.

The SCAA began a long process of consultation towards revising the curriculum for 2000, with a series of consultations and conferences on the wider aspects of the curriculum in 1996. The Chief Executive of the authority was now Nick Tate (who had so adroitly 'rescued' the History Working Party's proposals for MacGregor). Some of these proposals and discussions will be the subject of the final chapter of this book.

But SCAA itself had a shorter shelf-life than its predecessor: it was merged with the National Vocational Qualifications Council in September 1997, to form the Qualifications and Curriculum Authority (QCA), which was charged with oversight of all education and training, and resultant qualifications (thus matching the merger of the Department for Education with the Department for Employment, that had been made in July 1995).

But by the time that the QCA started work, there was a new Labour Government. The Prime Minister, Tony Blair, had made education an important part – he might say the most important part – of his election campaign. Following the Conservatives' predilection for three-word policy slogans in education (for example, 'Choice and Diversity'), the Labour slogan became 'Standards, not Structures', which meant a refusal to change the structures for schooling that the Conservatives had introduced – grant-maintained schools, city technology colleges and the like – and to concentrate on raising the standards of achievement reached by pupils. The curriculum was one area, however, where the new Education and Employment Secretary, David Blunkett, did decide to make structural changes. In a drive to improve standards of literacy and numeracy in primary schools, the National Curriculum was relaxed so that schools need only in future follow the core curriculum subjects and information technology (which had become detached from technology as such at the time of the Dearing review). Schools should be 'mindful' of the foundation subjects, and be able to show inspectors evidence of work in them, but the prescribed content and targets would be abandoned from September 1998. Task Forces on literacy and numeracy introduced a much greater degree of control over the teaching content and methods of English and mathematics teaching. All schools were expected to follow prescribed literacy hour and mathematics hours schemes, that specified to a degree unseen before the type of teaching (whole class, group work, etc.), the amount of time given to each activity within the hour, and the vocabulary and concepts that were to be introduced and mastered, term by term.

The story of curriculum change in England over the twentieth century is marked, and continues to be marked, by conflict. There are conflicting ideas over what education is for, and what it can be expected to achieve, and these have led to a series of attempts to define the curriculum that can achieve these aims. However, through all of these changes, through the oscillations between central and local control, there has been the perception that the curriculum is important, that it marks out what kind of society and culture is wanted for the next generation. Education is about how we reproduce our culture, how we transmit from age to age the non-genetic part of our nature. This is part of the political struggle that has always gone on, about who 'we' are, and about what is 'our' cultural nature. Various protagonists throughout this account have sought to preserve existing certainties (or to return to those of an earlier age), or to ensure that the next generation does not repeat the follies of its elders. All of them were certain that the curriculum was essential in social reproduction: this will be the focus of the next chapter.

6   Curriculum and Reproduction

The central theme of this chapter is the relationship between an educational system, and particularly its curriculum, and the wider society within which the system is located. While most of this volume is concerned with the curriculum that is written down – what Jackson (1968) termed the 'preactive curriculum', this chapter focuses on what he called the 'interactive curriculum: what Young (1977) calls 'curriculum as practice', rather than 'curriculum as fact', or Grundy (1987) 'praxis', rather than 'product'. In Chapter 1, I drew upon the metaphors of the garden and cultivation to characterize the curriculum. Another common analogy is that of reflection: an educational system, many have said, inevitably reflects the society in which it is located.

Emile Durkheim characterized education as 'the image and *reflection* of society. It imitates and reproduces the latter in an abbreviated form; it does not create it' (1897, p. 372; emphasis added). For him, education was 'the means by which society prepares, within the children, the essential conditions of its very existence ... the man whom education should realise in us is not man as nature has made him, but as the society wishes to be, and it wishes him such as its internal economy calls for. ... Society draws for us the portrait of the kind of man we should be, and in this portrait all the peculiarities of its organisation come to be *reflected*' (1956, pp. 64–5; emphasis added). This functionalist view is still common: 'all societies have the task of passing on to the next generation the knowledge and skills regarded as particularly worthwhile; ... societies achieve this by means of ... education' (Lawton and Gordon, 1996, p. 10). Although Durkheim's model was not wholly static – his work *The Evolution of Pedagogy in France* (1938) shows both how educational changes can lead to wider social modification, and how changes in such social structures as occupational patterns can lead to modifications in schooling – it emphasizes stability, and sees society as essentially homogeneous. The reflection is mirror-like and results in self-replication (1897, p. 372). We learn who we are to be: we are what we have learned to be.

By contrast, John Dewey proposed a largely transformative model of education. The school processes should promote social equality, so that 'each individual gets an opportunity to escape from the limitations of the social group in which he was born, and come into living contact with a broader environment' (1916, p. 20). Education also had a developmental role for the individual: 'it creates a desire for continued growth and supplies the means for making the desire effective in fact' (p. 50). These egalitarian and developmental functions partly derived from Dewey's view of knowledge as something to be constructed by the learner as an active experimenter, provoked into inquiry by the teacher. (Dewey's model can also be seen as reflective, reproducing his perception of American society – 'mobile and full of channels for the distribution of change occurring anywhere' (Dewey, 1900, p. 88).) More recently, John Rawls has similarly argued that education has such egalitarian and developmental functions: 'resources for education are not to be allocated solely or necessarily mainly according to their return as estimated in producing trained abilities, but also according to their worth in enriching the personal and social life of citizens, including here the less favoured' (1971, p. 107).

Education as an Agent for Social Transformation

Many observers have argued that, whatever the ambitions the egalitarians and liberals have for education to transform society, this has not happened. Christopher Jencks, for example, argued that education had not been an equalizing influence, and that not only have the better-off appropriated far more than their share of publicly funded educational resources for their children, but that even if all pupils had the same educational resources, there would be no substantial change towards equalities of income as a consequence (1972) (but also see Apple, 1990, p. 39). From a rather different perspective, Raymond Williams argued that 'the common prescription of education, as the key to change, ignores the fact that the form and content of education are affected, and in some cases determined, by the actual systems of decision and maintenance' (1961, p. 120): political (decision) and economic (maintenance) structures tend to prescribe the composition of the curriculum and the systems by which it is delivered in ways that minimizes the possibility of societal or economic change. Michael Apple develops this further, concluding that schools contribute to inequality because they are intentionally organized to unequally distribute particular kinds of knowledge (1990, p. 43). Williams and Apple both hold that the educational systems in respectively Britain and the United States are designed to duplicate social and economic inequalities.

Some empirical studies would seem to demonstrate that they can do this (and nothing but this) very effectively. The very substantial analysis by Coleman and his colleagues of educational inequality (Coleman et al., 1966) concluded that the pervasive inequality found in the United States' educational system was not a consequence of the uneven (and racist) distribution of resources, but followed 'inequalities imposed on children by their home, neighbourhood and peer environment ... carried along to become the inequalities with which they confront adult life at the end of school' (p. 325). Levels of educational outcomes reflected the socio-economic locality of the school. Schools were able to do little to change underlying structural inequalities, and such socialization that schools were able to provide was into the culture of home, neighbourhood and peers, and not into anything broader or more common. Alternative studies suggested that individual schools might make a difference to educational attainment. In the study of English secondary schools by Rutter and others – longitudinal, unlike Coleman's – it was suggested that there were aspects of a school's activities that *did* influence academic attainment: the atmosphere of cooperation, the organization of coursework and the quality of pupil–teacher relationships were important variables that were within the control of the school. Adjusting for social class factors, Rutter suggested that some schools achieved significantly better than others, and that a superior learning environment was not simply equatable with schools that were materially better equipped (Rutter et al., 1979). These features fall broadly within the wider definitions of curriculum provision:

> the 'informal' programme of so-called extracurricular activities as well as all those features which produce the school's 'ethos', such as the quality of relationships, the concern for equality of opportunity, the values exemplified in the way the schools sets about its task and the way in which it is organised and managed.
>
> (DES, 1985a, para. 11)

Rutter did not, however, suggest that influences outside the school were the strongest factors in the maintenance of inequality. The factors he identified are most often found in schools with larger numbers of well-motivated students: these schools would attract and motivate good teachers, and attract pupils from relatively privileged homes, and thus the cycle of reproduction would be maintained. A later study by Coleman et al. (revising his 1966 data) reached very similar conclusions (1981), as did a study of English primary schools by Mortimore and his colleagues (1988).

Studies of educational success in the UK consistently show correlations with social background, suggesting that while individual schools may be able to make a difference, the preponderant effect of the educational system is to replicate the status quo. Thus, for example, Halsey and others compared the educational progress of boys from a working-class background to boys from the 'service class': over the 1945 to 1980 period, the service class youth was ten times more likely to still be attending school at age 18, and eleven times more likely to attend University (1980). The Committee chaired by Lord Swann reported that while 13 per cent of white school leavers were achieving one or more A level success, only 5 per cent of West Indian origin pupils were reaching this level (DES; 1985i). Data collected in the late 1990s about young students entering University education, based on the neighbourhood from which they come, suggest that 74 per cent of 18–21-year-olds from very high-income professional backgrounds (average highest family income of £29,000); 34 per cent of young people from white-collar families living in owner-occupied suburban semis (average income £17,800); and just 9 per cent of young people from blue-collar families in council properties (average income £12,700) will attend University (Woodrow, 1998).

The Reproduction of Social Inequality

Michael Apple argues that this reproduction is not a conspiracy to deprive, but a 'logical necessity' to maintain the unequal social order (1990, p. 40). Given the nature of the political economy of the contemporary western State, and the way in which this affects every aspect of the organization of everyday life, then a schooling system which credentializes a particular proportion of the population roughly equivalent to the needs of the division of labour (and de-credentializes the rest) is an almost natural way of maintaining the economic and cultural imbalance on which these societies are built. Apple goes on to suggest that because education legitimizes the economic and social order, it is an *active* force, and not merely engaged in passively mirroring society (p. 42).

The content of education, the ethos in which it is presented, and the structures through which it is delivered are all part of the intimacy education has with the socio-economic order of society. Education delivers the economic hierarchies necessary for each generation, using its curriculum and structures to produce and reproduce different forms of official knowledge in different social orders, and to inculcate acceptance of the uneven power structure that lies behind this as normal and common sense.

Gramsci, writing in the 1920s, also suggested that the social reproduction that was effected by schools was considerably more complex than a simple mirroring. He acknowledged that while 'the child's consciousness is not something "individual" (still less individuated), it reflects the sector of civil society in which the child participates'. This social reproduction was effectively done by the child's family and neighbourhood, and not (necessarily) by school. In most cases, Gramsci argued, the organization and culture of the school was at odds with the needs of the working-class child. 'The individual consciousness of the overwhelming majority of children reflects social and cultural relations which are different from and antagonistic to those which are represented in the school curriculum' (Gramsci, 1971, p. 35).

Berger and Luckman were later to work from an essentially similar proposition, when they argued that while parents (primary socializers) are not seen as institutional functionaries, secondary socializers (such as schools) provide the child with a distancing capacity: the school represents institutionally specific meanings which may be in conflict with those of the primary socializers. Social interaction in school is formalized: teachers are 'institutional functionaries with the formal assignment of transmitting knowledge' (1966, p. 162). Teachers give the curriculum a spurious objectivity through the social control of schooling, compared with the inevitable subjectivity in the content of primary socialization. Home knowledge, they argue, is left outside when entering the classroom. The child necessarily lives in the world as defined by his parents, but teachers try to posit the artificial knowledge of school against the 'natural reality' of knowledge acquired thorough primary socialization.

Gramsci's premise was that the proper function of schooling was to produce a politically democratic society, with equal participation by its members: his analysis of educational change (in Italy, eighty years ago, but nevertheless germane today) was that the growth of differentiated schools – and differentiated school curricula – perpetuated social differences. Traditional schools were oligarchic: those for the children of the ruling classes produced those destined to rule in turn.

> Each social group has its own type of school, intended to perpetuate a specific social function, ruling or subordinate. ... The multiplication of types of vocational school thus tends to perpetuate traditional social differences; but since, within these differences, it tends to encourage internal diversification, it gives the impression of being democratic in nature. ... But democracy ... must mean that every 'citizen' can 'govern' and that society places him in a position, even if only abstractly, in a general condition to achieve this. Political democracy tends towards a coincidence of the rulers and the ruled, ensuring for each non-ruler a free training in the skills and general technical preparation necessary to that end. But the type of school which is now developing as the school for the people ... is organised ever more fully in such a way as to restrict recruitment to the techni-

cally governing stratum. ... We are really going back to a division into judicially fixed and crystallised estates rather than moving towards the transcendence of class divisions.

(Gramsci, 1971, pp. 40–1)

What Gramsci is concerned with here is less the formal curriculum of what is taught – which, as he acknowledges, can be a common curriculum that advocates diversity, but the culture and ethos of the school. Ivan Illich encapsulated this insidious aspect of schooling in the phrase 'the hidden curriculum'. Far from having the function of developing a democratic and participatory society, Illich argued that the main tasks of the school were in reality four-fold: they provided custodial care for children, freeing parent's time; they effectively distributed pupils into occupational roles; they transmitted the dominant value system; and they taught pupils to acquire socially approved knowledge and skills (Illich, 1973). The relationship between schools and society, he argued, was essentially one of producing the economic requirements of society – and in particular, disciplined workers (at all levels), who were aware of and accepting of the political and economic hierarchies. Illich's argument is set within his wide-ranging critique of contemporary society, where he argues that modern economic development has removed from previously self-sufficient individuals the skills that they need, and made them instead dependent on professional experts (doctors, teachers, employers). Schools encourage passive consumption of the existing social structure, in the unconscious manner in which their procedures inculcate discipline, obedience and conformity. As he summarized it, schools teach children 'to know their place, and to sit still in it' (p. 74).

The nature of the hidden curriculum was summarized well by Valance: 'those non-academic but educationally significant consequences of schooling that occur systematically but are not made explicit at any level to the public rationales for education' (Vallance, 1974, p. 7). No open rationalization of the practices of schooling could publicly acknowledge and defend the insidious infusion of values, the tacit political socialization into a culture of docility and acceptance, or the reproduction of class structures. The theorists who followed Illich focused on the way in which social control was imposed through the form of school organization, rather than through its formal curriculum content. This is so deeply embedded and hidden that it generally passes completely unrecognized by both the pupil passing through school or the teacher who uses the control to determine the pupil's experiences in school (MacDonald, 1977).

The Hidden Curriculum and the Needs of Capitalist Production: Stan Bowles and Herb Gintis

One of the best known expositions of the nature and workings of the hidden curriculum in the context of the political economy was put forward by Bowles and Gintis (1972, 1976, 1988). To them, education is simply a response to the capitalist system, transmitting technical and social skills (through the overt curriculum), and inculcating discipline and respect for authority (through the hidden curriculum). The social relations of the means of production *correspond* to the social relations of schooling, and this, they argue, is no coincidence.

> The school is a bureaucratic order, with hierarchical authority, rule orientation, stratification by 'ability' as well as by age, role differentiation by sex (physical education), home economics, etc., and a system of external incentives (marks, promises of promotion, and threat of failure) much like pay and status in the sphere of work.
>
> (Bowles and Gintis, 1972, p. 87)

It is not just that schools reproduce the personality types required by capitalist production ('those at the base of the hierarchy requiring a heavy emphasis on obedience and rules, and those at the top, where the discretionary scope is considerable, requiring a greater ability to make decisions on the basis of well-internalised norms' (p. 87)) – this is the very *purpose* of the school. Alienation and anomie are *necessary* outcomes of this schooling, not merely incidental to the incompatibility of the cultures of the primary and secondary socializers (Gramsci, 1971; Berger and Luckman, 1966).

Following from this argument, schools become mechanisms both for cultural distribution and for class reproduction: the two are indivisible. The subtle hegemony that a ruling class exercises over the legitimization of acceptable cultural knowledge is employed through the control of the knowledge-producing and knowledge-preserving institutions of that society (Apple, 1990). Only a particular version of reality is selected and distributed, a selected social construction which will serve the interests of only a segment of society (Mannheim, 1936). The question then becomes, as Whitty puts it, 'how and why reality comes to be constructed in particular ways and how and why particular constructions of reality seem to have the power to resist subversion' (1974, p. 125).

The connections between technological change, production, capitalist organization and the educational system are examined by Bowles and Gintis. Using their USA data, they compare the institutional background to the development of modern capitalist industry and the development of system of schools. While conceding that there are some benefits in schooling, such as the elimination of illiteracy, and access to intrinsically self-fulfilling learning experiences, they argue that the expansion of schooling has been a response to economic needs, and not in order to initiate or promote social reform: 'Schools are destined to legitimate inequality, limit personal development to forms compatible with submission to arbitrary authority, and aid in the process whereby youth are resigned to their fate' (1976, p. 266). They argue that there are explicit links between education's central role in reproducing the political structure of the capitalist production process and the legitimization of the rights vested in property: 'education is directly involved in the contradictory articulation of sites in advanced capitalism and is expressed in terms of the property/person dichotomy: education reproduces rights vested in property, while itself organised in terms of rights vested in persons' (Bowles and Gintis, 1981, p. 56). The inability of education to promote personal development is not because of the content of the curriculum, which has little part to play: it is the form of the educational discourses that determine what is reproduced.

The situation is, however, not *necessarily* closed, Bowles and Gintis argue. There are contradictions in the system that allow for the possibility of re-negotiating more egalitarian consequences, because the dominant – almost the only – mode of discourse provided in schools is that based on natural rights.

> This contradictory position of education explains its dual progressive/reproductive role (promoting equality, democracy, toleration, rationality, inalienable rights on the one hand, while legitimating inequality, authoritarianism, fragmentation, prejudice and submission on the other) and is, in part, a reflection of the stress in liberal discourse on procedure over substance. But it provides as well the tools by means of which it can be transformed into an instrument in the transition to socialism ... the goal of progressive educational reform must be framed in the structural boundaries of liberal discourse, and can be simply expressed as the full democratisation of education. These goals can be divided into two complementary projects: the democratisation of the social relations of education and the reformulation of the issue of democracy in the curriculum.
>
> (Bowles and Gintis, 1981, p. 57)

But this possibility for optimism is tempered by what they see as the stranglehold of the capitalist system. 'To reproduce the labor force, the schools are destined to legitimate inequality, limit personal development to forms compatible with submission to arbitrary authority, and to aid the process whereby youth are resigned to their fate' (1976, p. 266). Bowles and Gintis chart the development of the American educational system from the late eighteenth century to demonstrate their thesis. Thus they link the expansion of capitalist production in the first half of the nineteenth century to the ascendance of 'a self conscious capitalist class [that] came to dominate the political, legal and cultural superstructure of society. The needs of this class were to profoundly shape the evolution of the educational system' (p. 157), leading to a system of labour training the costs of which were born by the public. They quote contemporary educational administrators consciously modelling school organization on the principles of the divisions of labour; and argue that most larger employers supported public education because of its hidden curriculum, rather than for any desire for cerebral advancement. For example, this 1854 school board seems more concerned with work habits than anything else:

> The object of education is by no means accomplished by mere intellectual instruction. It has other aims of equal if not higher importance. The character and habits are formed for life ... of attention, self-reliance, habits of order and neatness, politeness and courtesy ... habits of punctuality'
>
> (quoted in Bowles and Gintis, 1976, p. 169)

The growth of corporate capitalism, in the late nineteenth century, required a more highly differentiated and hierarchically organized labour force: Bowles and Gintis relate this to the urban school reform movement and the inevitability of a school system that domesticated a labour force for the corporate order based on standardizing, testing and the bureaucratic tracking of pupils. The educational system creates a method that appears to be fair and just to allocate individuals to particular social and economic positions, but it does so at the behest of larger social and political forces: the same educational system inculcates people to accept as legitimate the limited roles in society that they are allowed (see also Meyer, 1977).

MacDonald has pointed out that the same hierarchical, rule-dominated organization of schools was equally a characteristic of the pre-industrial school (1977). She argues that there is a more complex relationship between the educational system and the social setting, best examined by distinguishing the systems for social reproduction from those of cultural reproduction. The latter, though dependent on the former, is able to maintain a certain degree of independence.

Cultural Capital and its Reproduction: The Work of Pierre Bourdieu

Pierre Bourdieu's theory of cultural capital includes both cultural production and reproduction in schools. The cultural capital, or *habitus*, of the middle class is expressed through its habits of thought, assumptions and complexions, that are particularly cultivated and expressed by the school system: the school inculcates, partly through the formal but particularly through the informal curriculum, 'not so much with particular and particularised schemes of thought as with that general disposition which engenders particular schemes, which may then be applied in different domains of thought and action' (Bourdieu, 1971, p. 184). This cultural capital is used as a mechanism to filter pupils to particular positions within the hierarchy of capitalist society. Schools re-create the social and economic hierarchies of the society in which they are embedded, by using processes of selection and teaching: but by judging and comparing these activities against the habitus of the middle class, they effectively discriminate against all those children who have not had access to this. 'By taking all children as equal, while implicitly favouring those who have already acquired the linguistic and cultural competencies to handle a middle class culture, schools take as natural what is essentially a social gift, i.e. cultural capital' (Dale et al., 1976, p. 4). As Bourdieu puts it, 'the cultural capital and the ethos, as they take shape, combine to determine behaviour and attitude to school which make up the differential principle of elimination operating for children of different social classes' (Bourdieu, 1974, p. 36). Applying the same cultural criteria in an equal way favours those students who have been previously socialized into the particularly favoured culture:

> students from different social milieux owe their ... nature to the fact that the selection that they have undergone is not equally severe for all, and that social advantages or disadvantages have gradually been transformed into educational advantages and disadvantages as a result of premature choices which, directly linked with social origin, have duplicated and reinforced their influence.
>
> (Bourdieu, 1974, p. 37)

Treating cultural capital in the same way as one would analyse economic capital shows how (and why) our dominant cultural institutions are organized and operate to allow those who have inherited cultural capital to do better, in just the same way as inherited economic capital favours economic success. 'Like economic capital, cultural capital (good taste, knowledge, ability, language) is unequally distributed through society and by selecting such properties, schools serve to reproduce the distribution of power within the society' (Dale et al., 1976, p. 4). The implications of the unequal distribution of cultural capital will be considered below, when we examine Bourdieu's notions of Pedagogic Action (PA) and Pedagogic Authority (PAu).

Bourdieu and Passeron argue that education has a particular or special function in the transmission of the cultural hierarchy: it can reproduce particular realities in particular social classes, and thus preserve the cultural and other differences between classes. They argue that traditional analyses of education tend to separate cultural reproduction from its functions of social reproduction: they 'ignore the specific effect of symbolic relations in the reproduction of power relations' (Bourdieu and Passeron, 1990, p. 10). Functionalist analyses, such as that of Durkheim, assume that

> the different P[edagogic] A[ction]s at work in a social formation collaborate harmoniously in reproducing a cultural capital conceived of as the jointly owned property of the whole 'society'. In reality, because they correspond to the material and symbolic interests of groups and classes differently situated within the power relations, these P[edagogic] A[ction]s always tend to reproduce the structure of the distribution of cultural capital among those groups or classes, thereby contributing to the reproduction of the social structure.
>
> (Bourdieu and Passeron, 1990, p. 11)

This is a very wide-ranging claim. It implies that the 'nature vs. nurture' debate is not really relevant, because we largely do not choose our identity – or indeed, *cannot* choose our identity. 'We receive the cultural identity which has been handed down to us from previous generations. ... As we grow older, we modify the identity we have inherited. The identity is not intrinsic but the scope for changing it is circumscribed by the social expectations of the group with which we are associated. By our actions we informally reinforce our inherited group affiliation' (Robbins, 1990, p. 174). Bourdieu and Passeron's model claims – insists – that our social identity, our membership of groups, are maintained by adopting tastes and lifestyles that serve as identifying images, with no intrinsic value other than to serve to maintain the coherence of the group to which we belong.

We are formally socialized by the system of education. The state establishes a schooling system to give the particular training or instruction necessary for the changing labour market. The schooling system also seeks to build in the whole population of the State an identity or association with the nation-state, that is in some way parallel to, or equivalent to, the group or class affiliations. States are themselves artificial or invented constructs (see, e.g. Colley, 1992; Hobsbawm and Ranger, 1983) that seek to construct uniform social identities within their synthetic boundaries. Robbins, in his commentary on Bourdieu, argues that while we are taught *some* things in school (largely in the formal curriculum) that are not necessarily part of this social purpose, for the most part schools are involved in the transmission of *arbitrary* culture and knowledge. These

> do not help people reconcile their group identity with a national identity, but instead throughout, ... distinguish people on supposed merit or ability. The equalisation of opportunity provided by state education and by the recognition of 'innate' intelligence is a sham. The system simply provides a series of awards or qualifications which, as much as hairstyles, are reinforcements of our previous group identity. The content of courses is such that only those who have already been initiated into the language of school discourses by their earlier socialisation are able to demonstrate 'ability'. Schools which, in response, alter their curricula in order to be able to recognise the merit of students who have been differently socialised, will tend to find that they become marginalised as institutions because they have 'poor standards'.
>
> (Robbins, 1990, p. 175)

Michael Young comes to a very similar conclusion in *Knowledge and Control* (1971). Power is unequally distributed in society: the system that allows this is created and maintained at least partly through the transmission of culture. There is a direct relationship between those who have 'access to power and the opportunity to legitimise certain dominant categories, and the processes by which the availability of such categories to some groups enables them to assert power and control over others' (Young, 1971, p. 8).

How does Bourdieu explain the production and legitimization of cultural goods? He distinguishes the agencies of cultural production (theatres, laboratories, universities) and the cultural agents (artists, scientists, writers) who together constitute an intellectual field (1971). The field, seemingly neutral, cohesive and independent, is located in an ethos of intellectual freedom and autonomy. In this way knowledge appears to be independent from the social context of those who produce it. But, Bourdieu argues, to work in a cultural field is in fact to submit to a demand that one adopts a particular cultural code: the categories of thought, perceptions, meaning that constitute and order the way the cultural agent views reality: their habitus (or what Basil Bernstein, as will be seen below, describes as 'mental structures'). Universities thus do not simply act as a guide to 'official' culture, but behave in ways that reinforce the social groups which support their choice of approved culture. Schools and Universities thus both conserve culture, and act to reproduce it: individuals are cultivated to have a specific set of values, tastes, thoughts – their habitus. Thus the organization and validation of knowledge becomes more important than the mere content of knowledge, the curriculum: what is important is not what the knowledge is, it is how particular knowledge comes to be validated as important and how it is used to have power-forming and power-augmenting characteristics.

Thus culture both classifies knowledge, but also, in its power-validating mode, classifies the classifiers: it discriminates between those who have the power of cultural legitimization, and those who do not. In *Reproduction in Education, Society and Culture*

(1990, 2nd edn) Bourdieu (with his colleague J.-C. Passeron) describes this process. All pedagogic action (PA), they argue, 'is objectively symbolic violence, insofar as it is the imposition of a cultural arbitrary by an arbitrary power' (p. 5). Such pedagogic action implies that it has pedagogic authority (PAu), so that pedagogic transmitters (including schools and Universities) are 'from the outset designated as fit to transmit that which they transmit, [and] hence entitled to impose its reception and test its inculcation by means of socially approved or guaranteed sanctions' (p. 20). The cultural values that are implicit in the formal curriculum, and pervade the informal curriculum, are in effect arbitrary selections. As MacDonald summarizes it,

> by controlling education the dominant classes are able to ensure the reproduction of the particular culture and the 'master-patterns' which underlie it. The culture which the school transmits is *not* therefore a collective cultural heritage but rather the culture of the dominant class.
>
> (MacDonald, 1977, p. 40)

Cultural reproduction through education is thus seen as one of the principal mechanisms to reproduce class structure. Bourdieu points out that such a process is ideally suited to contemporary States that formally deny the hereditary transmission of power and privilege (such as, for example in Bourdieu's case, France):

> among all the solutions put forward throughout history to the problem of the transmission of power and privilege, there surely does not exist one that is better concealed ... than the solution which the educational system provides by contributing to the reproduction of the structure of class relations and by concealing, by an apparently neutral attitude, the fact that it fulfils this function.
>
> (Bourdieu, 1971, p. 72)

This is the role of cultural capital. It is acquired by an individual from their family, through particular linguistic and social competencies ('style', 'manners', 'know-how'). These skills and expectations give the child the ability to read the code of the dominant culture, so that they can decipher and accumulate this culture. Pedagogic communication is termed 'magisterial' language, that of the transmitter. It is contrasted with 'popular' language, that of the working class. Children of this class, who have not acquired these skills for handling cultural capital from their family, begin school deprived of the ability to recognize and respond to the dominant culture that the school represents, transmits and for which it acts as arbiter. Privileged children arrive with the habitus to respond to academic training; the others are positioned on the wrong side of the cultural rift that segregates, for them, school discourse and home discourse, academic knowledge and everyday knowledge. The symbols that describe and delimit the dominant culture are imposed in such a way that subordinate groups are unable to decipher them: 'symbolic violence' is the power 'to impose meanings, and to impose them as legitimate by concealing the power relations which are the basis of its force' (1990, p. 4).

What sets out to be a criticism of the correspondence theory by Dennis O'Keeffe (1979) in fact turns out to be the exemplification of Bourdieu's cultural reproduction theory. O'Keeffe's challenge centres on the passivity of pupils and students that Bowles and Gintis imply. (Other have also criticized the denial of agency that runs through both their various works and those of Bourdieu (e.g. Kennett, 1973, p. 246; MacDonald, 1977, p. 45; Apple, 1990, p. 34).) O'Keeffe argues that middle-class students are active in making decisions about the curriculum. 'The curricular patterns we observe are not the passive, social investment outcomes of bourgeois manipulation. Very frequently they are active *consumer* oriented patterns' (p. 47). He exemplifies this by the ability of students to elect to study sociologists and others such as Marx (and presumably O'Keeffe), not necessarily because of any demand for knowledge about such writers and their views, but because such students can make real decisions about what they wish to study. He characterizes this as a 'consumption curriculum', where the middle classes combine educational consumption and investment – the educational system has been removed from the principles of the market, and as a result of this there is a very low sense of what are the real costs of educational curriculum decisions. O'Keeffe argues that the products of a sociological education find employment through 'the screening phenomena, whereby employers recognise talent through certification, often with scant regard to the specific content of curricular biographies' (p. 48).

The educational system, therefore, far from corresponding to the economic system of capitalism, is a mismatch: 'the public financing and direct provision of education leads to curricula and pedagogies almost certainly different from what would occur were education more capitalistically organised. The present system encourages ... experimentalism and consumerism' (O'Keefe, 1979, p. 51). But what O'Keeffe apparently fails to recognize is that 'sociological knowledge' has, to a large extent, come to be authenticated as cultural capital by the pedagogic authorities, and – *pace* his references to middle-class choices – become one of the dominant paradigms that are used to differentiate classes. The pedagogic action that results in a sociology degree is precisely the ratification of a cultural ability to engage in a particular discourse, based around an accepted discipline, approved knowledge and discourses that an employer of graduates would require: there is no need for an employer to investigate the 'specific content of curricular biographies' because they seek to employ people versed in the culture and discourse of culturally approved knowledge, not specific skills that might be 'useful' to them in employment in a more direct fashion. The fact that the approved knowledge might be 'revolutionary' or 'anti-capitalistic' is irrelevant: it has been legitimated by the pedagogic authority as evidence of possession of cultural capital. The subject matter or content of the course could be seen simply as evidence of the repressive tolerance of the regime (Marcuse, 1964).

Codes of Class and Language: Basil Bernstein's Contribution

Bourdieu's work in France is in many ways paralleled in Britain by the writings of Basil Bernstein. They use a rather different terminology, and there are significant points of disagreement (e.g. Bernstein 1990, pp. 168–72). In one of his earlier articulations of his theme, Bernstein argues that children from different social class backgrounds develop different codes or forms of speech in early life, and this affects subsequent school performance (1971b). This is not simply about verbal skills, or different ranges of vocabulary, but concerns the systematic ways language is used, rather as Bourdieu regarded language as evidence of cultural capital. In a series of papers composed and published through the 1960s (later collected into a single volume, Bernstein, 1971b), he characterized the language of working-class children as displaying what he termed a restricted code (1962a, 1962b): he described this in much greater detail than did Bourdieu.

A restricted code will include many of the following characteristics:

- language tends to be used for communicating practical experiences, rather than for discussing abstract ideas, relationships, or processes;
- language is directed towards the group, instead of being geared to explanations of *why* behaviour follows the pattern that it does;
- there will be unstated assumptions made by the speaker, that s/he expects the listeners to be aware of, and thus infer understanding;
- the vocabulary, syntax and norms of the language will be tied to the local cultural setting of the community or district of the speaker/listener;
- these values and norms will be taken from granted, and not explicitly expressed in speech (1971b, p. 77–8).

Bernstein explained the transmission of this characteristic pattern of speech by arguing that working-class children tended to be socialized by parents using a system of direct rewards (or punishments) to correct their behaviour.

Contrasted to this was middle-class speech, marked by mental structures (or in Bourdieu's equivalent term, habitus) that characterized an elaborated code in which:

- the meanings of words can be individualized, to suit the demands of a particular situation or context;
- language therefore will be less tied to a particular setting, and context, and will be more capable of being generalizable, and of expressing abstract ideas;
- those who hold elaborated code patterns of speech are more likely to be able to meet the formal academic demands of schooling.

This form of language behaviour was transmitted, he argued, by middle-class parents controlling their children and socializing them by using explicit verbal reasons and principles which explained why the particular behaviour was required. Bernstein went to some pains to assert that he did not regard working-class speech, restricted code, as in any way deprived or inferior. The point he wanted to demonstrate was that such a code clashed with the academic culture of the school, while the middle-class child's mastery of the elaborated code meant that, for them, the school environment was more understandable, and one in which they could join and achieve success: 'one of the effects of the class system is to limit access to elaborated codes' (1971b, p. 176).

There has been some extended debate in Britain on these arguments. Joan Tough, for example, produced some empirical findings that suggested that working-class children did have fewer questions answered by parents, and were offered fewer explanations about how other people reasoned (1976). Tizzard and Hughes found slightly different results, but generally within the same framework, and concluded that much depended on the expectations of the adult or the school (1984). However, Labov argued that working-class speech really only differs from elaborated code in its grammatical characteristics, not in its ability to handle complexity: he described how Bernstein's restricted code had its own grammar and terms, and asserted that it was equally able to convey abstractions and generalizations (1978). This may well be true, but it misses the point: the essence of Bernstein's argument was not really whether one code was better than another, but that one code – the elaborated code – was the one utilized by academic culture, was the one that was used to transmit socially approved knowledge, was the one used to make judgments about ability and aptitude, and was the one effectively restricted to middle-class users.

Bernstein thus offers a powerful explanatory model that relates socio-economic class to under-achievement at school and in achieving status in later life. The restricted code speech attributes of a working-class child inhibit their educational chances. It is through education that individuals construct and assume their mental structures, and the formation of particular mental structures derives from the social division of labour (1975). A child who gets limited responses to questions s/he asks at home is likely to be discouraged from asking further questions, and therefore to be less well informed or curious about the wider world, and less able to formulate questions in school settings. The language of school, being essentially abstract and unemotional, will mean that the restricted code child will have difficulties in responding to school, both in teaching and in appeals to principles of school discipline. The teacher's talk will be difficult to comprehend, because it will differ from the child's accustomed usage. If the child tries to translate the teacher's language into more familiar terms, they may well fail to grasp the abstract principles that the teacher intended to convey. However, the child may have very little difficulty in coping with rote learning or drilling: this in itself would accord with some of the points that Bowles and Gintis made about the relationship between elementary education (traditionally, at least in the nineteenth century, the location of rote learning) and the role of the school in reinforcing economic class distinctions.

Bernstein returned to his analysis of cultural reproduction and resistance in *The Structuring of Pedagogic Discourse* (1990). The relationship between culture and the relationship between classes was not a simple correspondence: while class differences selectively identify particular aspects of culture in order to legitimate and reproduce class differences, and use the education processes to augment this partiality, educational discourses act to amplify a whole range of social inequalities as well as those of class. Education becomes simply the transmitter of all the relationships of social power:

> pedagogic communication is simply a relay for something other than itself. Pedagogic communication in the school, in the nursery, in the home, is the relay for class relations; the relay for gender relations, the relay for religious relations, for regional relations. Pedagogic communication is a relay for patterns of dominance external to itself.
>
> (Bernstein, 1990, pp. 168–9)

But, he then argues, if this is what is relayed, what is the medium that effects the relay? We tend to study only the surface features of pedagogic communication – the message, and not the structure that makes the message possible. We also, he argued, need to study the overwhelming similarities between different educational systems: 'The most outstanding feature of educational principles and practices is their over-whelming and staggering uniformity independent of the dominant ideology' (p. 169).

Most theories of reproduction (and specifically Bourdieu's), he argued, were not just deterministic, but were also unable to recognize or allow for cultural change. The only way that they would allow change to be possible in cultural reproduction would be for it to happen when the social basis for production had been transformed, in some unspecified future. But cultural reproduction theory offers a two-fold distortion of communications – the first distortion comes through the way that pedagogic discourse is deformed in the interests of the ruling group, while the second distortion is of culture of the subordinate groups. But, Bernstein asks, what then is the theory of *undistorted* communication? His answer is that 'the inner structure of the pedagogic *is* such a theory of pedagogic communication' (p. 171).

Cultural reproduction theory is thus concerned with

> messages of patterns of dominance. We are here referring concretely to what goes on in a school: the talk, the values, the rituals, the codes of conduct are biased in favour of a dominant group. These privilege a dominant group, so such codes of communication are distorted in favour of one group, the dominant group. But there is another distortion at the same time; the culture, the practice and the consciousness of the dominated group are misrepresented, distorted. They are recontextualized as having less value. Thus there is a double distortion. However, theories of cultural reproduction are essentially theories of communication without an explicit theory of communication.
>
> (p. 171)

Bernstein's concern is that the cultural reproduction theory of Bourdieu uses concepts that are unable to generate specific descriptions of the very agencies that are central to their concerns. But a theory that could successfully put agency before structure would be able to show how groups might actively resist and oppose pedagogic communica-tions, rather than being structured by them. Bourdieu and Passeron limited themselves to concepts of arbitrary authority, arbitrary communication, pedagogic authority, pedagogic work and habitus: these cannot on their own be used to derive descriptions of the agency of cultural reproduction. Why is this? Because

> they are concerned only to understand how external power relations are *carried* by the system, they are not concerned with the description of the carrier, only with a diagnosis of its pathology. Their concepts specify what is to be described, they call for description, but they are unable to provide principles for that description.
>
> (p. 172)

From this critique, Bernstein goes on to develop a model for the carrier: the control of official pedagogic discourse, he argues, is an official recontextualizing field. Official pedagogic discourse 'regulates the rules of production, distribution, reproduction and interrelations of transmission and acquisition (practice) and the organisation of their contexts (organisation)' (pp. 195–6). The 'field' originates, sustains and modifies the official discourse, and is made up of a core of officials, consultants and advisers – educational and economic. Bernstein argues that the official recontextualizing field is regulated by the state, and operates through Parliament and the Civil Service (writing in 1990, he noted that this might include the Department for Employment as well as the DES): these incorporate specialist services from agencies (such as the NCC). In addition to the official recontextualizing field is a pedagogic recontextualizing field – the University departments of education, colleges, schools, publishers, etc., who regulate the circulation of pedagogic theories and texts, including their production and reproduction.

Bernstein argues that these recontextualizing fields define two spheres:

- the categories, contents and relationships to be transmitted (the classification of the curriculum) – 'the "what" of pedagogic discourse' (p. 196), and
- the manner of pedagogic transmission (essential to the framing of the curriculum) – 'the "how" of pedagogic discourse'.

The first of these recontextualizes subjects or areas of study from intellectual fields or disciplines (such as chemistry, mathematics, history), or the expressive fields (such as music and art), and from skill-based fields (crafts, technology). The second element, framing, recontextualizes from social science theories educational transmission (such as psychology). Bernstein argues further that in most cases the producers who create the original discourse are different from those who recontextualize the pedagogic discourse ready for transmission.

Bernstein's model moves the context of this discussion, that of the interactive curriculum, into the realm of the preactive curriculum. In the following chapters we will examine three different forms or traditions of the preactive or written curriculum.

7 Content-driven Curricula

In Chapter 1 the metaphor of the baroque garden was used, to suggest that one possible design for the curriculum is as a construction of formally delimited zones of subjects or disciplines. This has been the dominant curriculum paradigm for most of English education in the twentieth century: the historical review of curriculum change shows the enormous resilience of these particular subjects. Bernstein's 1990 analysis suggests that this dominance of the official pedagogic discourse is the consequence of a core of officials, consultants and advisers, both educational and economic, recontextualizing the curriculum into disciplines (1990, pp. 195–6). This chapter examines the way that such a curriculum is composed of boundaries and frames, and examines the origins and persistence of the major disciplines. It then examines the various arguments that have been advanced to justify the various divisions. Although in many senses a subject-based curriculum is both traditional and the means of preserving tradition, the subjects themselves are not fixed, and the ways in which new disciplines emerge and find a justification within the array of subjects reveals that the arguments for a content-based tradition are varied, and make appeal to a number of ideologies other than the simple sanction of convention and custom. As new disciplines are accepted into the disposition of curriculum contents, the hierarchies of the subjects change, and new cores and peripheries come to be defined. The content-based curriculum, though often seeking its justification in appeal to traditional eternal verities, possesses a very real dynamic: 'the visible, public and changing testimony of selected rationales and legitimising rhetorics of schooling' (Goodson, 1988, p. 16).

This type of curriculum has been variously described by analysts (see *Table 7.1*). Blyth saw it in the primary school as the 'preparatory' curriculum, designed to lead to the traditional secondary (grammar/public) school curriculum (1967); Lawton (1975) as the 'subject-based' or 'knowledge-based' curriculum; and Goodson described it as the 'academic' curriculum (1987). It also has close parallels to Skilbeck's 'classical humanist' curriculum (1976) and Golby's 'liberal-humanist' curriculum (1989). These five writers distinguished this form of curriculum from two other varieties, which will be examined in succeeding chapters.

As Goodson points out, these three forms are ' "centres of gravity" in the argument about styles of curriculum ... representing three clear constellations of curriculum styles which recur in the history of school subjects' (1987, p. 26). The content-based curriculum has been the ground on which the official pedagogic discourse has been largely fought, the area from which 'from a whole possible area of past and present,

Table 7.1 *Classifications of curriculum types*

Blyth (1967)	preparatory	elementary	developmental
Skilbeck (1976)	classical humanist		progressivism
Lawton et al. (1978)	subject-centred/ knowledge-centred	society-centred	child-centred
Goodson (1987)	academic	utilitarian	pedagogic
Golby (1989)	liberal humanist	technocratic	child-centred progressivism
	Chapter 7 *Content-driven*	*Chapter 8* *Objectives-driven*	*Chapter 9* *Process-driven*

certain meanings and practices [have been] chosen for emphasis, [and] certain other meanings and practices ... neglected and excluded' (Williams, 1961, p. 205).

Boundaries and Frames

Bernstein proposed that curricula could be described by an *educational code*, which he used to characterize two broad categories (1975). The variety described in this chapter is of the *collection* type, in which units or divisions of knowledge are strongly bounded, and which have a hierarchical organization and transmission mechanism. The alternative *integrated* type of curriculum (considered here in Chapter 9) allows for interdependence between units of knowledge in a less rigid thematic approach, with less dependence on the relative positions of teachers and pupils. In 'On the Classification and Framing of Educational Knowledge' 1971a), he argues that the two key concepts of the code are classification and frame.

Classification is used to describe the relationship between the contents of the curriculum: it is concerned with the existence and strength of the boundaries that are constructed and maintained between subjects:

> Where classification is strong, contents are well insulated from each other by strong boundaries. Where classification is weak, there is reduced insulation between contents, for the boundaries between contents are weak or blurred. *Classification thus refers to the degree of boundary maintenance between contents.*
> (Bernstein, 1971a, p. 88, emphasis as in original)

Frame, on the other hand, is used by Bernstein to refer to the context in which knowledge is transmitted and received – the relationship between the teacher and the pupil. Frame refers to the strength of the boundary of what may or may not be taught – it refers us to the range of options available to teacher and taught in the control of what is transmitted and received in the context of the pedagogic relationship. Strong framing entails reduced options; weak framing entails a range of options. *Thus frame refers to the degree of control teacher and pupil possess over the selection, organisation, pacing and timing of the knowledge transmitted and received in the pedagogic relationship.*

(Bernstein, 1971a, pp. 88–9, emphasis as in original)

These two concepts create four possible types, of which, Bernstein suggests, only two are normally found in practice (*Table 7.2*).

Table 7.2 Typology of curriculum types, after Bernstein

		Classification The construction and maintenance of boundaries between curriculum contents; their inter-relationsh-ips and stratification.	
		Weak Contents blur into each other; boundaries are not distinct or well-maintained; hierarchy of content (if any exists) is unclear.	**Strong** Well insulated subjects with strong boundaries; subjects arranged in a well-accepted hierarchy of importance and value.
Frame The relative degrees of control possessed by the teacher and the pupil over the selection, trans-mission, pace, etc. of transmission and learning of knowledge.	**Weak** Unclear what is and is not appropriate subject matter for learning; teacher/pupil relationship one of discovery; pace of learning negotiated between the two.	**Integrated** Teachers cooperate with colleagues and pupils; authority is personalized; power of teachers is concealed; projects/topics are used to organize content; direction of learning is less focused and more open to negotiation.	
	Strong Teacher/system determines the appropriate material that has to be transmitted; pace of learning is determined by teacher/curriculum; teacher has all the necessary information to be learned by the pupil.	(Programmed learning is a possible example of this (Bernstein, 1975, p. 89). Content may be blurred, but the pupil has no control over what is learned.)	**Collection** Teachers are subject specialists, transmitting body of knowledge defined outside the classroom; subjects are clearly distinguished; pace and direction of learning are fixed by teacher.

Note: Shaded areas indicate predominant codes.   Source: Bernstein, 1971a, p. 87–90

He goes on to analyse the latter stages of various secondary collection-type curricula, contrasting the specialized nature of A level courses (a small number of subjects, which are normally related or cognate to each other) with the less-specialized post-16 courses found in the USA and continental Europe. He also suggests that the USA syllabuses tend to be structured around courses as knowledge units, while the continental European collection curricula are constructed from subjects.

At the time that Bernstein was developing this theoretical framework, he suggested that there was a discernible movement in England away from the collection code variety of curriculum towards integrated code. Sixthformers, he noted, were less likely to be taking related A level subjects (the example he gives is of a student taking A levels in Religion, Economics and Physics, as opposed to a 'pure' specialized course in Chemistry, Physics and Mathematics). University degrees were becoming more course-based, and less focused on single traditional disciplines. The school curriculum was developing integrated and cross-subject courses, aided by the innovations of the Schools Council: the headteacher's authority was becoming more collegiate as horizontal, integrative relationships between teaching teams developed (Bernstein, 1975, pp. 103–6; MacDonald, 1977, p. 25: but see Musgrove, 1971, p. 69 for an alternative view of this). Such a move can be shown schematically as in *Table 7.3*.

Collective codes operate wherever subjects are used to describe the curriculum: this distinction is at the heart of the 1980 dispute between the HMI's *View of the Curriculum* (DES, 1980b) and the DES's *A Framework for the School Curriculum* (DES, 1980a) (see Chapter 4). Where HMI argue for 'areas of experience' as the mode for defining the curriculum, they are arguing in particular for a weak classification, while the DES's attempt to prescribe a strong classification based on tightly timetabled subjects betrays also a set of underlying presumptions about the need for schools to

Table 7.3 *The movement from a collection code type of curriculum to an integrated code curriculum*

	Collection code	→	*Integrated code*
Content of curriculum	distinct subjects	⇨	enquiry-based approach to topics and themes
Organization of teaching/learning	fixed timetable	⇨	flexible timetable
Arrangement of pupil groups	streamed/setted by ability	⇨	mixed ability
Choice given to pupils	strictly limited	⇨	wide
Assessment of learning	single mode (usually formal written examination)	⇨	multiple mode (including coursework, teacher assessment)
Teachers' control of pupils	hierarchical	⇨	interpersonal
Teachers' roles	staff are independent of each other	⇨	staff relate to each other in interdependent teams

Source: After Hoyle, 1976, p. 20.

operate within a strong frame. The integrated model was advocated by HMI not only for primary pupils, but also for secondary schools, where HMI were professionally aware of the schooling of the 'below average' ('Newsom child') pupils, unlike the memories of the DES civil servants who drafted *A Framework* (even less their political masters, who approved its publication).

Given that the predominant mode in English education has been of the collection type, not withstanding some (usually short-lived) advocacy of a more integrated type, questions arise about the origins and persistence of this type. Why have this particular collection of subjects emerged? Noting the great similarities between the 1904 code and the 1987 National Curriculum, why is this particular collection so persistent? While the collection is clearly not immutable (as can be seen by the emergence of technology), there is clearly a certain inertia in the list. Is this inherent in the current social perceptions of the world and of learning, as the emergence of the 'world-wide' elementary curriculum (as shown by Meyer and his colleagues (1992): see Chapter 2)? Or are there more fundamental causes, related to the structure of knowledge itself? Or is this list a mere cultural artefact, a form of heritage that has become ossified through usage?

The Quadrivium and the Trivium

The traditional 'classical' curriculum was based on the implicit assumption that education was linked to the symbolic control of society, and not linked in any way to production. The manual processes necessary for production in the pre-capitalist, medieval world were reproduced instead through family and guild structures, through what Bernstein has called an 'invisible relay' (1990, pp. 147, 152). The education provided in this period was strongly related to the Church, and served to reproduce the control symbols of the ecclesiastical structures, as well as the discourses necessary for administration and diplomacy. The curriculum of the medieval University was constructed around a seven-fold collection of disciplines, which is said to date from Boethius in the sixth century (Lawton and Gordon, 1996). Each discipline was tightly bounded from the others. The first three of these 'seven liberal arts' were grammar, logic and rhetoric – the Trivium. After these had been studied, the Quadrivium followed – music, arithmetic, geometry and astronomy. The whole course traditionally lasted seven years. Durkheim's analysis of this organization of knowledge (1938) suggested that the Trivium was essentially concerned with the exploration of the word (which is God), while the subjects of the Quadrivium explore the world. Bernstein adds to this distinction the word being essentially concerned with the inner unity of the person, in a discourse of the sacred, while the exploration of the world (in an abstract sense) is concerned with the outer, organic solidarity of the social, in a discourse of the profane (Bernstein, 1990). He suggests that the dislocation of these two, the Trivium and the Quadrivium are an inherent Christian metaphor for the dislocation between the inner and outer, person and society, achieved through the Church's discriminating recontextualizing of ancient Greek thought: the 'dislocation is a metaphor of the deep grammar of Christianity and produced by it' (p. 151, also Bernstein, 1996, p. 23). This abstract form of education had no necessary connection with production in the pre-capitalist world, and its form became so entrenched that its forms can be seen to persist in contemporary classical humanist curricula.

This classical humanism can be seen as the oldest and traditionally highest esteemed of all the curriculum ideologies (Skilbeck, 1976). It is characterized today by a belief in a refined cultural heritage, and until the mid-twentieth century was seen as being reserved for the education of a relatively elite custodian class, some form of descendants of the Platonic guardians. This elite was able to lay claim to social power through its special knowledge of subjects, such as particularly the classics, which were perceived as bestowing privilege and rights – for example, to assume positions of leadership in the civil service, the armed forces, colonial administration, academia and the like. This most medieval classical heritage had successfully adapted the Trivium and Quadrivium to construct subjects that have lines of descent from the seven liberal arts. The Trivium's grammar, logic and rhetoric thus transmute into classical languages, philosophy and theology, and the Quadrivium's concern with the world and the social – music, arithmetic, geometry and astronomy – become mathematics and the social and physical sciences. The essence of classical humanism has remained essentially static since Plato's educational treatises *The Republic* and *The Laws*: it was based on the presumption that the search for knowledge would produce ultimate and permanent truths that would be both universal and timeless. Instruction in such a search for knowledge constituted necessary and sufficient education for the elite who were destined to rule.

This vision of an education for the rulers persisted through to most of the twentieth century. The nature of the knowledge, and its arrangement into different bodies, have shifted: in Chapter 3 the effects of the 1868 Taunton Commission were seen, where the then traditional grammar school curriculum was liberalized by the introduction of a spoken language, some natural sciences, history and geography, at the inevitable expense of Greek and Latin. Beliefs and practices – even those of recent origin – become ordained as though they were long-established traditions, and become necessary requirements of the 'well-educated' person.

Until quite recently, it has been axiomatic that such a cultural tradition was properly to be reserved for the relatively small elite who would require it. The mental discipline that would be engendered through such studies would fit one for public service and leadership: Gordon quotes an unidentified writer in the late 1880s on the necessary curriculum for those preparing to enter the Indian Civil Service as

> fairly good instruction in Latin and Greek … and a facility for composing verses [in those languages]; a thorough acquaintance with French and German. I should require, were it possible, that the young men selected should have the manners and self-respect of well-bred Englishmen; a good training in horsemanship; and … as an adjunct a course of veterinary study.
>
> (Quoted by Gordon, 1978, p. 123)

Bantock, writing in 1968, urged the maintenance of diverse curricula that acknowledged the distinction between the 'high' classical humanist culture and mass popular culture. He advocated traditional subjects 'for those who can cope with them', but for the rest, he argues that what is not needed is 'a watered down version of the same culture that is thought adequate for the brightest'. In place of such a 'high' culture, he suggests curricular activities based on what he calls 'the primary experience ... the face-to-face interests of the folk' (p. 62). To provide a common curriculum for all would be, for most pupils,

> the imposition of an abstract educational provision, derived from social and polit-ical principles of little relevance to the situation, on the living reality of children with their immense range of interests and capacities, deficiencies and handicaps, all of which need careful consideration in order to serve their best interests.
>
> (1968, p. 62)

This argument for a differentiated curriculum is based on the supposition that most pupils ought to be interested in a particular 'folk culture', qualitatively and struc-turally different from the 'high culture' that is reserved for the intellectual pupils (for whom is reserved the right to enjoy, to preserve, and to denote their ability and right to assume positions of power).

Subjects, to Bantock and the traditional classical humanists, are a key ingredient to the curriculum, for two oddly linked reasons. First, the subjects are 'the most fruitful and convenient mode of organising knowledge so that it can profitably be studied and can lead on to new understanding' – 'some such organisation is essential to allow expe-rience to be handled intellectually at all' (Bantock, 1968, p. 122). This clearly implies the existence of a canon of knowledge, classified into subjects that are logically ordered. But, second, the study of subjects is not the acquisition or accumulation of facts, but the application and problem-solving, the mental disciplines and skills that are acquired in the process of learning. This second argument seems to undermine the claims of the first: if such skills are to be developed, then the context or content that is used to develop them could be logically divorced from any encapsulation of the canon of knowledge-in-disciplines. Pring, considering the various principles that might be employed in the selection of a curriculum, distinguishes the former as selection based on *common culture* – the 'common heritage that would serve to promote some form of social unity ... to preserve a common background of values and meaning through a shared literary tradition' (1978, p. 141) (though one might here point out that 'common' in this context is only that which is common to a particular political-social class) – from the selection principle of mental powers, increasing analytic and logical thinking, in which 'it [did] not matter what you learnt so long as it had this intellec-tual mileage in it' (p. 142).

Classical humanism is no longer the preserve of those attempting to reserve a particular curriculum for the elite. White, for example, argued that such a curriculum, as the basis for access to power, should be available for all: 'all children should be compelled to study certain disciplines – history, physics, and so on. ... the separate disciplines should be seen as fitting people to be members of the good society' (White, 1969). Gramsci's arguments were rather similar: the essential knowledge of elite education should be available to all (Chapter 5). Lawton argues that 'the selection from a culture of a society' that constitutes the curriculum is essentially of classless knowledge, and that therefore to argue for a working-class curriculum, as Bantock does, is not possible (even if one could identify a single working-class culture) (Lawton, 1975, pp. 13, 45. But see also Ozolins, 1979). This was followed by the argument by HMI for a common curriculum, described in Chapter 4 (DES, 1977b), which although couched in the language of non-traditional 'areas of experience' nevertheless identified the subjects of the classical humanist curriculum as part of the necessary core. It was this same ideal of the essential classical canon (albeit couched in egalitarian terms) to which all pupils should be exposed to and judged by that led Kenneth Baker to insist on the ten-subject based National Curriculum in 1987 (Chapter 5).

The effect of the elevation of a curriculum that was invented for an elite, and used as a tool for control through the transmission of particular symbols and cultures, to become the curriculum for all is potentially alienating and divisive: this will be examined further in the final chapter. The classical humanist curriculum is the predominant form for most school education today, and Skilbeck usefully summarizes the key features of this tradition:

> Classical humanism has been associated with clear and firm discipline, high attainment in examinations, continuity between past and present, the cohesive and orderly development of institutions and of the myths and rituals engendered by those institutions, and it has been associated with redefined views about what it is fitting to do, feel, think, and with standards of performance in all spheres.
>
> (1976, p. 17)

Philosophical Rationales

Many of the arguments for the content matter of the classical humanist curriculum are based on little more than a self-evident appeal to tradition and common sense about the elements of high culture and its values. The body of high-status subjects appears as given, a settled canon of disciplines that need no further validation. One of the most significant attempts to justify the classical humanist curriculum, and to reflect on the elements that constituted it, was made by Hirst in 'Liberal Education and the Nature of Knowledge' (1965). He argued that the wide range of knowledge of which 'mind' is constituted can be reduced to seven fundamental 'forms of thought', each of which is a unique and essential way of understanding and knowing the world. A form of knowledge is a distinct way in which the individual's experience becomes structured, and this structure is formed around the use of publicly accepted symbols. Because these symbols have public meaning, the way in which the learner uses them can be tested, and the symbols become capable of elaboration and extension.

Each of the seven forms (mathematical, physical scientific, religious, literary and artistic, human (social) scientific, philosophical and historical) has its own particular central concepts that are unique to that form, and these concepts are related in a complex network of relationships that constitute a distinctive logical structure. Each form is able to make particular statements, or address particular questions, that are in most cases testable against experience, against criteria that are specific to that particular form of knowledge. The development of these particular techniques and skills for exploring and expressing experiences creates a body of symbolically expressed knowledge that constitutes the sum of the arts and the sciences (Golby, 1989, pp. 35–6). These forms of knowledge were closely related to existing school subjects, which Hirst argued were 'indisputably logical and cohesive disciplines' (1967, p. 44).

Hirst argued that everyone should, through education, experience each of these particular forms, and thus understand that mode of thinking. The curriculum, therefore, should be constructed from those subjects which best inculcated these seven forms of knowing. Such a rationale would suggest that, for example, physics would be better than botany as an introduction to the scientific form of knowledge. Hirst's curriculum is thus the same knowledge-based classical curriculum, argued from different principles that appeal to rationality rather than tradition. Hirst argues that he is not necessarily arguing for a discipline-based curriculum – 'fields of knowledge' such as agriculture or medicine could substitute for subjects, he argues – but in practice what he advocates is essentially a strongly-bounded collection-type curriculum.

This analysis has significant supporters. In the USA, Phenix (1964) has described nine 'realms of meaning' that are essentially parallel both to Hirst's forms of knowledge (though clearly not identical), and to the nature of the particular disciplines, each of which Phenix characterized as 'the characteristic activity of an identifiable organized tradition of men of knowledge, that is of persons who are skilled in certain specified functions that they are able to justify by a set of intelligible standards' (p. 317). King and Brownell (1966) described each academic discipline as 'a community of discourse', in which scholars share an identity created from their publications, conferences and concerns. Oakeshott (1974) uses the term 'idiom of activity', by which he means, in any given discipline, the knowledge of how to behave intellectually in an appropriate way: 'we come to penetrate an idiom of activity in no other way than by practising the activity, for it is through the practice of an activity that we can acquire the knowledge of how to practice it.'

Although these arguments support the kind of curriculum that Bantock argued for, they were also used by Hirst to suggest a rationale for a common curriculum. Hirst's analysis is directed towards the justification of the classical humanist curriculum for all: everyone should be introduced into the ways of knowing of each of the seven forms, and they should not be reserved for the elite. However, Pring argues that Hirst is in effect indulging in a form of philosophical reductionism in deriving just seven distinct and exclusive forms of knowledge (1976). The philosophical arguments for the content-based curriculum of subjects are largely derived from a particular initial view of education as a process of initiation, in which the learner is brought to *care* about the possession of particular knowledge defined as 'relevant': the learner is seen as a disciple, who comes to share particular tested modes of thought and conduct (Peters, 1965).

The Life-cycle of a Subject: Science and Biology

The second part of this chapter moves on to examine the origins of the subjects themselves. Subjects have developed, changed, and been supplanted by other subjects, despite the various claims made by classical humanists to longevity and to tradition, or appeals to rationality. Without wishing to reify subjects – there is a perhaps inevitable 'taking them for granted' in examining their origins (Seeley, 1966) – we can understand a great deal about the ideologies that underpin the content-based, subject-organized curriculum if we examine the processes by which they emerge into the pantheon of the collection of approved subjects, and the ways in which they achieve high (or low) status.

An instructive case study of the development of a subject within the school curriculum is provided by Layton's analysis of science as a discipline (1972, 1973), amplified by Goodson's account of the emergence of the particular science of biology as a separate and distinct subject (1987).

Layton suggested that there might be three stages in the emergence of a school subject from its first appearance to the time that it achieved the high status of academic 'official knowledge' (1973). The first stage was of that of useful knowledge, sufficient to satisfy both the interests and the needs of the pupils studying it. From this developed a period in which, while the 'useful knowledge' element remained important, there was much effort made by teachers of the subject to systematically and rigorously develop the subject's content and rationale. From these efforts, there began to develop some academic status for the subject, and this in itself became, for some pupils, a sufficiently important reason to study it. The third and final stage, Layton suggested, was arrived at when the most influential people in the subject were no longer the teachers in schools, but University scholars, who became the arbiters of what does and does not constitute the subject. It was they who determined the boundaries of the discipline, and became what Bernstein later called the official recontextualizing field. The teachers of the subject in the school at this stage have the role of transmitting the knowledge, and the pupils that of absorbing it. Goodson points out (1988) that this process is one of the school teachers – who had effectual control of the subject in the early stages – choosing to hand this over to outside powers: he comments that 'it is not so much domination by dominant groups as solicitous surrender by subordinate groups' (p. 193).

Layton's description of the first stage in the teaching of science concerns what was called 'the science of common things', taught in elementary schools in the 1840s. This was practical, utilitarian science: its chief advocate at the time, Richard Dawes, described it as 'drawn from things which interest at present, as well as those likely to interest them in future – such as a description of their clothing, how it is manufactured, etc., the articles which they consume, from whence they come, the nature of the products of the parish which they themselves and those about them are helping to cultivate' (quoted in Goodson and Dowbiggin, 1994, p. 44). Layton characterizes science at this point as a 'callow intruder', which

> stakes a place in the timetable, justifying its presence on grounds such as pertinence and utility. During this stage learners are attracted to the subject because of its bearing on matters of concern to them. The teachers are rarely trained specialists, but bring the missionary enthusiasms of pioneers to their task. The dominant criterion is relevance to the needs and interests of the learners.
>
> (1972, p. 165)

This curriculum area was effectively destroyed by the Revised Code in 1862. Goodson and Dowbiggin suggest that this was no accident: the elementary school curriculum was reformed and restructured at this point to undermine efforts to provide a real educational experience for lower classes. Layton describes an investigation at the time by the British Association into what form science education should be for the upper classes, and quotes the chair of the enquiry's comment that 'it would be an unwholesome and vicious state of society in which those who are comparatively unblessed with nature's gifts should be generally superior in intellectual attainments to those above them in station' (Layton, 1973, p. 41). Science had become common in most grammar schools since the 1840s, though it was virtually absent from the public schools at this time, which despised it because it was seen, at this point in its history, as utilitarian (Wiener, 1981, p. 17).

When science re-emerged in the secondary schools of the 1880s, it was in its second stages, in which

> a tradition of scholarly work in the subject is emerging, along with a corps of trained specialists from which teachers might be recruited. Students are still attracted to the Study, but as much by its reputation and growing academic status as by its relevance to their own problems and concerns. The internal logic and discipline of the subject is becoming increasingly influential in the selection and organisation of the subject matter.
>
> (Layton, 1972, p. 165)

This was a variety of pure laboratory science, now generally accepted as the 'correct' form. Utilitarian purposes and rationales for the subject were subdued, and more emphasis was put on scholarship and research as an intellectual discipline in its own right. Abstract scientific concepts assumed a greater importance than everyday experience, as the University departments assumed a greater involvement in the definition of what school practice should be examined: as Goodson and Dowbiggin put it, 'the context of professional practice [in the curriculum was] ... structured in ways which fostered institutional ties with bureaucratic organisations whose hegemony in the definition of culturally valuable knowledge was difficult to counteract' (1994, p. 45; also Millar, 1985).

Thus Layton's third stage is arrived at:

> the teachers now constitute a professional body with well established rules and values. The selection of subject matter is determined in large measure by the judgements and practices of the specialist scholars who lead inquiries in the field. Students are initiated into a tradition, their attitudes approaching passivity and resignation, a prelude to disenchantment.
>
> (Layton, 1972, p. 165)

Most science education today – at both school and undergraduate level – is undertaken in a passive way, in which students are not required or expected to read or study the work of scientists, but to work through texts prepared specifically for their course and level (Cooper, 1984, p. 46). Unlike social science or humanities students, who are expected to study original works that will outline contrasting and even opposing views 'scientific education ... is conducted entirely through textbooks ... the undergraduate acquires the substance of his field from books written especially for students' (Kuhn, 1970, p. 345; also Hodson, 1988).

The sciences were, in the nineteenth century, essentially seen as being four in number: physics and chemistry being strongly in the lead, with botany and zoology some way behind. Goodson's case study of the development of biology points out that at this time biology 'hardly existed as an identifiable discipline' (1987, p. 41) Advocates of the sciences tended, in Layton's second stage, to stress both the intrinsic value of each subject as disciplinary training, and also the utilitarian aspects of the subject. This utilitarian phase, Goodson suggests, is a necessary stage that a subject must pass through: to gain a real foothold, a subject must demonstrate these 'dual characteristics' of serviceability and erudition. While both chemistry and physics had a substantial pedigree of potential utility (Tracey points out that the achievements of industrial revolution 'all point to the utilitarian value of a knowledge of physics and chemistry for boys, if not for girls' (1962, p. 429)), botany and zoology had, at this stage, fewer such claims. Layton gives examples of claims to usefulness for these subjects that were attempted at the time – for example, helping with the extermination of insects destroying timber in docks.

Tracey's comment above is a useful reminder that science remains a highly gendered discipline (DES, 1980c; Kelly, 1985). Measor (1983) argued that girls become socialized into particular attitudes towards the kinds of knowledge and activities that are considered appropriate for women's sexual identity: in this respect, science – and particularly physics and chemistry – are seen by many girls as masculine. Measor observed that in some schools girls use this perception to establish their own identity and status by consciously rejecting studying science, or at least not taking it seriously. Some of them also put pressure on their peers to do the same. Hammersley (1984) suggested that children who were socialized in this way into gendered attitudes to subjects will, first, be more favourable towards knowledge that is considered appropriate to their sex; second, behave either incompetently or in an ignorant manner in these disciplines, in order to emphasize their sexual identity; and third, do these to a greater extent in situations where they feel insecure about their sexual identity, or where there is competition for inter-sex relationships. Physics and chemistry in particular continue to be avoided by girls in situations where options can be made, and correspondingly more take the more 'feminine' science of biology.

But biology was not, until relatively recently, seen at all as a mature subject, handicapped as it was with the image of a hobbyist pastime that was essentially no more than an accumulation of descriptions. Such a perception began to change at the end of the nineteenth century, with developments, for example, in bacteriology with the work of Pasteur, and in marine and agricultural biology. These developments demonstrated the subject's 'utilitarian potential [and this] was an important factor in determining its early progress' (Tracey, 1962, p. 429). Slowly, biology came to be accepted as an examination subject: it was not generally accepted as a matriculation subject until the late 1920s. 'It was the decade after 1930 which, more than any other, saw biology gain an established place in the secondary school curriculum' (Jenkins, 1979, p. 123), as it was realized that 'biology was capable of economic application and exploitation in industries such as fishing, agriculture and forestry, and in medicine' (Tracey, 1962, p. 423). Its academic status remained relatively weak, however: it was essentially a fusion of elements of botany and zoology. The growth in the number of candidates offering biology as a matriculation subject was remarkable, however, as *Figure 7.1* demonstrates (based on Goodson, 1987, p. 45).

Biology emerged finally as a high-status unitary science in the 1960s, driven by both the development of ecology as a rigorous experimental science (linked to field studies movements, Goodson 1987) and to the striking developments in molecular biology and the work of Watson, Crick and others, which provided 'at last the rationale for claiming parity of esteem with the physical sciences' (p. 51). Goodson points to the parallels between the development of biology in the twentieth century and science in the nineteenth: from its origins in the lower years of the secondary school as a continuation of the 'natural history' tradition of the primary school; through a growing appreciation of its economic uses and potential, in which new careers open up in which a biological training was seen as valuable. This gave the subject its second arena, in the sixth form, but one in which it was still marred as being vocational rather than academic from the 1930s through to the 1950s, and having a lower, utilitarian status. The academic status remained elusive while botany and zoology retained their hegemony in the University departments: hard science status did not come until the 1960s.

It was this growing acceptance of the discipline by the Universities that led to the changing status of the subject in schools. As was also true in the case of geography (examined in the next chapter), it appears that this was not so much the Universities dominating the secondary schools, but the active encouragement of biology teachers in the schools to legitimize the subject. Subgroups in the schools, Goodson

Figure 7.1   *Percentage of candidates offering science subjects, Northern Universities Joint Matriculation Board*

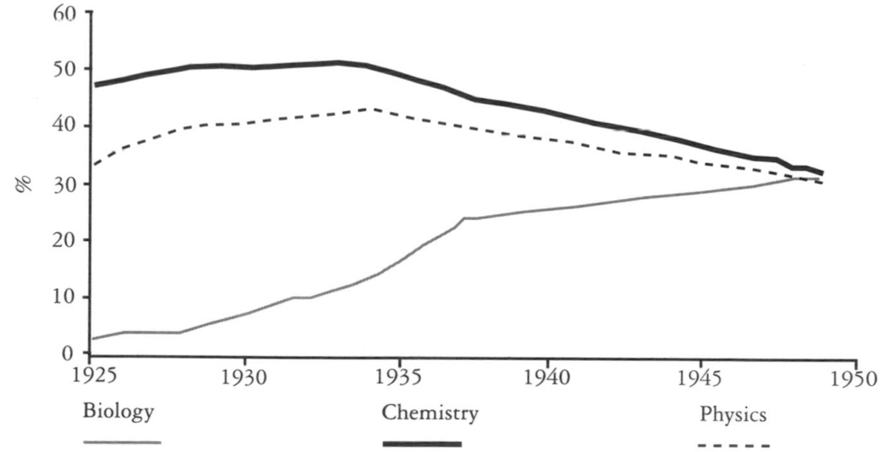

Source: Based on Goodson, 1987, p. 45.

suggests, 'conspire to increase the control over the definition and direction of subjects by university scholars' (1987, p. 193), in exchange for status and career development within the school. As Bernstein suggests, subject teachers seek a high degree of boundary maintenance for their subject: strong classification leads to a high status subject, with a strong frame. The University stamp of academic legitimacy confers such a strong classification, and gives external authority to the subject's status. As Reid observes, the importance of this is not the development of a subject that is capable of public evaluation, 'but the development and maintenance of legitimating rhetorics which provide automatic support for correctly labelled activity' (1984, p. 75). The main task of subject teachers in working to advance or defend their subjects is to select the choice of suitable identifiers, and to persuade the public with a convincing and eloquent justification for this. 'Teachers have been encouraged to define their curricular knowledge in abstract, formal and scholarly terms in return for status, resources, territoriality and accreditation' (Goodson, 1987, p. 192). The content-based curriculum is inherently reinforced by the subject-based organization of the secondary school, which reinforces the transmission model of learning: as one exponent put it, 'the important task of every day is to bring about a personal confrontation between teacher and pupil, at the end of which a lesson has been well and truly learned' (Hewitson, 1969, p. 132).

Hierarchies of Subjects

In a content-based curriculum, with strong classification of subjects, the emergence of a hierarchy of disciplines is inevitable. Strong classification is usually linked to strong framing, and strong framing creates school structures that favour hierarchical structures of departmentalism. Departments focused around subjects inevitably jockey with each other for resources and status, and generate rhetorical statements that bolster their subject's credentials at the expense of others. Subject departments will use any currently available educational and political discourse in order to sustain this: utilitarian, social and pedagogical arguments will be used to establish a foothold on the ladder, but to move up the hierarchy academic credentials are seen as key, because high-status, apparently disinterested authorities external to the school can be used to determine the subject boundaries that validate the classification.

The National Curriculum's hierarchy is based on this set of distinctions: high-status knowledge is formalized within the distinct definitions of the foundation subjects, with the highest status for the core subjects. Low status knowledge is relegated to the cross-curricular themes and other elements (often not worthy of description, and thus unbounded, non-classified) within the area of the whole curriculum. However, this could be seen as merely formalizing the pre-existing ranking of subjects. Despite the experimentation found in schools in the two decades before the introduction of the 1988 Act (see Chapter 4; Richards, 1998, p. 67), there was a de facto hierarchy, even in the department-less primary school. Alexander contrasts the primary school's 'Curriculum One' (the basics: high priority, teacher-directed, utilitarian rational knowledge, progression, etc.) to 'Curriculum Two' (the 'other' curriculum: low priority, heuristic child-initiated, empiricist anti-knowledge stance, random learning experiences, etc.) (Alexander, 1984, p. 77).

Goodson advances his overall thesis first in *Defining the Curriculum* (1984b). First, subjects are not monolithic, but should rather be seen as shifting amalgamations between areas, in which process school subjects become established. Second, there is a continual pressure from subjects with less esteem, which begin by stressing their pedagogic and utilitarian traditions, towards asserting and creating an academic tradition for themselves. Third, the curriculum debate is generally a conflict between different subjects over aspects of status, resources and territory (pp. 28–9).

Goodson's analyses the forces that create these hierarchies in *School Subjects and Curriculum Change* (1987). He traces back the rules that are used to define high status knowledge. Once the 1904 Revised Code had been supported by the School Certificate system, the curricular system was used by subject teachers to sustain and advance their own positions. While the initial rules for what constituted high-status knowledge reflected the dominant interests at that time, Goodson argues that 'teachers' self-interest in the material conditions of their working lives' (p. 193) sustained and developed the system.

Goodson thus reverses the explanations of Peters (1965), Hirst (1967) and Hirst and Peters (1970). Their argument had been that an intellectual discipline was created by a community of scholars, normally working in a University, which was then 'translated' for use as a school subject. Goodson admits that while 'it is persuasively self-fulfilling to argue that here is a field of knowledge from which an 'academic' school subject can receive inputs and general direction' (1987, p. 5), in practice many University disciplines *follow* the evolution of school subjects, and serve to legitimate the subject. He argues that academic subjects are linked to external examinations, and that these confer important status on the subject. This status is translated into specialist teachers, places on the school timetable, and leads to the various activities that distinguish subject groups: categories of examination, specialist degrees, and training courses. Goodson also suggests how important it is for a subject to have a 'department' in the school:

> the subject is the major reference point in the work of the contemporary secondary school ... the teacher is identified by the pupil and relates to them mainly through his or her subject ... teachers are normally arranged in 'subject departments'. The departments have a range of 'graded posts' for special responsibilities and for the 'head [of] the Department' ... the subject provides the means whereby salary is decided and career structure defined, and influence on school policy is channelled.
>
> (1987, p. 31)

Able pupils were linked to academic examinations, and from this link developed pathways to resources, graded posts and career prospect. To gain these, teacher groups had to demonstrate their subject's claim to an academic tradition: this meant ensuring that Universities legitimated the subject with departments and chairs, and acted as guardians to the definition of the subject. It also led to the paraphernalia of testing intelligence and aptitude, that could be used to ensure that this costly academic curriculum could be bestowed on the 'right' pupils. Goodson terms the link between academic subjects, examinations and 'able' pupils a 'triple alliance', that perpetuated this system of content-based tightly-bounded subjects into the comprehensive school system of the 1970s and 1980s (p. 194).

Repeated studies of the practice of schools have shown the process by which resources are channelled to higher-status subjects: for example, Byrne observed that not only did high-status subjects seem to need more time in the school's timetable, but they also needed – and got – 'more staff, more highly paid staff and more money for equipment and books' (1974, p. 20). Ball's study of 'Beachside' school (1981) also showed the effects of this hierarchy on the pupils. The pupils were acutely (and accurately) aware of the precise status of each subject, and they also recognized how they were divided into groups to match particular types of curricula. The hierarchy of subjects was all-pervasive: 'the most experienced teachers spent most of their time teaching the most able pupils ... academic achievement tended to be the single criterion of success in the school' (p. 18). Beachside's hierarchy of subjects was directly linked to perceptions of pupil ability. At the top were the traditional 'O level' subjects – mathematics, English, languages, sciences, history and geography – all of which had 'an academic orientation in common: they are concerned with theoretical knowledge. They are the subjects for the brighter, the academic, the band 1 pupil' (p. 140). Below this came the practical subjects – technical studies and metalwork at O level, then the traditional CSEs and, finally, for the least able pupils, the subjects that were 'lowest of all in status, new Mode III CSE'. At one end of the school spectrum the staff and pupils were engaged in a curriculum that was 'planted in revered academic tradition, adapted to teaching from a pool of factual knowledge and has clearly defined, if often irrelevant subject boundaries'; at the other end of the spectrum was an entirely different low-status curriculum, that was 'experimental ... focusing on contemporary problems, grouping subjects together and rejecting formal teaching methods' (p. 104).

The changes in secondary school organization that were brought about by the ending of the tripartite system of 1944 had little real impact on the curriculum. The content-based curriculum continued unchallenged in its position of esteem, and was taught alongside the low-esteem pedagogic and utilitarian curricula that will be examined next. In these other traditions, the curriculum was an 'attempt to align school work to the environment of ["non-academic"] children'. The Norwood Commission (Board of Education, 1943), on which the 1944 Act had been based had identified 'the categories of curricula and pupil clientele, [which were now to be] merged or prioritized in the comprehensive schools' (Goodson, 1988, p. 121). The school system was still divided 'into two sections, one geared to a system of external examinations, the other less constrained ... it is the consequence of innovation into these two separate sections rather than the curricula themselves which may be producing a new means of sustaining old traditions' (Shipman, 1971, pp. 101–2).

Curriculum Status and Pupil Status

The Norwood Report had identified three groups of pupils, and matched each to a particular curricular tradition. The content-based, high-status subject curriculum was allocated to the pupil who was:

Table 7.4 Percentages of pupils leaving school at age 15 characterizing school subjects on scales of usefulness and interest

(1) Boys

	Useful		*Useless*	
Interesting	metalwork	63		
	woodwork	60		
	English	51		
	mathematics	48		
	science	56		
	PE/games	44		
	technical drawing	43		
	geography	40		
	current affairs	39		
	arts and handicraft	23		
Boring	mathematics	19	religious instruction	30
			foreign languages	26
			music	48

(2) Girls

	Useful		*Useless*	
Interesting	housecraft	82		
	English	69		
	commerce	61		
	needlework	51		
	current affairs	42		
	PE/games	30		
	geography	28		
	science	27		
	foreign languages	23		
Boring	mathematics	22	music	34
			history	22
			foreign languages	20

Source: Schools Council, 1968, p. 60.
Note: Subjects scoring less than 20 per cent in any one cell are omitted.

interested in learning for its own sake, who can grasp an argument or follow a piece of connected reasoning; who is interested in causes, whether on the level of human volition or in the material world; who cares to know how things came to be as well as how they are; who is sensitive to language as expression of thought; to a proof as a precise demonstration; to a series of experiments justifying a principle; ... interested in the relatedness of related things, in development, in structure, in a coherent body of knowledge.

(Board of Education, 1943, p. 2)

The utilitarian, goals-based curriculum, to be considered next, was reserved for those pupils 'whose interests and abilities lie markedly in the field of applied science or applied art' (p. 2), with an altogether more simple, and less defined or bounded, curriculum for the pupil who 'deals more easily with concrete things than ideas ... [who] may have much ability, but it will be in the realm of facts ... [who is] interested in things as they are ... [but finds] little attraction in the past or in the slow disentanglement of causes or movements' (p 3).

The concept of utility in the curriculum, or of an objectives-driven curriculum designed to develop specified capabilities, has particular appeal for many pupils, parents and politicians. A survey of young school leavers, conducted for the Schools Council in its early period, asked pupils to categorize the subjects that they had encountered in their schooling along a spectrum of useful to non-useful, and again along a spectrum from highly interesting to boring. The results of this (*Table 7.4*) show that the content-based curriculum was perceived by these low-achievers as a 'useful' curriculum. Its utility, however, probably resided less in the content of what was taught, than in two other factors. The first was the stress that teachers continued to place on the 'usefulness' of their subject. The strategies that subject teachers used to gain academic status for their subjects were conducted with an audience of academics and policy-makers: with the very different audience of less able pupils, then a different strategy was always used, of stressing the relationship of the subject to everyday life, and the application it would have to this. Second, there was probably a shrewd recognition by most pupils that high-status subjects were useful precisely because of their high status: they were 'useful' in getting better paid and more interesting jobs. It is in this way that 'the tyranny of subjects is firmly established ... an externally imposed order, based on the sacredness of subjects' (Hunt, 1970, p. 48).

8 Objectives-driven Curricula

The content-driven curriculum, with its sharply delimited divisions into high-status subjects, and its emphasis on academic credentials and validation, seems to be the vehicle *par excellence* for the transmission of Bourdieu's cultural capital to an elite group of students. To insist on its application to the whole school population, as did the English National Curriculum, might appear to be an egalitarian move, accessing elite cultural capital to all. As Moon and Mortimore commented, 'the secondary curriculum ... appears to be based on the curriculum of a typical 1960s grammar school', and 'the primary curriculum was put forward as if it were no more than a pre-secondary preparation' (1989, p. 9). But there are alternative perspectives on the nature of this national curriculum. First, most subjects can also be presented in an instrumental fashion: indeed most subjects (or topics and themes) can be justified in any number of ways. Bowles and Gintis quote the nineteenth-century Boston Schools Committee to demonstrate how a curriculum activity as instrumental as needlecraft *could* in nineteenth-century elementary schools be portrayed as character building and developing an assiduous disposition (1976, p. 168): 'The industrious habits which sewing tends to form and the consequent high moral influence which it exerts upon society at large may cause its introduction more extensively in all the schools.'

This chapter will thus cover some of the same school subject matter as the previous chapter, but this time from the perspective of instrumentalism: for many children, the traditional humanist curriculum is presented to them as utilitarian – both in the sense that there is a form of usefulness in acquiring credentials in such subjects because it brings access to careers and professions otherwise unavailable, and in the sense that most subjects can be portrayed in some way that demonstrates utility ('What is the *use* of Latin sir?' (Nigel Molesworth, in *How to be Topp*, G. Williams and R. Searle)). While the end result may appear to be similar, the intentions and processes of the instrumental curriculum are rather different, however.

One variant of the objectives-driven curriculum is the reconstructionist curriculum identified by Skilbeck (1976). This social-need led curriculum version of the objectives-driven curriculum – the claim that 'education, properly organized, can be one of the major forces for planned change in society' (p. 11) was perhaps less typical of established industrial societies (one form was propounded by Nyerere in Tanzania, for example (1968, 1970), though it was also found in Benn and Simon's advocacy of comprehensive schooling in Britain (1972). Reconstructionists have taken the Enlightenment goal of rationality for education, arguing that 'attempts to plan and organize individual and social experience according to agreed ends and using agreed social procedures', particularly through educational processes, will lead to 'the deliberate cultivation of rationality, of problem-solving procedures, adaptability and flexibility and a generalized capacity to face up to the problems of practical life' (Skilbeck, 1976, p. 12).

In these kinds of curricula – whether reconstructionist or otherwise – objectives that meet specific needs for competencies – of society, of the economy, or of the individual – are specified in advance, and a curriculum is drawn up to achieve these objectives. Abilities and capabilities necessary to meet the needs of contemporary life are specified and used to justify the collection of subjects that constitute the curriculum. The justification depends not on the academic worth or otherwise of the subject, but in its ability to deliver the particular skills that are judged necessary. It is not essential that there are strict boundaries to subjects, so the classification code could, in theory, be weak. The frame, however, necessarily remains strong, because the dominant pedagogic model remains one of transmission from the expert teacher to the novice pupil. In practice, the classification does also tend to be strong, because the teachers who have obtained the strong, externally validated definition of the subject's boundary are the same individuals as those who control the instrumental curriculum and specify the objectives that are to be realized.

Variant forms of the classical humanist curriculum are thus created to be offered to those pupils judged less able, or less suited to receive the high cultural capital of the elite: commercial French, travel and tourism studies, popular culture, and the like. (Ironically, these examples are themselves now also in the process of transmogrification into academic subjects, albeit in the name of 'relevance' and of 'capabilities'.)

This model of the curriculum can be justified in various ways. Academic subjects may be based, as the Norwood Report asserted (Board of Education, 1943), on complex conceptual reasoning, and thus be inappropriate for all pupils. Inhelder and Piaget (1958), for example, suggest that the ability to think conceptually is limited to older pupils, and not to all of these: a curriculum that made less intellectual demands, and put more emphasis on instrumental and concrete goals, could be said to serve these pupils better. Many pupils expect and demand vocational relevance in their schooling: whether it is real transferable occupational skills or credentials that can be used in the job market, they expect to see a direct correspondence between their 'work' in school and their future work. And on grounds of fairness and justice, it could be argued that if the instrumental curriculum parallels the academic curriculum, then the problems created by the tripartite school can be avoided, or at least mitigated: since it is difficult to divide pupils accurately into different streams, it is at least possible to allow students to switch from an instrumental variant of a subject to the academic form (and vice versa) if this later appears to be better matched to their abilities.

In one sense the traditional academic classical humanist curriculum was always vocational: possession of a classical education essentially marked out the gentleman from the worker (Eggleston, 1978), and foreign languages were directly vocational and utilitarian, but gave access to specific high-status vocations that were professional and effectively limited to the upper classes (Williams 1961, p. 163). It is because of this potential confusion that Goodson preferred to refer to the 'utilitarian' curriculum, rather than the 'vocational' curriculum when referring to 'low status practical knowledge. ... Utilitarian knowledge thus becomes that which is related to those non-professional vocations in which the majority of people work for most of their adult life' (Goodson 1987, p. 27). The academic curriculum has always therefore had a specific vocational cachet. Banks's 1955 study of the secondary modern school suggests that as the proportion of artisan and lower-middle-class children in schools increased, secondary schools necessarily gave greater attention to vocational needs, but that while they tried to amend the traditional academic curriculum to admit directly vocational or utilitarian subjects, these were persistently viewed as low status.

> The persistence of the academic tradition is seen as something more fundamental than the influence, sinister or otherwise, of teachers and administrators. It is the vocational qualification of the academic curriculum which enables it to exert such a pressure on all forms of secondary education.
>
> (Banks, 1955, p. 238)

The utilitarian–classical divide is thus blurred. Williams pointed out that all educational systems represent 'a compromise between an inherited selection of interests and the emphasis on new interests. At varying points in history, even this interest may be long delayed, and it will often be muddled' (Williams, 1961, p. 172). Secondary modern pupils, and those in the comprehensive streams of the comprehensive schools, saw this clearly. As Measor reported, mathematics and English were perceived by all students as being of major importance, but simply because they were needed to obtain work. She observes the

> largely instrumental attitudes that almost all of the pupils had towards their secondary school curriculum. ... They wanted decent jobs, they recognised the contribution that schools could make towards their future job aspirations, they recognised the need for school-based qualifications to achieve those aspirations. Therefore school, or certain parts of it, the vocational parts, were useful.
>
> (Measor, 1984, p. 215)

Through much of the twentieth century vocationalism in education has had a low status. Craft skills were developed through the subjects of cookery, needlework and typing skills for girls, and metalwork and woodwork for boys in the secondary modern curriculum, and were characteristic of the academic–vocational divide. The distinction between the vocational and the progressive, or process-driven curriculum was also wide:

> progressivism was firmly on the academic side of the curricular divide, where it was locked in combat with traditional, classical humanist versions of education. Vocationalism did not impinge on progressive preoccupations at all. However, these unlikely partners became bedfellows in the new vocationalism which emerged towards [the] end of [the] 1970s
>
> (Bates et al., 1998, p. 112)

This chapter will explore the nature of recent demands for relevance and competencies in this instrumental curriculum, and the emergence of the 'new vocationalism'. Against this, it will examine older objectives-led curricular models of Tyler, and examine the case study of geography as an area that has consistently found it problematic to define its boundaries with other subjects, and made frequent references to its utility in maintaining its position.

Demands for Relevance and Utility

The antipathy to making the nineteenth-century public school curriculum relevant to professional requirements has been charted by Wiener (1981), and the way in which the elite were thus deprived of access to a scientific and technical background forms the background of his thesis, which was in turn so influential on Sir Keith Joseph's conduct of curriculum policy in the early 1980s. The liberal education of these schools was incompatible with utility. But Wiener quotes one exception, Dean Farrer, who wrote in 1868 that a scientific education would be useful.

> No sooner have I uttered the word 'useful' than I imagine the hideous noise which will environ me, and amid the hubbub I faintly distinguish the words, vulgar, utilitarian, mechanical. ... I meekly repeat that it would be more useful – more rich in practical advantages, more directly available for health, for happiness, for success in the great battle of life. I for one am tired of this 'worship of inutility'. One would really think it was a crime to aim at the material happiness of the human race.
>
> (1869, quoted in Wiener, 1981, p. 19)

A belief in utility as the defining factor in selecting a curriculum challenges arguments that curriculum construction is a matter of debate. Utilitarianism, as proposed in the Benthamite 'calculus of pleasures', attenuates discussion of social outcomes, individual development and epistemological arguments about the curriculum in favour of a calculation of overall advantage. Golby identifies this as the 'technocratic tradition' (1989, p. 30) in the curriculum, in which positivism proposes that planning by objectives will result in a rational curriculum.

Ralph Tyler was one of the principal exponents of managing the curriculum by setting objectives that were capable of evaluation. His analysis was deceptively simple: define clearly what are the desired outcomes of education, and do so in terms of the specific desired behaviour that is expected after the educational process is completed, and then the curriculum that will be the means to achieve that end will also be defined. The most technically apposite way to achieve these behavioural changes will be the 'best' curriculum. The means are determined by the ends. Tyler was scathing about attempts to describe the curriculum in terms of lists of knowledge to be covered:

> objectives are sometimes stated as things the instructor [*sic*] is to do. These ... may indicate what the instructor plans to do ... [but] the real purpose of education is not to have the instructor perform certain activities but to bring about significant changes in the students' patterns of behaviour.
>
> (Tyler, 1949, p. 44)

The ultimate purpose of education is not to 'cover' particular content, or to achieve generalized patterns of behaviour (how, Tyler asked, could we ever know if an aim such as 'to develop critical thinking' had been achieved?). Objectives had to be stated in terms that specified both the kind of behaviour and the specific context in which that behaviour was expected to operate, the competencies that were to be both demonstrable and capable of evaluation. Tyler's structure was filled in by educational theorists such as Bloom and his colleagues, whose *Taxonomy of Educational Objectives* (1956) categorized the precise specifications of knowledge that schooling should ensure be understood by pupils.

Tyler went on to give five principles to the selection of learning experiences by objectives:

1   students must have experiences that give them the opportunities to practise the desired outcome;
2   students need to achieve satisfaction through the behaviour that is the desired outcome;
3   it must be within the student's capabilities to achieve the desired behaviour;
4   different educational experiences might be used to attain the same objective; and
5   the same educational experience might have several different outcomes.

Having identified the necessary learning experiences, a coherent programme for their delivery was needed: to be effective, such a programme must be organized to achieve continuity through the reiteration of the material, through breaking down the material into a logical progressive development of the understanding or skill, and integrating experiences so that the student gets a unified view and can develop his or her behaviour in an integrated manner.

An essential element in Tyler's competency-led education was the evaluation of educational outcomes, to see exactly how far the objectives were being realized. Thus the curriculum-maker must define behavioural objectives, and then ensure that the students have an opportunity to demonstrate their ability to display that behaviour. This might be by actually testing the behaviour, or if this is not possible, by inferring the behaviour from some analogous and correlated behaviour.

The arguments against this form of reductionism are summarized by Golby (1989). In one sense, the desired objectives are taken as read: Tyler's model gives no room for guidance on how aims and objectives can be generated, assessed, rated or judged to be desirable. The contention that all learning outcomes can be evaluated by behavioural outcomes is problematic. While this is true in, for example physical performance, where a statement of behaviour ('can vault over 1.60 metres') is one in which the evidence for the behaviour also constitutes the behaviour itself (see Hirst, 1965), in higher order learning it is not likely to be the case that behavioural evidence *alone* will be either the only or sufficient evidence of learning: particular evidence of learning is not necessarily pre-specifiable, and there may be a wide range of evidence that learning has been achieved. Golby argues that achievements in these areas 'are so complex that they can only be judged contextually by one who has knowledge ... of the areas of achievement', which seems to substantiate Bourdieu's charge that pedagogic authorities control the validation of cultural capital and of testing its inculcation (Bourdieu and Passeron, 1990). Objectives-driven models assume that one can predetermine the shape to which a learner will be moulded. Whilst training processes may aim at uniformity of outcome, many intellectual and aesthetic activities involve imagination and other qualities that are difficult to describe in behavioural terms. Tyler claimed that 'every kind of human behaviour which is appraised for its part as an educational objective must be measured or summarised' (1949, p. 89), but such systematic technical evaluation of a learning programme is not possible in anything of a higher order than training. Finally, the whole objectives-led model of curriculum planning elevates the objectives at the expense of any subject matter. It does not seem possible to achieve a balance between content and objectives: any weight given to objectives seems to subordinate curriculum content.

Despite such concerns, ideas of giving primacy to utility in determining the curriculum was taken up by various elements of the 'new right' in the 1980s. Their voices were for various kinds of utilities, however: some for a curriculum that would be useful to society, others for economic usefulness. Thus, for example, Oliver Letwin, political adviser to Keith Joseph, argued that 'the strict duty of every school is to ensure that, by the end of their school days, every pupil has what I shall call a grounding ... an understanding of those things which it is necessary to understand in order to take a properly independent part in the life of our society' (1988, p. 70). Pupils need to be taught to read and comprehend, so they can make choices about matters such as finding jobs and managing their homes, make sense of newspapers, and hold independent and informed attitudes to government. This, Letwin argues, is the duty of those who care about a liberal democracy in which people are permitted to make choices. Further,

> the idea that a school's aim is to train people for jobs is equally noxious. ... Jobs are done to provide those who do them and their customers with economic benefits. ... Schooling ... is making a direct contribution of its own to the sustenance of a civilised existence.
>
> (Letwin, 1988, p. 73)

The alternative view of a narrowly utilitarian curriculum was also powerful, as is seen in the constant pressure for utilitarian subjects, despite their continuing failure to achieve a high status. Industrialists' advocacy of utilitarian training, in order to meet the manpower needs of the changing industrial economy ran through the 1970s and 1980s, although they were at their most acute at moments of perceived crisis in the economy and society (Goodson, 1987; Stronach, 1989.

Objectives-driven Considerations in the Formation of School Subjects

Goodson (1987) examined the development of geography as a secondary school subject, which provides some evidence of how utilitarian arguments can contribute to the shaping and development of a school subject. The nature of geography as a discipline has always been seen by some as problematic: it is sometimes described rather as a 'field of knowledge'. David Gregory pointed out that the Victorian view of geography was that it developed skills and knowledge that were needed for trade, for diplomacy and for military strategy, and thus was wholly utilitarian – but that this very characterization 'appeared to make a command of geography vital both for the maintenance of the Empire itself and for the ascent of men to the most acclaimed positions of profit and power within it' (Gregory, 1978, p. 21). In the twentieth century other uses developed: geographical skills aided spatial and regional planning, and had political implications. Ahier's analysis of elementary school textbooks of the late nineteenth and early twentieth century suggested that geography was taught as part of general training for citizenship, and by the 1920s and 1930s was developing an appreciation of British dependence on trade (1988, p. 165): the utility here is political and social, rather than personal, in the development of attitudes towards the colonial territories as 'dependent' (the reciprocity of the dependency being masked by the view of Britain as 'the workshop' of the Empire).

Geography did not have the same academic or University status. MacKinder, the eminent late-Victorian geographer, was active in attempting to raise the subject's academic profile from the very tentative place that it held in Universities and schools in the late nineteenth century. He asked, 'can geography be rendered a discipline, instead of a mere body of information?' (MacKinder, 1887). One important recognition was achieved when it was included in the list of secondary school subjects in the 1904 Board of Education recommendations, and thereafter several examination boards began to include geography, although some of them only allowed it as a subsidiary subject.

MacKinder realized that one critical step would be to persuade universities to establish Schools of Geography: these would sustain the teaching of the subject in schools, and create a base around which the discipline could be founded and delimited. This was no straightforward task: even in the early 1990s there were occasional references to Secretary of State John Patten's degree in geography as being somehow not in a 'real' subject. Goodson quotes a writer in the *Times Educational Supplement* in 1975, that 'some senior members of our ancient universities can still be found who dismiss it as a school subject' (Goodson, 1987, p. 61). There were fierce disputes over the boundaries of the subject, and attempts were made in universities and schools in the 1920s and 1930s to ensure that it excluded climatology, meteorology and geology: disputes that were echoed in the 1980s, when the National Curriculum Science Working Party met before the Geography Working Party was appointed, and appropriated the earth sciences before the geographers could set out their case.

The weak classification of the subject, using Bernstein's terms, was evident from the disputes that have followed the subject since the first University schools were established. There were long debates over whether the area should be located with the arts or the sciences, and the indeterminacy of the subject added to its marginality. In schools, the rationale for the subject's inclusion in the curriculum remained its usefulness: the Hadow report, while acknowledging the value of geography as an 'instrument of education' in 'developing an attitude of mind and a mode of thought', nevertheless stressed the utility of the subject: 'travel and correspondence have now become general; the British dominions are to be found in every clime; and these facts alone are enough to ensure that the subject shall have an important place in the school timetable' (Board of Education, 1926). The Norwood Report on the secondary school curriculum (Board of Education, 1943) commented that while geography might be defined as 'the study of man and his environment from selected points of view' there were also other subjects with legitimate interests in the area: 'natural science, economics, history, the study of local conditions as regards industry and agriculture might also be concerned with environment'. The problem with geography was, the Committee noted, 'the expansiveness of geography ... enthusiasts for geography may be inclined sometimes to extend their range so widely as to swallow up other subjects ... widen their boundaries so vaguely that definition of purpose is lost' (pp. 101–2; see also Honeybone, 1954). David quotes Professor Frank Debenham (Cambridge University), that 'Teachers of established subjects objected to this new *omnium gatherum* of a study, which threatened to invade their boundaries' (1973, p. 64).

The general usefulness and application of geographical studies over a wide range of studies continued to mean that its boundaries were ill-defined. This lack led to some defensiveness by geographers, some of whom seemed to fear that developments in the subject might lead to its metamorphosis to another discipline, or worse. When the 'new geography' movement was launched in 1963 by Chorley and Haggett, the 'old' geographers felt that they had to defend the 'integrity' of their subject's boundaries. The President of the Geographical Association claimed that Chorley and Haggett's *Frontiers in Geographical Teaching* (1967) was 'creating a problem that will ... lead towards subject fragmentation as fringe specialisms in systematic fields proliferate and are pursued independently to the neglect of the very core of our discipline – a core that largely justifies its existence' (Garnett, 1969, p. 369). Geography was, she continued,

> a unique 'bridging subject' and as a keystone in educational curricula, so concerned within itself with the integration of knowledge that, surely geographers should be the first to express an interest in taking a lead in such interdisciplinary studies. Yet at times I have gained an impression that the reverse seems to be the case.
>
> (ibid.)

Goodson concludes his analysis of the subject by suggesting that there may be a stage prior to those described by Layton (1973), In this first stage, says Goodson

> teaching was anything but 'messianic', for the subject was taught by non-specialists and comprised 'a dreary collection of geographical facts and figures'. The threshold for 'take-off' on the route to academic establishment ... was [when it was proposed that] the geography teacher is to set the exams and is to choose exams that are best for the 'common acceptance' of the subject.
>
> (Goodson, 1987, p. 78)

Geography is idiosyncratic and information based, and places initial stress on personal, pedagogic and utilitarian values: but this itself makes the subject expansive, and consequently more like a world citizenship course. The outcome was ultimately similar to the solution reached in science: [make] 'the geographers in the Universities' and then 'the piecemeal changes [made] in pursuit of school relevance could be controlled and directed. The definition of geography through the universities instead of the schools (78/79) began to replace the pedagogic or utilitarian bias with arguments for academic rigour' (Goodson, 1987, pp. 78–9).

The subject was not, Goodson argues, dominated by powerful forces, but by teachers' own material self-interests. The suggestion that there is 'domination by the universities fails to characterise a complex process' (p. 193); but, as in the case of science, ' "academic" sub-groups in school subjects clearly do conspire to increase the control over the definition and direction of subjects by university scholars' (p. 194), a conspiracy between academic school groups and Universities, made at the expense of both the pedagogic and the utilitarian tradition.

The 'New Vocationalism'

Goodson proposed a relatively simple dichotomy. On one side is the 'academic' curriculum, designed 'to smoothly educate a meritocratic minority ... meanwhile disenchanting the majority. The social class status quo is thereby preserved along with the requisite ratio of managers to workers' (1987, p. 197). On the other side are both the pedagogic and the utilitarian traditions, linked to 'the working world of industry and the everyday world of the learner' (p. 197). But the 'new right' had a more complex collection of educational policies than this might suggest. Whilst many of these were utilitarian and objectives-driven, some, like those of Letwin (1988, above), were decidedly not technocratic or vocational. Others were, and these were instrumental in the development of a newer and more subtle form of vocationalism (Quicke, 1988).

The objectives-driven nature of the National Curriculum testing regime is, to some extent, masked by the content-led definition of programmes of study for each of the subjects. Quicke points out that a genuine academic curriculum is unlikely in this context (using 'academic' to mean a curriculum that seeks to develop critical thinking through 'the controversies and arguments within traditional subjects, and which is constructed and taught in a manner which connects with the culturally located experiences of pupils' (p. 82). Rather, he suggests, there will be increasing instrumentalism, as even the most academically able pupils study in order to achieve credentials, instead of learning for its own sake. Whilst the new right generally claimed to be opposed to relevance or utility as an organizing factor in curriculum policy, there were frequent implicit references to needs for this, as seen, for example, in the reference to 'the challenges of employment in tomorrow's world' in the National Curriculum consultative document (DES, 1987h, p. 2). This is the group identified by Dale (1998) as the 'industrial trainers' (see Chapter 5). This liberal ideological stance, developing into what became known as the new vocationalism, identified increased industrialism and industrial competencies as the potential source of a more meritocratic society. Using the curriculum to enhance the capabilities of human capital began with the development of the Technical and Vocational Education Initiative in 1972, and the 'industrial trainers' were supported in this development by various groups within the new right for various reasons (including, Quicke suggests, the fact that the MSC-led initiative helped weaken the powers of the Local Education Authorities, and because such privatized, employer-based training might draw off those pupils who either cannot or will not be educated in schools). But vocationalism, as Quicke recognizes, was by no means the only thread in the new right's thinking on the curriculum: there was a parallel demand for relevance that focused on the child, and this neo-liberal strand will be examined more closely in Chapter 9.

The 'new vocationalism' had its origins in the late 1970s (Bates et al., 1984; Spours and Young, 1988; Stronach, 1989; Yeomans, 1998), and its development into 'controlled vocationalism' (Bates et al., 1998) shows how far the skills-led, objectives-driven curriculum moved from the ideals of the reconstructionist, social-need led curriculum of Skilbeck (1976). The 'old vocationalism' of the secondary technical school and the secondary modern school (and further education colleges) had low status and was highly marginalized in the educational system. The apprenticeship model of training, and the influence of the Industrial Training Boards, ensured that control of provision was in the hands of the employers, and that its focus was on occupationalism: training young people for specific niches within the employment market. What Skilbeck (1976) and Bates et al. (1998) identify as progressivism had very little impact on this vocationalism: it was effectively limited to a smattering of liberal studies, grafted on to technician courses. This changed dramatically with the rapid rise in youth unemployment in the years immediately following Callaghan's Ruskin speech, and the ending of the idea of a life-time's work in a single occupation. Vocationalism in education changed from preparation for a specific trade, as apprenticeships evaporated, to develop into a more generalized training in 'transferable skills' for work in a much broader spectrum of occupations (Chitty, 1991).

The plethora of schemes that emerged in the 1980s – the Certificate in Pre-Vocational Education (CPVE), TVEI, and the Youth Training Scheme (YTS) – were accompanied by revitalized accreditation of courses run by the City and Guilds and the Royal Society for Arts (RSA), and new accrediting bodies such as the Business and Technical Education Council (BTEC), and, in schools, the development of 'careers education' out of the careers guidance provision (National Curriculum Council, 1990d). One important characteristic of these manifestations of the new vocationalism was that they drew on what had hitherto been characteristics of progressive, process-driven curricular ideologies (Bates et al., 1998). The influence of the early activities of the Schools Curriculum Industry Project (SCIP) can be seen as pervading all these initiatives: Lightfoot and Jamieson had in particular pioneered the introduction of experiential learning, integrated approaches to organizing curriculum knowledge and skills, employing the teacher and adults other than teachers as facilitators, and student-centred learning (Jamieson and Lightfoot, 1982). Jamieson was later to admit that these approaches were a conscious borrowing from progressive primary school practice (Jamieson, 1984; Jamieson and Watts, 1987; also Crawford, 1999). This coming together of vocational and progressive ideologies in the 1980s could be interpreted as 'a general trend in education, from union leaders and labour politicians to classroom teachers. ... to use the opportunities that have sprung up around the modernising project to consolidate progressive trends and block the right's advance' (Jones, 1989, p. 93). The movement was variously seen as a bridging of the division between academic and vocational schooling (Young, 1993), the basis for a partnership between academic and progressive educationalists (Hodkinson, 1991), and a reconciliation of vocational and liberal humanist education (Pring, 1995). *Figure 8.1* shows a rather simplified visualization of these relationships.

This early phase of development was characterized by a loose relationship between economic values and liberal values: the vocational thrust may have implied that education was becoming secondary to economic instrumentalism, but the liberal values that were implicit in the experiential and integrated approach were included by those responsible for the programme as a balance to this (Jamieson, 1985; Ross, 1992). SCIP activities required pupils to negotiate, to make choices, to use teachers and adults as resources rather than as authorities; this was picked up on and extended in both the early TVEI programmes and the Youth Opportunities Programme (forerunner to

Figure 8.1   The new vocationalism: theorizing the relationship between three curricular models in the early 1990s

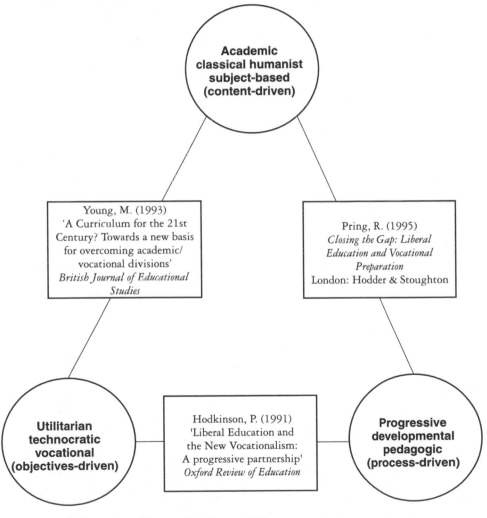

Source: Loosely based on Gleeson and Hodkinson, 1995.

YTS). This balance was achieved, at least in part, because of the loose regulation and control of the curriculum through most of the 1980s. As it was realized what the educational professionals had managed to inject into these programmes, so changes were introduced into the YTS to remove personal and social education, and to emphasize employer-led vocationalism. 'Obedience was seen as an important quality in trainees, to make them more employable' (Bates et al., 1998, p. 114).

The National Council for Vocational Qualifications (NCVQ) was established in 1986, and began to control the new NVQs, particularly by insisting that the criteria for assessing detailed outcome were specified in the validation procedures for the new courses. This form of assessing behavioural outcomes and competencies owes much to the work of Tyler, discussed earlier in this chapter. A second phase of the new vocationalism had begun, with employers more closely integrated into the new regimes in Further Education – now subjected to payment by results schemes that rewarded recruitment, retention and examination outcomes. With the 1988 Education Reform Act and the establishment of the National Curriculum Council, the selection of educational knowledge and behavioural outcomes was being more tightly specified at all levels of the educational system.

Bates et al. refer to the third phase of the new vocationalism as 'controlled vocationalism': 'the locus of control over content had shifted firmly to the government and its agencies ... with the explicit objective of improving Britain's economic competitiveness' (1998, p. 115). Nevertheless, certain progressive elements can still be detected in the nature of the GNVQs, even though 'each of these carries the imprint of the restructured relations between education and the economy' (ibid.). Specifically, GNVQs are designed to be 'vocational A levels', and (supposedly) have parity of esteem with the traditional academic qualifications, but it remains to be seen if GNVQs are recognized in practice in this way (Hodkinson, 1998). There is also an element of student choice over the curriculum, with options and modules that could be said to empower students, and allow them to assume a greater degree of control over the direction and content of their learning. Again, this 'progressive' element must be qualified: research by Hodkinson suggests that in the reality of the FE situation, 'many lower status options only become choices if something perceived as better cannot be achieved, and then they often do not feel like choices at all' (1998, p. 164). Finally, the GNVQ system is said to encourage self-directed learning, and to empower students by giving them a greater degree of control over the pace and nature of their learning. The rhetoric implies a weak framing of the curriculum, with the teacher in a supportive and collaborative role, rather than an instructional one. Again in practice this is not so clear: the reality is that the responsibility for learning is devolved to the student, but the objectives remain predetermined. The title of Bloomer's report on his research quotes a student's response that encapsulates this: 'They tell you what to do, and then they let you get on with it' (Bloomer, 1998, p. 167). This use of the term 'empowerment' was also found in the National Curriculum documents in its earlier phases: Craft (1995) dissects the various guidance papers published in 1990 that outline the 'Whole Curriculum' (National Curriculum Council, 1990a, b, c, d, e, f), and concludes that the National Curriculum allows pupils to develop a high degree of autonomy and control over their learning: but this view is contested (Ahier and Ross, 1995b; Ahier, 1995).

The pedagogic drive towards student self-responsibility in the GNVQs is 'geared towards occupational socialisation' – far from balancing the vocational thrust (*pace* Jamieson, 1985, above), it 'reinforces the vocational objectives' (Bates et al., 1998, p. 117). This is perhaps inevitable from any curriculum initiative that is based around pre-specified competencies and objectives, as the critiques of Tylerism have suggested. This is a rather different kind of autonomy than is found in the earlier 'progressive' educational model of the 'new vocationalism' (see, for example, Watts et al., 1989).

Autonomy is used in rather different ways in the three major curricular models that we are examining. *Figure 8.2* attempts to offer a schematized version of the differences. The traditional autonomy of the content-driven (or academic, or classical humanist) curriculum model is reserved for the few who have mastered the discipline and can demonstrate their control over the defined cultural capital (Bourdieu and Passeron, 1990). When the subject has been demonstrably accomplished, one is in effect licensed to practice it (Oakeshott, 1989).

The objectives-led curriculum and the progressive curriculum have both rather different conceptualizations of the term autonomy. For both of them, it is something that

Figure 8.2   The different meanings of autonomy within three curricular models

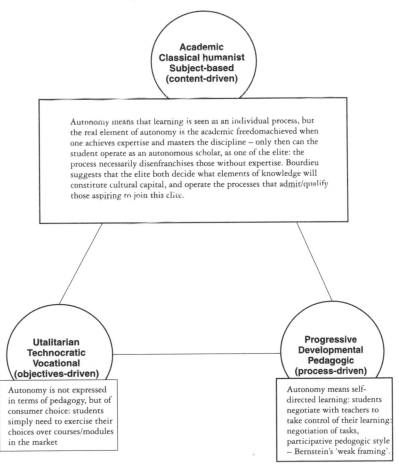

the learner – that all learners – ought to acquire in the processes of learning. But, while for the progressive this means pupil-centred learning, with the negotiation over tasks, the use of the teacher as a guide and facilitator rather than as an authority (Bernstein's (1975) weak framing model), for the 'controlled vocationalist' it is more of a consumerist autonomy, the freedom to choose a different course, to select modules and learning styles from a specified range, towards pre-selected objectives (Bates et al., 1998).

The three models of curriculum have characteristics other than autonomy which variously distinguish them. For example, the academic tradition sees knowledge as a distinct body of data, hierarchically arranged, which needs to be acquired. The progressive tradition is that education is a process: rather than knowing *what*, one should know *how* – and in particular, learning how to learn (about knowledge) is more important than knowing knowledge itself. For the objectives-driven curriculum, knowledge becomes a simple commodity.

The models also show various similarities, as well as differences. *Figure 8.3* describes some of these. The pairings that are possible between them all suggest that there may be three different axes around which they can be analysed.

- One axis might be have at one end a form of egalitarianism, that sees all students as being (to a degree) responsible for their own learning, and 'owning' their education, with an elitist, subject-centred approach at the other end. Such an axis would distinguish the Academic (content-driven) from both the Utilitarian (objectives-driven) and the Progressive (process-driven).
- Another axis would be based on differing views of knowledge: at one end the conceptualization of knowledge as a fixed entity (whether for its own sake or as a commodity to be acquired for utilitarian goals), and at the other end knowledge as something that one has to learn about accessing and understanding, rather than acquire in its own right. Such an axis differentiates the Progressive curriculum, process-led, from both the Academic and the Utilitarian.
- A final axis might be around attitudes to marketization and instrumentalism. Both the Academic and the Progressive model have a marked dislike of the instrumentalism of the Utilitarian curriculum.

But, despite these various cross-cutting axes, each model does have its own distinguishing features: towards the role of teachers, and towards the purposes and nature of assessment, for example.

Demands for Utility and Teachers' Preoccupations with Progressivism

We have so far examined both the content-led, academic curriculum model (the baroque garden of Chapter 1), and the objectives-led utilitarian/vocational curriculum (the dig-for-victory garden). The third curricular form has necessarily been alluded to in these analyses, and will now form the focus of the next chapter. This third variant has variously been described as the pedagogic curriculum in secondary schools (Goodson, 1987), the developmental curriculum in primary schools (Blyth, 1967) (sometimes also as the child-centred curriculum (Lawton *et al.*, 1978; Golby, 1989)), and also as the progressive curriculum (Skilbeck, 1976; Golby, 1988). Its distin-

Figure 8.3   Ideological rivalries and alliances between three curricular models

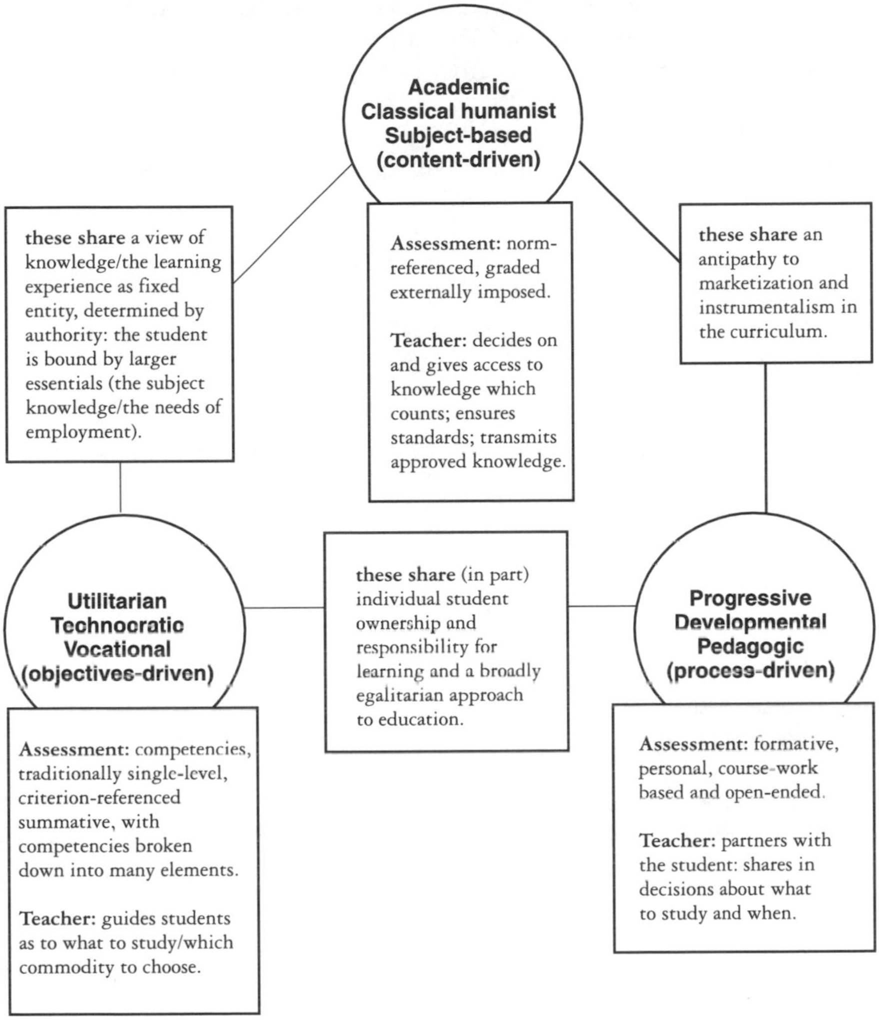

**Academic
Classical humanist
Subject-based
(content-driven)**

these share a view of knowledge/the learning experience as fixed entity, determined by authority: the student is bound by larger essentials (the subject knowledge/the needs of employment).

Assessment: norm-referenced, graded externally imposed.

Teacher: decides on and gives access to knowledge which counts; ensures standards; transmits approved knowledge.

these share an antipathy to marketization and instrumentalism in the curriculum.

**Utilitarian
Technocratic
Vocational
(objectives-driven)**

these share (in part) individual student ownership and responsibility for learning and a broadly egalitarian approach to education.

**Progressive
Developmental
Pedagogic
(process-driven)**

Assessment: competencies, traditionally single-level, criterion-referenced summative, with competencies broken down into many elements.

Teacher: guides students as to what to study/which commodity to choose.

Assessment: formative, personal, course-work based and open-ended.

Teacher: partners with the student: shares in decisions about what to study and when.

Source: Based (loosely) on Bates et al., 1998.

guishing characteristic seems to be that it is principally concerned with, or guided by, the *processes* of learning. As *Figure 8.3* suggests, it can often be sharply distinguished from the traditional academic/classical humanist curriculum, and was often therefore aligned with the utilitarian curriculum: the two sometimes formed an uneasy alliance in the secondary modern schooling system, and in many comprehensive schools: a simple dualism made categorization and description easier. Thus Shipman could write of 'a schools system that is still clearly divided into two sections, one geared to a system of external examinations, the other less constrained ... it is the consequence of innovation into these two separate sections rather than the curricula themselves which may be producing a new means of sustaining old traditions' (1971, pp. 101–2). On the one hand was the academic tradition, 'planted in revered academic tradition, adapted to teaching from a pool of factual knowledge and has clearly defined, if often irrelevant subject boundaries' and on the other an area that was 'experiential … focuses on contemporary problems, groups subjects together and rejects formal teaching methods' (p. 104).

The process-driven progressive curriculum does, however, have some clearly defined differences from the utilitarian/vocational curriculum, and this is evident not least in the differing views of the pupils, their parents and their teachers. In 1968 the Schools Council conducted a survey of the objectives of schooling, as perceived by these three groups. The focus of the study was particularly on the views of those leaving school at 16, and their parents and teachers (Schools Council, 1968). A list of possible objectives of schooling was presented, and each individual was asked to indicate which they felt to be 'very important'. *Table 8.1* shows the responses.

Table 8.1 Proportions of school leavers, their parents and their teachers saying that various school objectives were very important

	Pupils 13–16		Parents		Teachers	
	%	rank	%	rank	%	rank
Careers						
examination achievement	70	6	72	6	20	17
things of direct use in jobs	75	5	33	15	27	14
as good a job/career as possible	85	1	89	2	35	12
information about different sorts of jobs	78	=3	74	=4	57	=5
information about starting work	61	8	65	8	42	=9
Everyday life						
running a home	65	7	55	11	42	=9
money management	79	2	74	=4	52	7
sex education	50	10	50	12	42	=9
writing easily	78	=3	90	1	59	3
Self-development						
personality and character	45	=11	54	10	93	1
to help one behave confidently and at ease	58	9	78	3	78	2
Interest and awareness						
what is going on in the world	45	=11	56	9	58	4
plenty of subjects to widen interests	39	13	49	13	22	16
spare time interests and hobbies	20	15	47	14	51	8
school clubs	33	14	67	7	57	=5
drama	9	16	15	16	33	13
poetry	5	17	10	17	24	15

Source: Schools Council, 1968, p. 43.

It is clear that the responses given by each group show very significant differences of viewpoint. *Figures 8.4, 8.5* and *8.6* show the rank order of each group, in histogram form. The various objectives have been categorized, to highlight the major variations. Objectives that are, it seems, largely to deal with either the pedagogic or progressive curricula have been shown in white: instilling confidence, developing personality, the fostering of interests and hobbies, aesthetic activities such as drama, and so on. The more instrumental objectives are shown in darker grey or black: black is used for the vocational instrumental objectives (getting a good job, information about work, things of direct use in work), while the dark grey signifies instrumental objectives that are more to deal with the life skills needed by a young adult (handling money, running a home, sex education). Some objectives seem to possibly span more than one category (or may be differently categorized by different groups). Thus examination success may be seen as both academic/pedagogic or as instrumental in seeking employment: these are therefore categorized in lighter greys (as are such objectives as 'writing easily' and 'knowing about what's going on in the world').

The pupils are clearly most driven by their impending entry to the labour market: instrumental vocational objectives dominate their thinking (*Figure 8.4*). Their parents are less clear: they have similar concerns, but also wish to see their children with a wider range of skills and social characteristics (*Figure 8.5*). But their teachers have very different ambitions: their concern is with much less instrumental concerns (*Figure 8.6*), and it is to this process-driven progressive curriculum that we now turn.

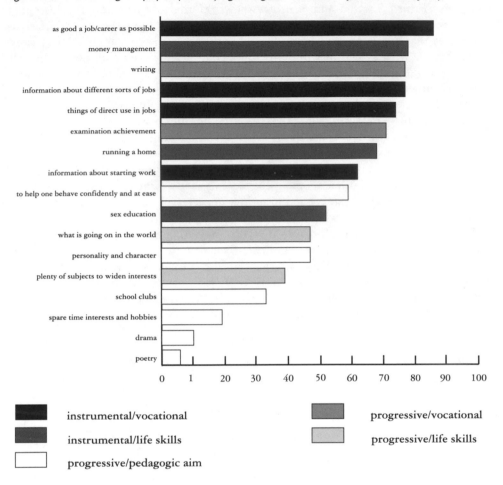

Figure 8.4 Percentage of pupils (13–16) agreeing each school objective as 'very important'

as good a job/career as possible
money management
writing
information about different sorts of jobs
things of direct use in jobs
examination achievement
running a home
information about starting work
to help one behave confidently and at ease
sex education
what is going on in the world
personality and character
plenty of subjects to widen interests
school clubs
spare time interests and hobbies
drama
poetry

0   1   20   30   40   50   60   70   80   90   100

instrumental/vocational   progressive/vocational

instrumental/life skills   progressive/life skills

progressive/pedagogic aim

Source: Schools Council, 1968, p. 43.

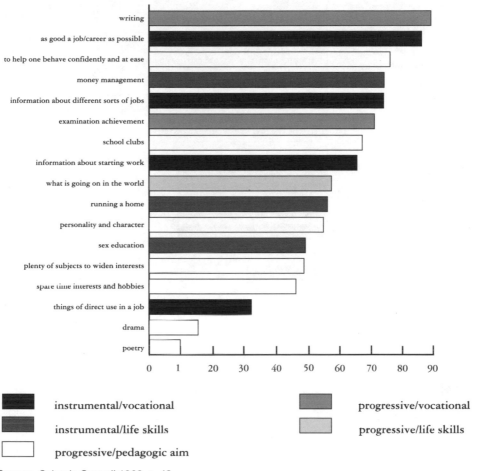

Figure 8.5 *Percentage of parents of pupils agreeing each school objective as 'very important'*

Source: Schools Council 1968, p. 43.

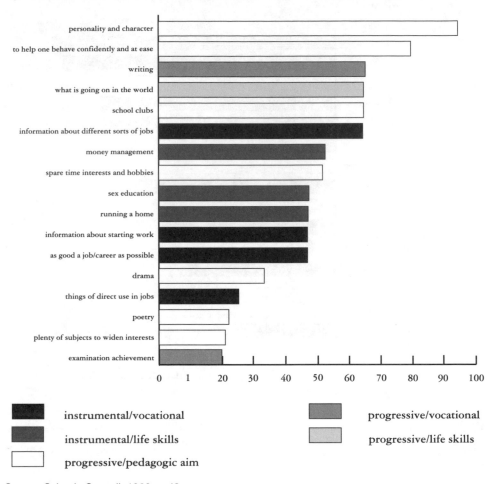

Figure 8.6   Percentage of teachers agreeing each school objective as 'very important'

instrumental/vocational

progressive/vocational

instrumental/life skills

progressive/life skills

progressive/pedagogic aim

Source: Schools Council, 1968, p. 43.

9   Process-driven Curricula

The landscape garden was, in some senses, designed as a revolt against the formal gardens of earlier generations. The catch in this is that, however naturalistic it appeared, it *was* designed: it was an artifice, created to appear how it was imagined the countryside might look had it been undisturbed by humans. But, first, there was no inert state of nature before the arrival of people – the landscape is always in a state of flux, subject to ecological and environmental swings; and, second, there is no way of knowing what might have been without a human population. These factors are as true of education and the idea that children should be allowed 'to develop' as they need, at the rate, direction and pace they need. Children are from birth members of a wider society, and they inevitably interact with that society. Durkheim suggested that 'the man whom education should realise in us is not man as nature has made him, but as the society wishes to be' (1956, p. 65); but there is no such thing as 'man as nature has made him': no society can prevent its activities having an effect on the children living within it. All education necessarily must take place within a social setting, and this social setting will constrain, shape and mould the learning that takes place. Nurse and priest impose on the child, 'the child imposes on the man' (or woman) into which she or he will grow (Dryden, *The Hind and the Panther*).

This chapter will look first at progressivism in English schools, and then consider the antecedents to be found in the theorists (and practitioners) who first advanced theories of structuring learning processes. It will then relate these back to the other two major curricular models that have been discussed.

Naturalism and the Curriculum

Rousseau provided the first sustained advocacy of a process of learning that would reflect the natural development of the learner. In this, the curriculum would be effectively determined by the needs and interests of the learner, and the pace of their learning. *Emile* described a fictional child, whose learning is guided and facilitated by a tutor. Because individual children vary in their aptitudes and interests, their learning needs to be tailored to meet their particular needs. But nevertheless Rousseau generalizes about the learning process: all children, he argued, were naturally curious and inquisitive: not necessarily about what teachers might want them to learn about (such as customary forms of knowledge of subjects, or learning for the sake of learning), but about their surroundings, and things in which they have a natural interest. He argued that a first principle should be 'that the first impulses of nature are always right' (Rousseau, 1964 [1762], p. 56). Rousseau contrasted his belief in the goodness of the natural state to the corruption that he saw as characteristic of society: he had, commented Skilbeck, a 'romantic iconoclast attitude towards the values and rules of traditional culture' (1976, p. 7). The child had therefore to be insulated from society, and raised in an environment carefully controlled by the tutor.

Rousseau's second principle was that the child was naturally good (an equally challenging assertion to contemporary society's belief in original sin). Moreover, children's thought processes were less formed than adults' thought processes, and not comparable to them: 'childhood has its own ways of seeing, thinking and feeling: nothing is more foolish than to try and substitute our [adult] ways' (Rousseau, 1964 [1762], p. 54). The tutor must therefore adapt to the capacity of the child (p. 144): too many educators concentrate 'on what a man ought to know, without asking what a child is capable of learning' (p. 1). This emphasis on the *processes* of learning is underlined by Rousseau when he complains of the conventional teacher 'you teach science: I am busy fashioning the necessary for its acquisition' (p. 90).

Most of the essentials of a child-centred, process-based approach to the curriculum are present in Rousseau's work: the child will develop naturally, given a suitable environment; the child's development is best self-directed; the role of the teacher is to enable learning, not to transmit knowledge; and the learning process should be organized for individuals, not class-sized groups. But Rousseau takes this last point to the extreme that he is prepared to isolate the child from all others, so that all areas of learning – mathematical understanding, language skills, scientific understanding, moral behaviour – are developed by the artful and well-informed teacher. The teacher, through a carefully engineered exploitation of experiences of everyday life, devises a highly structured, orderly and disciplined regime. The freedom Rousseau proposes is conditioned by the constant surveillance the tutor has over the child. School was not a community for learning: Rousseau distrusted the potentially polluting effects of others (Skilbeck, 1976).

Rousseau's conception of nature is problematic: he writes as though a state of nature is possible, and that the child has a nature that will develop if unchecked by society: yet all human activity is socially conditioned, all knowledge socially constructed. Isolating the child from society will necessarily lead to asocial behaviour such as the lack of the development of communicative skills. Rousseau's ideas, though they raised enormous enthusiasm and support at the time of their publication (Darling writes that booksellers found it more profitable to rent out copies of *Emile* by the hour rather than to sell them (1994)), were modified substantially by those who followed him. A direct line of descent can be traced from Rousseau through Pestalozzi, Froebel and Dewey to Teachers' College Columbia and the New Education Fellowship, while Pestalozzi and Froebel introduced communal settings to Rousseau's ideas, recognizing children as social beings, and therefore making education as a social activity (Skilbeck, 1976).

Pestalozzi's school at Yverdon aimed to harmonize the subject matter to be taught to the capacity of the child to learn, through a process of research into how learning in any particular area actually occurred – the mixture of sensory experiences, memory and imagination necessary. Practical activities dominate his approach: mathematics taught through the handling of real objects, counting and grouping them, for example

(Pestalozzi, 1802). Learning through play was not explicit in this, but is an implicit principle through his various accounts of practice: nature walks, games, singing, the handling of objects.

Froebel visited Pestalozzi's school, and worked there for two years. Froebel's contribution was to further emphasize the practical handling of materials, but not simply because this was a better way to aid the learning processes of the young, but because of a strong theism that Froebel sought to inject. Practical work was God's way: such work 'gives outward form to the divine spirit within him [man], so he may know his own nature and the nature of God' (Froebel, 1826, in Lilley, 1967, p. 65). But play becomes explicit as a necessary process in learning: 'because he learns through play a child learns willingly and learns much. So play, like learning and activity, has its own definite period of time and it must not be left out of the elementary curriculum (Froebel, 1840, in Lilley, p. 167).

Dewey's contribution was at a variety of levels. As a teacher educator, he legitimated child-centred learning to generations of American teachers. He showed how learning could take place through group activities, such as performing plays, cultivation of gardens and running classroom shops, in which the teacher facilitated and participated children's activities, rather than organized and led them. Learning was closely related to experience: it makes knowledge useful to the child, and therefore memorable; practising knowledge through activity reinforces the learning process. It was Dewey who first characterized this process as 'child-centred': 'the child becomes the sun around which the appliances of education revolve; he is the centre about which they are organised' (Dewey, 1900, p. 51). Dewey's philosophy – unlike that of his predecessors – was secular: his 'view of human development was conceived in terms of open-ended social interaction rather than as a quasi-mechanical unfolding process (Darling, 1994, p. 27).

Such an attitude towards the processes of learning has implications that are not limited to the primary school. Skilbeck (1975) argues that a school-based curriculum, in which teachers and learners develop the curriculum to be learned together, based on the learners' interests and capacities, has a number of virtues. Appraising the learners' needs will free the teacher from the constraints of both content-based curricula and objectives-based curricula: instead the teacher will be able to set objectives and targets for learning. This will be onerous and demanding for teachers, and schools will need to support them in developing curricula. Skilbeck argues that the Schools Council played a major role in developing such curricula, particularly in the way in which most of the Councils devolved activity to teachers (in contrast to the management-dominated US national projects, which he characterized as objectives-based and being designed to be 'teacher-proof' (p. 22)).

This progressive ideology came under increasing attack in the 1970s. The various groups on the right – traditional, neo-conservative and neo-liberal – advocated curricular policies that were either academic or vocational: both of these rejected the process-based approach. For some of these, it was a project to restore the authority of the State and traditional social values, for others, it was an attempt to counter the anti-instrumentalism of the progressive movement. The Hillgate Group's *Whose Schools?* (1986) became the most concise statement of attack. They argued that educators had lost the confidence of parents. Neither LEAs nor teachers were trusted, because of their obsession with ideologies of the 'child-centred' and 'curriculum reform', and the need to make learning 'relevant' to the child. The solution they proposed was to give parents the power to select schools, and thus lessen the power of the LEAs and of child-centred 'experts' (Quicke, 1988).

Child-centred Education in the English Primary School

Contemporary child-centred education, or progressive education, is no longer based on the naive assumption that educators must not interfere with children's development, or that such development will not be deeply affected by the social context in which the child develops. They do argue that the nature of the learning that takes place should not be solely at the requirement of society, but should take into account the personal interests, motivations and aptitudes of the child, albeit that these very interests, motivations and aptitudes will in part be constructed between the society and the child. The Plowden Report asserted that this was central: 'no advances in policy ... have their desired effect unless they are in harmony with the nature of the child, unless they are fundamentally acceptable to him' (CACE, 1967, p. 7). Equally, they are concerned that the learner is not restricted to the acquisition of prior knowledge, and its organization and arrangements into particular forms, but learns instead *how* to acquire knowledge, *how* to understand it, rather than knowing *what* knowledge has been codified. In this sense, process-driven curricula do have an objective (to acquire the skills of synthesis and analysis, of evaluation and generalization, of communication and reception of ideas and knowledge), and they do have a content (to learn through such activities and knowledge-sets that will achieve this objective). But the underlying motive is to develop processes (Blyth, 1988c). Such a focus on process means that progressive educators are particularly concerned with how children learn: what are the better ways of inculcating learning? Is one sequence better than another: *does* it matter what you teach them first? (Boswell notes that Dr Johnson observed 'Sir, it is no matter what you teach them [children] first, any more than what leg you shall put in your breeches first.')

Process-led curricula are thus posited around five central positions, each of which can be traced back, in some form, to Rousseau:

- children will develop naturally, given a suitable environment
- children's development is best self-directed
- subject/discipline divisions are artificial
- the role of the teacher is to enable learning, not to transmit knowledge
- the learning process should be organized for individuals, not class-sized groups.

Taken together, these five lead to the maxim

- the curriculum should enable the student to understand the world in her or his own terms, through her or his own enquiries.

These positions are (of course) contested by advocates of both content-based and objectives-based curricula. Peters (1969) and Stones (1971) have both challenged Plowden's assumption that the 'natural' child has an inherent propensity to mature.

From where does this nature come from? Will it develop without some guidance, and if not, who should be the guide? Decisions about what should be selected are too important to be left to the learner, it is argued, and it is both inefficient and a risk to leave it to the learner to discover the major forms of knowledge. The resources are simply unavailable to provide the level of support that would be needed for effective child–teacher interactions. Society has particular needs to be met by its members, and quite rightly requires its educational system to channel learning towards meeting these needs.

Although the term 'child-centred' implies that progressive or process-led curricula are primarily directed at younger children, in some kind of preparatory stage that will lead them to develop into requiring the content- or objectives-driven curricula when they are older, the progressive or pedagogic tradition is found through all stages of education, not just in the nursery or infant school. The British system has fostered a particular child-centred ideology, advocated and encouraged both in the Hadow Report (Board of Education, 1931) and in the Plowden Report, *Children and their Primary Schools* (CACE, 1967). Darling (1994) reminds us that the Scottish Education Department's Primary Memorandum (SED, 1965) propounded the same position, and pre-dates Plowden (see also Cunningham, 1988; Proctor, 1990; Thomas, 1990). How extensive the practices suggested in Plowden actually became is sometimes disputed: Alexander (1984) suggests that they were not so common as supposed (and effectively derided the ideology and language which tended to surround child-centredness), while the survey of teaching styles made by Galton et al. (1980) suggested that most primary teachers very effectively used a mixture of pedagogic styles, including those that embodied child-centred approaches, but not to the exclusion of more formal styles. The elements of such teaching are in part directly curricular – there is a tendency to integrate, not to let subject boundaries 'interfere' with the directions in which a curious child may wish to explore (and therefore a weak classification (Bernstein, 1975)) – but also, inevitably, organizational: learning is organized in small groups, with a high interactional content, negotiated with the teacher, rather than prescribed, and at a pace that is not wholly established by the teacher (and therefore a weak frame (Bernstein, 1975)).

Two popular beliefs developed following the Plowden report. First, it was believed that the processes described happened in almost all primary schools all the time, as the Plowden Report implied was desirable, rather than as one element in the repertoire of the good primary teacher, used in greater and lesser degrees according to the judgment of the teacher, the ethos of the school – and the needs of the children. Second, the belief arose that this was somehow not 'real' education. This may in part be ascribed to most adults remembering their subject-based secondary education more clearly than their primary education – and perhaps those adults in the administrative and political classes responsible for the direction of educational policy remembering their own preparatory school tradition, which would not have been in the process-led category. The central role of play in learning was popularly misunderstood, and examples of highly unstructured curriculum and organization (such as William Tyndale school in the mid-1970s) were taken up by the authors of the Black Papers and the popular press to press this further (Blyth, 1988b). Alexander (1984) claimed that many primary teachers were themselves unclear about the progressive tradition, citing many texts for primary teachers that showed what he saw as a child-centred ideology, with an accompanying and illogical rhetoric to support it.

The attack on primary progressive education was advanced with evidence from Bennett's work *Teaching Styles and Pupil Progress* (1976). This was a study of the progress of primary pupils under different teaching regimes: Bennett found that children in 'formal' classrooms made the most progress in reading, mathematics and English comprehension, while those taught in 'informal' classrooms progressed least. The book attracted considerable attention in the media and in educational circles: so much so from the latter that Bennett found it necessary to re-examine his data more rigorously. On doing so, he discovered (Aitkin, Bennett and Hresketh, 1981) that the initial findings considerably exaggerated the significance of differences: in English comprehension, formal classes did show more progress, but in mathematics there was no significant difference between formal and informal styles, and in reading there was greatest progress in informal classrooms. This re-evaluation did not attract the media attention of the initial report.

Other commentators defended the child-centred curriculum. Blyth, for example (1990) suggested that a 'dentritic' model of the curriculum, which began in the early years as a relatively undifferentiated set of learning experiences (that were none the less learning activities carefully structured by the teacher) and branched into greater degrees of complexity as the child developed, so that (for example) a broad environmental programme at age 8 became gradually differentiated into history, geography, social studies and science at age 11, and the science branch divided into biology, chemistry and physics by about age 13. Such a curriculum neatly bridges the divide between process-driven curricula with younger children, and content-driven curricula in secondary education. However, there was a progressive tradition within secondary education, particularly in parts of the comprehensive schools, which will be examined in the following section.

Despite the public and political perceptions, progressive, child-centred primary education remained relatively intact during the establishment of the National Curriculum, at least in the sense that Kenneth Baker repeatedly insisted that his proposals and the work of the National Curriculum Council were not intended to be prescriptive about classroom practice or pedagogy, or how teachers elected to deliver the curriculum. The attack came a little later – it might be cynical to observe that it took place as soon as all the statutory orders were in place for all ten subjects. In 1992 the Secretary of State commissioned a report – billed as a 'discussion paper' – on *Curriculum Organisation and Classroom Practice in Primary Schools* (Alexander et al., 1992). The three authors (dubbed the 'three wise men' by the media) were carefully selected: Jim Rose, the chief primary HMI, Robin Alexander, professor of education at the University of Leeds and critic of 'the primary ideology', and Chris Woodhead, chief executive of the National Curriculum Council. Their paper suggested what the government wanted to hear: discovery learning was dismissed and subject-based learning promoted in its place, greater subject specialism for primary teachers was advocated, and more whole-class teaching suggested in place of individual and group work. Their message can be summarized: 'over the past few decades the progress of primary pupils has been hampered by the influence of highly questionable dogmas which have led to excessively complex practices and devalued the place of subjects in the curriculum' (p. 1). 'Thousands of teachers have unthinkingly subscribed' to ideology: they were accused of being 'amenable to indoctrination' (p. 3).

The new orthodoxy was imposed; the newly formed Office for Standards in Education (Ofsted), set up at almost the same time, devised rigorous enforcement schedules to monitor primary schools' implementation of the new regime. The change of government in 1997 did nothing to change the situation; far from promoting the progressive, process-driven models of the curriculum, that had been the cause of the left a decade earlier, or even allowing some degree of pluralism, the attack on progressive education intensified. Highly defined programmes for teaching literacy and numeracy were introduced in 1998 and 1999, in which teachers were firmly encouraged to adopt particular didactic teaching styles. There was very little room for the consideration of learning processes in devising the primary curriculum (Riley 1992).

The Progressive Tradition in English Secondary Education

The progressive tradition, in which the teacher adopts the stance of facilitator rather than instructor, was not confined to the primary school. As the 1968 Schools Council *Survey of Young School Leavers* cited at the end of Chapter 8 shows, there was a strong secondary school teacher movement that challenged both the utilitarian teaching-by-objectives model and the academic content-based curriculum (*Figure 8.6*). Various secondary school-based ethnographies of the 1970s identified teachers within this philosophy. For example, Rubinstein and Simon wrote of

> the tendency ... towards the development of the interdisciplinary curricula, together with the use of the resources approach to learning, involving the substitution of much group and individual work for the more traditional forms of class teaching ... this movement in itself promotes new relations between teachers and pupils, particularly ... the teacher's role ... from that of ultimate authority to that of motivating, facilitating and structuring the pupils' own discovery and search for knowledge.
>
> (Rubinstein and Simon, 1972, p. 123)

The Schools Council Humanities Curriculum Project (directed by Laurence Stenhouse) made the position of the teacher as facilitator or reconciler even more explicit: the teacher, the Project directed, needed to 'accept the need to submit his teaching in controversial areas to the criterion of neutrality ... the mode of enquiry ... should have discussion, rather than instruction, as its core' (Schools Council/Nuffield Foundation, 1972, p. 1).

Such a curriculum always carried the potential stigma of being perceived as the low-status alternative to both the academic and the utilitarian curriculum. Goodson suggested that those pursuing a child-centred approach to education would always stress the personal, the social and common-sense views of knowledge. An approach in such a style,

> with its emphasis on the individual pupil's learning process, can be characterised as the pedagogic tradition within the English curriculum. Child-centred or progressive education does not view the task of education as preparation for the

'ladder' to the professions and academia or as an apprenticeship to vocational work: rather education is seen as a way of aiding the child's own 'inquiries' or 'discoveries', a process facilitated by the 'active' methods which move the pupil away from the role of passive recipient to one of active agent in the learning process.

(Goodson, 1987, p. 28)

Much curriculum development took place in the 1960s and early 1970s, as was outlined in Chapter 4. Integrated styles of learning were particularly taken up as part of the 'ROSLA movement' – the strategy adopted to meet the particular needs of pupils who would previously have left school at 15, but were now held for a further year in compulsory education by the raising of the school leaving age. For students such as these, the Newsom Report (CACE, 1963) had defined what was, in effect, a pupil-centred curriculum. 'Four words – practical, realistic, vocational choice – provide keys which can be used to let even the least able boys and girls into an educational experience which is genuinely secondary'. From this developed a secondary school curriculum that developed basic learning skills as an initiation into the adult world of work and leisure for those pupils judged not capable of taking the then current CSE and GCE examinations. One example of this was the Interdisciplinary Enquiry project (IDE) developed by the 'curriculum laboratory' at Goldsmiths College (University of London). This was an outright assault on the idea of a subject-based, time-fragmented curriculum for these pupils, in which, it was argued,

> the arbitrary division of knowledge into subject-syllabuses encourages a didactic form of teaching with the pupil's role reduced to passive assimilation. Any enquiry resulting from keen interest shown by children ... inevitably takes them over the boundaries of the subject into another.
>
> (Goldsmiths College, 1965, p. 4)

Shipman analysed the potential of curricula such as these in optimistic terms at this time. There were, he argued, great opportunities with the 'new curriculum, involving topic centred approaches, interdisciplinary enquiry, projects taking the children outside the school and experience of social service and working conditions' (1971, p. 103). They would, he suggested, 'probably increase the motivation of the pupils and give them insight into the working world around them'. However, there were possible dangers:

> they are often lacking in real academic discipline and at worst can be a potpourri of trivia chosen because they are believed to be of interest to the young. But regardless of their worth, they could separate the education of the Newsom child from that of the future elite as effectively as when these groups were educated in different schools or systems.
>
> (Shipman, 1971, p. 104)

Other researchers had similar reservations about the social consequences of such a curriculum innovation, whatever the epistemological virtues of the approach. Burgess made a study of how the informal curriculum was used in secondary schools with the less able pupils. Burgess observed these courses in action in a comprehensive school, watching the non-examination stream of 'Easter leavers' and their teachers. The pupils' own views are summarized in the title of one of Burgess's articles describing the study: 'It's not a proper subject, it's just Newsom' (Burgess, 1984; the observations were actually made about ten years before this date). The school – pupils and teachers alike – used the descriptor 'Newsom course' to identify this particular curriculum. For both groups, the Newsom course was

> regularly compared with work in academic subject departments against which the Newsom course was timetabled. Newsom had been given departmental status but lacked the resources and staff that were given to other departments. Indeed, Newsom teachers were qualified in subjects, and taught in subject departments. There was, as the pupils indicated, no qualification to teach Newsom, apart from experience and a desire to work with non-academic pupils.
>
> (Burgess, 1984, pp. 196–7)

It was, Burgess concluded, a non-subject, with very little content or subject matter that was transmitted. The methods of teaching that were adopted were generally perceived as unconventional: there was virtually no book-based learning, and the material used in classes tended to rely very heavily on the teachers' own experiences. The teachers also displayed very informal attitudes towards the standards of discipline they expected of the Newsom pupils, very different from those of the rest of the school and curriculum. There were no opportunities for public examinations that would result in qualifications for the pupils. This ethos was at odds with the dominant ideology of the school, which governed the non-Newsom pupils. All pupils, Newsom and non-Newsom, recognized that 'the major message of the school curriculum was that conventional subjects count, while non-subjects were of less value' (Burgess, 1984, p. 197). The assumption that everyone shared was that 'real' teaching – teaching with status – was based on subjects and the transmission of knowledge, whether this was academic knowledge or skills-based knowledge.

Steven Ball's studies of 'Beachside Comprehensive' confirmed this hierarchy of curricula within the single school: 'The most experienced teachers spend most of their time teaching the most able pupils ... academic achievement tended to be the single criterion of success in the school' (Ball, 1981, p. 18). There were three clear levels, he suggested. At the top were courses based around the traditional O level subjects – maths, English, the languages, sciences, history and geography – 'an academic orientation in common: they are concerned with theoretical knowledge. They are the subjects for the brighter, the academic, the band 1 pupil' (p. 140). Below this, in the middle tier, were the utilitarian courses, the practical subjects – technical studies, metalwork at O level, and, at the lower end of this level, the traditional subjects at CSE level. At the bottom were the non-examination subjects, the 'lowest of all in status, new Mode III CSEs' in which assessment was by teacher-marked course work.

Dimensions of Curriculum Analysis

The three curricular traditions that were outlined early in Chapter 7 (*Table 7.1*) have now been discussed in some detail. Each type has its own particular characteristics, and they tend to be regarded in some ways as polar types. That is, many of those engaged in curricular discussion treat one or other of the types as desirable, and everything else as undifferentiated and undesirable. Thus, for example, there is an 'academic–non-academic' axis for debate, in which debate groups around those advocating a classical-humanist style curriculum and those against it. These three sets of polarities can be shown diagrammatically, as in *Figure 9.1a*.

Figure 9.1a   Three polarizing axes for curricular debate

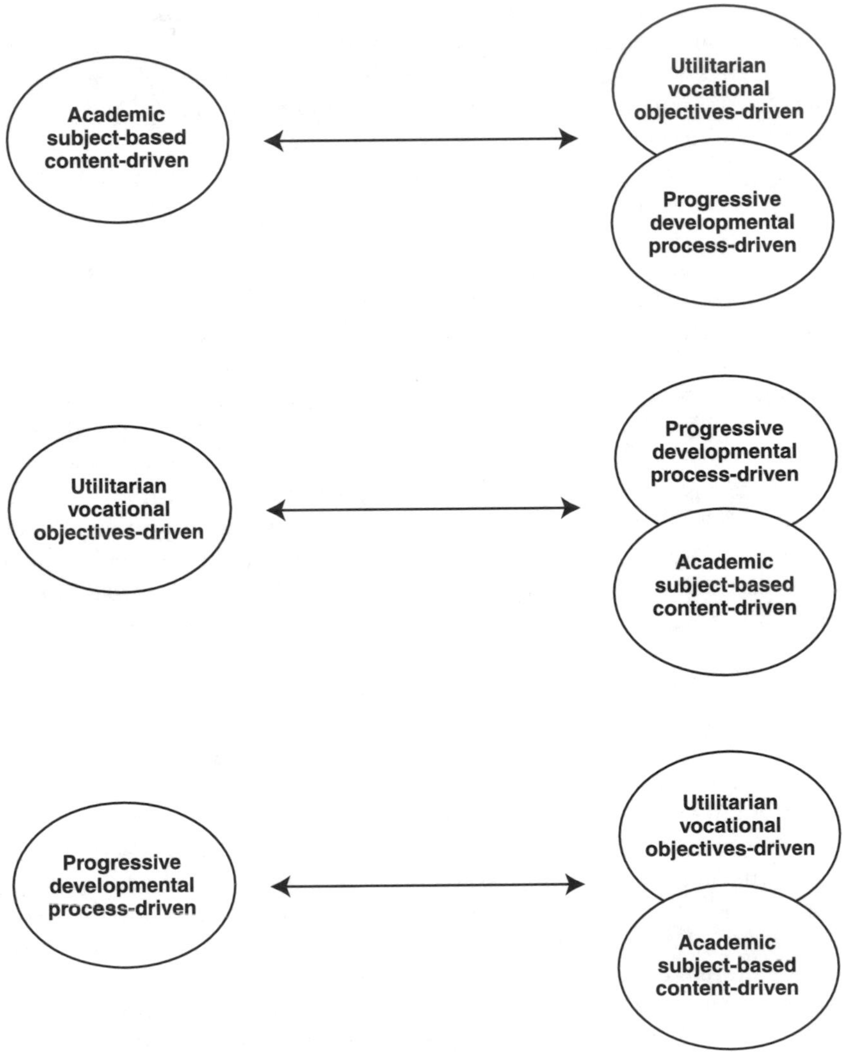

In each case, the contention is between one particular form and 'the other', in which 'the other' embraces proponents of quite different forms. In the example of the academic content-driven curriculum (the first axis shown in *Figure 9.1a*), the other end of the axis, on the left, is a coalition of the utilitarian, objectives-driven curriculum and the progressive, process-driven curriculum. Yet at other moments, in other altercations, either of these two may themselves become separated and in opposition to another coalition as 'the other'.

With three different axes, three different types of curriculum definition, one might expect to be able to represent various positions and movements as taking place within some form of three-dimensional matrix. *Figure 9.1b* shows such a hypothetical matrix, with each of the three types being located at the end of one of three axes that move in three dimensions. If this were so, it would in theory be possible for any particular curriculum ideology to be located at any point within the matrix: one could, for example, imagine a curriculum that combined various proportions of all three elements – say fairly strongly progressive, moderately academic, and weakly vocational.

Figure 9.1b Schematic arrangement of polarizing axes

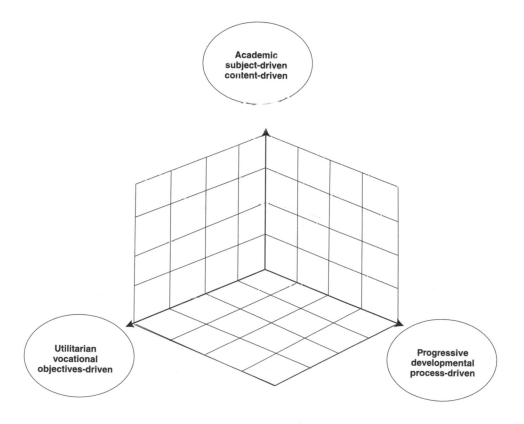

But the effect of the peculiar form of polarity described above means that this does not appear to happen. Instead, curricular positions appear to be located about the axes themselves, or on the plane surfaces between any two of the axes. Instead of a three-dimensional model, what appears to happen is that a confrontation develops between a position at one end of one of the axes, and either a point on one of the other axes, or a point on the plane surface opposite that axis. For example, the contention might at one time be between the academic/content-driven position and the utilitarian/ vocational position, in which case the alternative axis, the progressive/process-driven would be *hors de combat*, simply ignored in the debate (though the advocates of this position might be allied with one or other of the two major protagonists: which would depend on whether the first or the second axis in *Figure 9.1a* was dominant). Much of the curricular debate of the twentieth century seems to have been in this form. Indeed, the tripartite system that evolved in the mid-century seemed almost to allow the three different curricula to develop in parallel, although disputes about relative status persisted. It would be possible to show some kind of development in the career of a learner: Blyth's suggestion of a 'dendritic' curriculum (1990) could be shown as a child beginning school with an undifferentiated curriculum at the end of the progressive/process-driven axis (bottom right of *Figure 9.1b*). As the curriculum became more differentiated in the upper primary school, so the dominant curriculum form might be seen as progressing across the surface between the academic and the progressive axis, moving towards the academic apex. Later in schooling, a student might remain on the academic axis, or might migrate towards the utilitarian pole, moving across the surface between the academic and the utilitarian (to the bottom left of *Figure 9.1b*).

The analysis of curriculum history developed in Chapters 4 and 5 suggests that the situation became considerably more complex, particularly in the period following Callaghan's Ruskin speech. Different positions became more sophisticated as divisions and alliances developed between proponents of the different polar types. There developed a new imperative, to find a common curriculum, as opposed to continuing to accept the tripartite division that had been dominant. *Table 4.6* attempted to summarize the positions of various political groups that had evolved around the curriculum in the period just before the National Curriculum was designed: while the dominant discussions were between members of the various forms of the new right, and a general professional opposition to them, other variants and positions were described, both within the left and the 'old' right.

It is now possible to use the model that has been developed to locate these political positions. *Figure 9.2* is a tentative attempt to do this, using the typology developed in Chapter 4. Some groups are found at the three respective poles. Thus the academic position is advocated by the old traditional right (A), the classical humanists who argued for a particular elite education that accorded status only to the established disciplines inherited from the past. The same position, or one very similar to it, was also held by some members of the traditional old left (E), who held that a traditional curriculum, provided that it was accessible to all, would provide a meritocratic-based ladder of advancement that would allow individual members of the working class to progress. Callaghan himself was in this group: Chitty, following an interview with Donoghue (Callaghan's senior policy adviser), claims that the Prime Minister 'believed

passionately in the need for rigorous educational standards to enable working-class youngsters to rise' (Chitty, 1989, p. 68).

The vocational position was held by the right industrial trainers (B), propounding a strictly utilitarian view of education as a preparation for economic production. The progressive position was held by part of the new left (shown here as H), with an ideology centred on developmental learning processes. The term 'new left' is used here in terms of 1985, and is in no way analogous to the 'New Labour' of 1997: the position of New Labour today is rather similar to the 'left 1' group of 1985 (G), who held an industrial training position, rather similar to the right industrial trainers at B, but with also some strong progressive/developmental associations.

The new right of the mid-1980s was, as has been noted, divided. In *Figure 9.2* they are shown as taking up different positions on the surface between the Academic and

Figure 9.2   Relationship between political positions/groupings on the curriculum and curricular debate

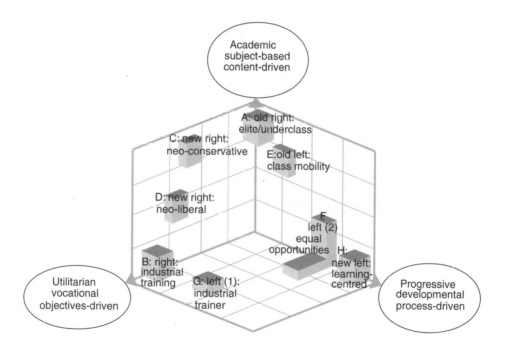

the Utilitarian axes. The neo-conservatives (C) are more strongly Academic – but have a measure of utility about them; the neo-liberals (D) are more strongly Utilitarian, but also have some regard for the subject-based traditional classical humanist position. These two groupings provided the principal debate within the Conservative Government in the mid-1980s: the polarity of debate lay between them and 'the other' – in this case, all those not shown as on the surface supported between the Academic/Utilitarian axes (Johnson, 1995).

In each of these cases, the debate tends to be held along a line that stretches from the point indicated on the figure to the point at the end of the opposite axis: thus the various 'new right' positions (C or D) are held as polar opposites to the Progressive/process-driven position; the industrial trainers of the right (B) or left (H) are on a line of debate that opposes the Academic/content-driven position.

The other form of the left, described as 'left 2' (F) who had strong equal-opportunities, egalitarian motivations, and who sought to use education as a means of social transformation, are slightly less easy to classify in this typology. Firmly progressive, though somewhat less so than the 'new left' group (H), they sometimes displayed some Academic/anti-utilitarian traits, and at other times some Utilitarian/anti-academic objectives. They have thus been shown in *Figure 9.2* in a rather unsatisfactory position, ambivalent between these axes. The equal opportunities/left 2 position thus sets up its polar opposite sometimes the Academic position and sometimes the Utilitarian, which is why its own position seems to alternate between the two opposite planes.

These models, and the positions shown in the figure, are proposed as a tentative step towards trying to provide an explanatory archetype of a complex relationship between curriculum types. The relationship seems peculiarly complex because of its continuing bi-polar presentation, even though there are clearly more than two positions available. But it may offer some help in tracing the various movements and debates, particularly those that have characterized educational analysis in England since the mid-1970s.

Nation-building and Curriculum

This is a particularly English debate, and the examples used in this book have been almost exclusively from that debate. The characteristics of national identity are of particular importance to the content and shape of the curricular debate, and it is to this final area that we will turn in Chapter 10.

Goodson observes that the selection of the content of particular subjects – and the selection of the subjects themselves – suggested that ideas and concerns about national identity were regarded as more important than possible industrial or commercial considerations.

> The national curriculum ... can be seen as a response to the 'nation at risk' at two levels. First, there is the general sense of the nation-state being in economic decline and subject to globalisation and to amalgamation in the wider European Community. There the response is paradoxical. Nation-building curricula are often favoured over commercially 'relevant' curricula. The solution may therefore exacerbate the problem. ... Secondly, given that the UK is clearly a divided

nation, investigation of the national curriculum allows insights into precisely *which* nation is at risk. ... elite and middle class groups ... have the greatest historical connections to the 'traditional subject'.

(Goodson, 1994, p. 104)

The ways in which the curriculum may influence social reproduction may be contested, but the fact that it does have an influence on the nature of future society is no longer an issue. The curriculum has a role in shaping future identities. If social identities and cultures were secure and static, then the role of education in this would not be at issue, but this is not the case, either in Britain or much of the rest of the world. Social mobility, migration, increased awareness of gender, environmental concerns, social exclusion and class: all continue to contribute to a general challenge to traditional verities. Even if there was once a notional stability – and what stability and coherence there was may have been at best an invention – it does not continue today. Society is plural and fragmented. This is not a cause of concern for many people: the multiple identities that we are now able to take on have done much to liberate groups that have been hitherto suppressed. But for many others, it has been of concern that inherited and established patterns and groupings are breaking up. One of the motivations behind the national curriculum has been the desire to use the educational system to weld together the various parts of society, to ensure that a 'whole' society was reproduced in the future.

Searching for a common identity has its dangers. Some members of the polity will resist the imposition of a dominant culture on them; others will resist what they will see as the hybridization of tradition. Perhaps more importantly, the only way to create a common identity is to distinguish 'the other': to create a group that is outside, that is used to make 'us' different from 'them'. Sometimes 'the other' is created by hiving off a particular sector – the underclass, the ethnic or linguistic minority, the welfare-dependants. In order to create a commonality between the rest, groups such as these are isolated and demonized as the other. A synthetic idea of 'society' or 'the nation' is created by stigmatizing the outsiders, those who do not belong. Another strategy, equally divisive and dangerous, is the nationalistic path: 'the other' is here identified as the foreigner, whether resident here or across the Channel. Whichever tactic is adopted in the search for an elusive national identity, the curriculum plays a pivotal role. The final chapter of this book examines the search for identity through the curriculum.

10 Forging the Curriculum: Nationalism, Identity and the English Curriculum

Nations have traditionally employed symbols and metaphors to signify what they wish to show as their distinctive characteristics. Englishness has been variously represented by the Cross of St George (now in face-paint form), John Bull and, perhaps rather unfortunately, by Roast Beef. This final chapter is an attempt to explore some of the symbols of nationality that are embedded in, or associated with, our curriculum, and to suggest that these may present some problems in terms of values and of equality.

A critical examination of our current preoccupations with national identity will be related to the UK's relationships with other States (and to the nature of the UK itself), and the State's relationship with its citizens and their presumed duties to the State. From this, it will be suggested that contemporary representations of the nation are used to generate individual and national identities, and that the curriculum has a central role in this. This will be related to the language and rhetoric of the various National Curriculum documents, and to materials from the Schools Curriculum and Assessment Authority (SCAA), its successor, the Qualifications and Curriculum Authority (QCA), and their officers. The argument which will follow from this is that the curriculum is being utilized to invent a new form of national identity, in the face of a range of other offerings of identity, and that this identity attempts:

- to define its citizens primarily as individuals owing obligations and duties to the State, and that these duties are prior to and independent of any rights, and
- to minimize alternative identities (of class, ethnicity or gender – or regional and supra-national affinities).

This argument is particularly interesting during a period of moral panic in the British press and Parliament. We have witnessed, over the past few years, a series of debates on the role of schools in teaching 'moral values', on the teaching of 'citizenship', and on the nature of the nation (whether rebranded as 'cool' or otherwise).

National Identity in the Early Twenty-first Century

It was not easy, even in the heyday of nineteenth-century nationalism, to define what was mean by national identity. Nations were often based on some notion of unity, or of consanguinity ('think with your blood!', Bismarck was supposed to have commanded), or of some shared culture, or appearance, or language. None of these seems to be either

150

a necessary or a sufficient condition, however. The United States manages without consanguinity, for example – though it currently seems to see language as a defining issue, as can be seen in the moral panic about the possibility of non-English speakers forming a majority. But Canada manages, more or less, without a common language: with 75 per cent of the population living within a hundred miles of the US frontier, what makes Canadians Canadian is that they are not Americans.

Walker Connor suggests that nationalism is no more (and no less) than a psychological phenomenon: a perception held by a group of people that they hold some major homogeneous characteristics (1978, p. 379). Emerson refers to the nation as the

> terminal community – the largest community that, when the chips are down, effectively commands men's loyalty, overriding the claims both of the lesser communities within it and those that cut across it or potentially enfold it within a still greater society.
>
> (Emerson, 1960, pp. 95–6)

This is rather similar to, if more emphatic than, Norman Tebbit's definition of 'which team do you cheer for?'.

Benedict Anderson argues that such nationalisms are no more than *Imagined Communities* (1991), held together by invented traditions. Eric Hobsbawm and Terry Ranger's collection of papers on *The Invention of Tradition* (1983) details the ways in which many national entities, sometimes of apparent great antiquity, present fictional traditions that are 'exercises in social engineering which are often deliberate and always innovative' (p.13). One study of French modernization convincingly suggests, for example, that most rural and small-town dwellers in France did not conceive of themselves as members of a French nation as recently as 1870, and many still failed to do so as late as 1914 (Weber, 1979).

Linda Colley (1992) examines the creation of the British State, following the 1707 Act of Union between England (and Wales) and Scotland. (The current United Kingdom, despite the politicians' rhetoric of 'a thousand years of history', 'cricket on the village green, old maids cycling to Holy Communion, warm beer', etc., dates back only to the implementation of the Government of Ireland Act in 1922.) Colley suggests how the idea of Britain-as-a-nation was effected (or forged, in both meanings of the word) by the ruling elite identifying characteristics that might persuade the English and the Scots (or at least most of the more powerful members of these communities) that they had a common identity. Factors such as their common Protestantism, their mercantilism, and their interests in the pre-1779 and post-1779 empires were utilized to define the new British, post-1707, with a shared nationality that was largely defined in terms of negatives – largely, not being (continental) European.

So even this nationalism of the 'old' nations was largely created (or socially constructed), rather than having any natural existence. The feudal and peasant societies that entered the modern period in the sixteenth century created themselves as nations because they had a need for an homogeneity that was otherwise missing (Gellner, 1964). This is why much of the subject of history (in both as a 'school subject' and as the 'subject matter of history') is so important to nationalism: nationalism needs selectively to make use of the past in order to define and control the present. When Shakespeare, in *Henry V*, introduces Scots, Welsh and Irish soldiers to the English campaigns in France, he is addressing the needs of nationalism in the Elizabethan England of the late 1590s, *not* describing any 'real' national affinities in 1415: equally, Laurence Olivier's 1944 film of the play was clearly produced to address the national needs of Britain in the World War.

Two current popular beliefs clearly hold sway: first, that the pre-1945 major nations were homogeneous, and second, that the consensus of values that held the nation together has now been lost in some way. It is held by politicians and curriculum-mongers alike that we need to reassert national identity, and that schools have a particular and vital role to play in this process. Thus Nick Tate, Chief Executive of SCAA, wrote:

> In England ... we seem almost evasive, inclined to understatement, embarrassed by any public display of concern about identity. And yet it is this which underlies many of the documents on three aspects of the Schools Curriculum and Assessment Authority's curriculum proposals ... a key role of a national curriculum should be the explicit reinforcement of a common culture: pupils first and foremost should be introduced to the history of the part of the world where they live, its literary heritage and main religious traditions. They should be taught these things with the sensitivity a more diverse society demands; they should be taught other things too; but the culture and traditions of Britain should be at the core. Seen in this light, the central role of British history, Christianity and the English literary heritage are axiomatic.
>
> The SCAA recommendations come off the fence on this issue. The proposals for British history, standard English and the English literary heritage are designed to reinforce a common culture. A national curriculum, we imply, is more than just a recipe for meeting economic needs, vital though these are; it is more than just the means to facilitate the infinitely varied life of choices of collections of isolated individuals. It also plays a key part in helping society maintain its identity.
>
> In a society which cannot afford to be complacent that it is defining itself clearly, the future of our common culture is also at stake.
>
> (Tate, 1994, p. 11)

The contemporary idea of the nation *has* changed, in all the nations of the world – it has been changing since the early 1950s – because of a range of factors.

Some of these factors are social, such as increasing migration, changing gender roles, increasing affluence and education, the development of a variety of youth cultures and a general challenging of traditional values (and indeed, in postmodernism, of the very idea of values). Other factors are political and economic. The creation and promotion of new states has inevitably led to some reappraisal of the nature of the older nations, largely because many of the older nationalisms had been defined in distinction to 'the other'. Thus Britain/England was largely defined as '*not* continental Europe', the United States as '*not* the Old World', and so on. Other challenges to the old nationalisms have emerged from both the growth of supra-national organizations (such as the European Union), and the move towards emphasizing regions within nations (current EU policy and practice). There have been further changes in the concept of nation since 1990, as the end of the Cold War has allowed suppressed ethnic and cultural tensions to emerge, and a new and often angry face of nationalism to emerge. In 1950 the suggestion that there would be more than 150 independent nations by 1975 would have seemed preposterous: the idea in 1990 that there would be approaching twenty new states in Europe alone by 1995 would have seemed bizarre. The point of this is not simply that there are now new nations: it is that each nation is defined in the context of all the other nations, so that the invention of new nations means that each of the old nations needs to redefine itself. There has also been a continuous re-ordering of national economies in the various league tables of prosperity: there has been relative economic growth and decline, and such changes in position have required States to devise new explanatory narrations to explain these.

All of these tendencies can be seen as requirements on nations whose identity is under threat to redefine their authority and re-assert their hegemony over their citizens: this is both from the need modern states have to have a cultural homogeneity (following Gellner, 1964, 1983) and is part of the way in which states use nationalism to incorporate the masses into social structures (Nairn, 1977). As the characteristics of a particular nation change then new 'traditions' need to be invented to justify the older nation's continuance and exclusivity. Contemporary nationalism continues to emphasize the notion of 'the other' as an appeal to some kind of loyalty or primordial attachment. As homogeneity is seen to fade in the kaleidoscope of fragmentation between particularist and international tendencies, those whose own positions are tied to the idea of the nation will demand that national identity be re-forged. This leads to the re-invention of traditions and heritages. New bonds must be devised and be portrayed as ancient. A narrative needs to be written – and re-written – that forges the nation together in the face of the estrangements and alienations of contemporary societies.

Representations of the National Culture

Introducing a UNESCO-sponsored survey of social studies teaching in schools around the world, Howard Mehlinger pointed out that

> Every country employs a wide range of social institutions to induct new members into its society, transmit the cultural heritage to the young and to develop in its people a feeling of national pride. The major means for accomplishing these goals is through educational institutions ... [and] within the schools, the major responsibility falls on the social studies programme.
>
> (Mehlinger, 1981, p. 25)

Culture is many-faceted. A 'national culture' might include, for example, the selection of a specific body of literature that was said to represent or even embody particular characteristics: a canon. Anderson (1991) suggested that the attainment of universal (or near-universal) literacy is an important and necessary function of contemporary nationalism and nation-construction. The definition and transmission of a language, through the formal mechanisms of education, thus includes the identification of a canon of literature that demarcates and identifies the culture, and the definition of an educational curriculum represents an undertaking to both reify and transmit this to new and younger members of the nation. There may be arguments about what should be the content of the canon, and even if there should be a canon – but content there must be in a curriculum, and the content that is selected will, in a sense, contribute to and be part of that culture. The evolving nations of the sixteenth century, Gellner submitted, needed 'second order teachers and intellectuals necessary to produce the ground-level teachers' who would transmit this literacy and its literature (1964, p.159). Music, art and literature are clearly culturally-rich subjects, around which particular debate has taken place; mathematics, science and technology are commonly perceived as having a lesser (or even no) cultural content (although there is a minority who would see these subjects as being not only as culturally rich as the others, but also equally and wholly social constructed).

But it is the social subjects that encompass culture most strongly, and particularly encompass national culture (note, in contrast, how art and music, and to a lesser extent literature, are placed in wider cultural groupings, such as western art, the western European literary tradition, etc.). Social studies – history and geography in particular, but also sociology and economics – inevitably make *selections* of data in the construction of curricula. The curriculum architects in these subjects may (sometimes) argue that the content is subservient to the processes being learned, but the content is nevertheless critical. It will inevitably define who 'we' are, and what 'our society' is, generalizing about activities, creating boundaries, borders and categories, selecting moments from the past that seem to have particular significance, making assumptions about (for example) possessive individualism and 'rational' economic behaviour – all of these items will tell 'us' who 'we' are. And the 'we' is not just an amorphous collection of individuals, but becomes the class, the school, the district, the nation.

The subject of geography necessarily defines social space and territory, given its concern with boundaries (national and physical), zones of activity and notions of regionality: these are inevitably part of the process of identifying people with places, in terms of the identity and nature of a nation. Thus Nick Tate complains that the current geography curriculum lacks 'a specific requirement to study the geography of England or the United Kingdom as an entity in itself' (Tate, 1996). Geography, Tate asserts, should (*inter alia*) 'develop pupils' sense of national identity and pride in their own country'. Likewise history necessarily constructs social groups to help explain and analyse the past, such as the middle classes, entrepreneurs, the north east, the French or the Picts, and whether socio-economic or cultural, such categories can very easily be utilized in the construction of 'nationalities'.

Through these subjects, a definition is created, an identity for the learner to put on. This happens whether the child studies 'their' society or that of others, because when studies are made of 'other' societies (for whatever motive), children are comparing and contrasting, and thus asserting the way that their culture does things differently, how their past is another country. From the very first directive of a teacher to the youngest children, that '*we* do things in this way in *our* class' an identity is being constructed for the individual, an identity as a member of a collectivity is being asserted.

The Curriculum as a Narration of the Nation

It was argued in Chapter 6 that one of the primary purposes of education can be seen as the reproduction of a hegemonic culture (Bourdieu and Passeron, 1990). The pedagogic authority represented by the State will seek to produce structures and curricula that are designed to maintain national identity, particularly at moments when national authority might seem to be in question. Bernstein expressed part of this when he wrote that 'how a society selects, classifies, distributes, transmits and evaluates the educational knowledge that it considers to be public reflects both the distribution of power and the principles of social control' (1971a). If existing power structures and distribution are to be maintained, knowledge, and the particular kinds of knowledge that constitute cultural capital, must be selected and transmitted to particular groups. Such cultural capital must be identified, protected and valued over other cultural phenomena. Authorities need to assert their identity and control, and, in the context of the arguments presented in this paper, they need national and cultural symbols to do this, and they need control over the way in which they are transmitted. The international data on national elementary curricula collected and analysed by the team led by John Meyer (Meyer et al., 1992), referred to in Chapter 2, are particularly instructive: they can be read as suggesting that the nationalistic elements of the curriculum (history and geography) were generally in decline world-wide, over the period 1900 to 1975, when compared with the rise of the generally non-nationalistic subject of social studies. In the late nineteenth century the primary focus of history and geography had been on 'instilling a spirit of national strength and pride', placing 'great emphasis on the outstanding heroes of the nation's past or the particularities of the national identity' (p. 124). The rise of social studies, and the associated decline in geography and history, was a consequence of the decline of 'national' identity elements in the curriculum, so that 'the social science curriculum commands less attention than subjects like mathematics or science ... [and is] of secondary importance' (p. 125). But the data also reveal a post-1975 move towards a renaissance of the history/geography categories, and a swing from social studies. This marks the return of using the curriculum to relate new national identities (Ross, 1995a). These subjects are value-laden, even when stripped of content: their very methodologies imply particular views of the organization of knowledge that have implicit values (linear, temporal, spatial, relational, causal).

The view of cultural transmission as one of the essential functions of an educational system is widespread, and can be seen in the practices both of formal (school-based) education and informal (home and community-based) education. It applies equally to secular education and to religious or faith-based education. It is as true for those who regard culture as a version of received truth as it is of those relativists who view all knowledge as a social construct. In the late nineteenth century, and up to the middle of the twentieth century, many sociologists argued that socialization – such as that which was imparted by the national schooling systems – made an essential contribution to the development of the national solidarity that was necessary in an increasingly differentiated society (for example, Parsons, 1966; and the 'nation building' theorists analysing the new states of the 1960s).

As part of this culture, it can also be argued that schooling provides a mechanism for the transmission of those hegemonic values necessary to maintain the hierarchical structures of power associated with capitalism (for example, Bowles and Gintis, 1976). Schooling incorporates a hidden curriculum that reinforces the basic values and rules that maintain both social differentiation (between classes, in support of the capitalist distribution of wealth) and social integration (at the national level). John Ahier's (1988) analysis of history and geography textbooks shows both these forces also at work in the formal curriculum of geography and history.

Schooling – and perhaps particularly primary schooling – thus has an important role in narrating the 'new' nation, in transmitting the invented heritage of the new nation. As has been suggested above, history can be defined in ways that require teachers to select issues from the past that accentuate moments that can be seen as defining for the modern contemporary definition of the state and nationhood. Geography can be defined to justify frontiers, typologies of economic activity and transportation and settlement patterns that 'explain' differences between nations. Teachers and educational systems will be used in this process – and will in many cases willingly be used – to assert differences and to create new traditions.

Individualism, Equality and National Identity

Nick Tate (the Chief Executive of the SCAA and then the QCA) has asserted that schools and teachers need clear guidance on 'the transmission of culture, knowledge and guidance from one generation to the next' (Tate, 1996, §10). In his address to the conference which began the SCAA consultation on 'Curriculum, Culture and Society', Tate put forward what he called four 'big ideas':

1   'the fundamental purpose of the school curriculum is to transmit an appreciation of and commitment to the best of the culture we have inherited', in which the 'school curriculum is a key factor in maintaining continuity within society' (ibid., §16);
2   'the cultural dimension of the curriculum needs to be firmly and proudly based in a cultural heritage that has its roots in Greece and Rome, in Christianity and the many-sided traditions of European civilisation' (§19);
3   'the best guarantee of minority cultures ... is a strong majority culture which values itself and which signals that traditions and customs are worthy of respect' (§24); and
4   'a key purpose of the curriculum is to introduce young people to some of the characteristics of what has traditionally been known as 'high culture' (§28), because 'some works of art, music, literature or architecture are more valuable than others' (§25).

These seem to be particularly value-laden ideas: no doubt Tate would argue that they are deliberately so. But it must nevertheless be pointed out that each idea is imbued with quantities of cultural and intellectual baggage.

The first idea is clearly designed to preserve the existing social order, and almost every word begs a whole series of questions and problems. Who can define the 'best of the culture' (Matthew Arnold is invoked at one point (§29)? Who are the 'we' that is referred to? Does 'appreciation' necessarily involve 'a commitment to continuity'? Is continuity within society necessarily a virtue (are there *no* aspects of society that Dr Tate would seek to change?)?

The second idea is, on analysis, also a strange assertion. The Graeco-Roman tradition was, *inter alia*, based on pantheistic ritual, slavery, exploitation and an inability to compute. European civilization includes the appropriation, de-culturalization and degradation of most of the globe. At the same conference that Tate addressed, Anthony O'Hear claimed that education 'should be guided by a notion of universally applicable standards, particularly in the cultural and moral domains ... derived ... from the combination of Hellenism and Hebraism which form the core of morality and culture in Western Europe' (O'Hear, 1996). The 'idea' implies that 'our' culture has discrete, autonomous and timeless qualities, whereas it is a shameless magpie collection of material borrowed from around the globe.

Tate's third idea is no more than the tyranny of the majority. Is it really suggested that acculturation into a dominant culture will in any way preserve minority cultures, or imbue in the 'majority' a special regard for cultures which differ from it?

Tate develops his fourth idea, his battle with the cultural relativists, by contrasting examples of high culture – Schubert's *Ave Maria*, Milton and Vermeer's *View of Delft* – with what he thinks to be inappropriate cultural manifestations – Blur, Mills and Boon and 'dead sheep at the Tate' – and he argues that postmodernist thought holds that all of these are now being seen 'as cultural products to be understood, not in themselves and in terms of their value, but in relation to the structures and circumstances – including the gender, race and social class of the artist – within which they were produced' (Tate, 1996, §26). There are several oddities here. First, Blur, Mills and Boon and Hirst are as much products of European civilization and traditions as are Tate's preferred canon. Tate's selection is 'safe' because the items have the patina of age that makes them less contestable than items selected from contemporary culture. Second, it seems to be suggested that cultural artefacts can be understood and valued in themselves in some way that is divorced from their structures and circumstances. But it does not require a great degree of reflection to realize that individual items do not constitute a culture (high or popular), but that culture is composed of the sum of its parts. How can items be valued independently of each other? How could any such hypothetical value be transmitted other than by assertion and by rote? In fact, if one really seeks to 'transmit a culture' this is far more likely to be achieved through relating the artefacts of a culture to the ethos and surroundings within which they were produced – including the forbidden trilogy of race, gender and class.

How do these ideas relate to the development of a national cultural identity? Tate suggests that the curriculum's purpose is to transmit a particular cultural heritage – 'our' heritage, one that 'we' have in some way temporarily mislaid. Heritage is particularistic and individualistic: it gives proprietorial rights to individuals of a particular inheritance of the past, not to the common past of all humanity. Heritage is a particularly myopic view of history. Raphael Samuel has championed it in *Theatres of Memory* (1995) as a democratic/populist reclamation of the past: Samuel (1996) was recruited by Tate to make this pitch at the SCAA conference in February 1996 – to enable 'young people to develop a sense of ... civic and national identity' (Tate, 1996, §32). As Neal Ascherson (1995) pointed out, such use of heritage

> is a term of obligation, binding people not only to respect relics of the past, but also to understand them in one prescribed way as 'national symbols'. [Such a use] is not spontaneous. It is a form of manipulation, devised by politicians and quangocrats to make the tatty, dishevelled building-site of the present look more imposing.

Brian Cox (1992) contrasts the current curricular emphasis of 'a cultural heritage view' in the English curriculum orders, emphasizing as it does the requirement to lead children to an appreciation of fine literature, to the possibilities of 'a cultural analysis view', in which children would be helped towards a critical understanding of the literary culture of the world and in which they live: both, Cox argues, are essential.

The stress in the National Curriculum and its associated documentation – the original version, the Dearing review, the Curriculum Guidance papers and the *Culture, Curriculum and Society* conference papers – is on the individual: educating the individual independent of society, and educating 'the individual within a community and developing the individual's *sense of commitment to that community*' (Tate, 1996, §32, emphasis added). This reiterates the ways in which the cross-curricular themes consistently stress the individual over society (see Ross, 1995c).

There has been a long tradition in political writings about citizenship of linking rights to duties. Invariably – up to 1986 – the sequence seems to have been to place the rights of the individual before and independent of any duties s/he might owe the State. We are still urged (by some) to legislate for a Bill of Rights, and no one has yet suggested a concomitant Bill of Duties. It is Sir Keith Joseph who appears first to have reversed the order: in a DES press release accompanying the *Draft Statement on the Principles of Teaching Politically Controversial Issues in Schools and Colleges*, he took the reference to the need for pupils to understand the rights and duties of citizenship, and, in longhand, changed the wording to put 'duties' before 'rights' (DES, 1986d). Since then, duties have gradually assumed the ascendancy: Curriculum Guidance 8: *Education for Citizenship* (National Curriculum Council, 1990f), for example, focuses on obligations and 'negative freedoms' (Gilbert, 1995). This discourse of responsibilities has spread across the political spectrum, and has become a significant – almost central – aspect of Blair's redefinition of Labour Party beliefs (Blair, 1996). David Selbourne, in *The Principle of Duty* (1994), elevated duties above rights in a critique of the liberal order (though he does also allow that the society may have duties to its citizens). The stress on individualism and the individual's duties continues. The *Report of the National Forum for Values in Education and the Community* (SCAA, 1996b) uses the language of duties/ responsibilities and rights as shown in *Table 10.1*.

Other Possible Identities

We are all capable of multiple identities: the problem seems to be that the State's perceptions of the exigencies of the crisis in national identity require it to use the school curriculum to create and promote one national identity above all others.

Table 10.1 *Categorization of some aspects of the* Report of the National Forum for Values in Education and the Community

		Obligations/duties/responsibilities	Rights
Society	Values		We value ... collective endeavour for the common good of society.
	Principles for action	understand our responsibilities as citizens; obey the law and encourage others to do so; promote participation in our democracy; contribute to, as well as benefit fairly from, economic and cultural resources; support families in raising children and caring for dependants; help people know about the law and legal processes.	support people who cannot sustain a dignified life-style by themselves.
Relationships	Values		We value others ... [as] relationships fundamental to ... the good of the community.
	Principles for action	earn loyalty, trust and confidence; work cooperatively with others; be mutually supportive; respect the beliefs, life, privacy and property of others; try to resolve disputes peacefully.	
The self	Principles for action	try to live up to a shared moral code; make responsible use of our rights and privileges; strive for knowledge and wisdom throughout life; take responsibility for our own lives within our capacities.	make responsible use of our rights and privileges.
Environment	Values		We ... accept our duty to maintain a sustainable environment for the future.
	Principles for action	preserve balance and diversity in nature wherever possible; justify development in terms of a sustainable environment; repair habitats devastated by human development wherever possible; preserve areas of beauty wherever possible; understand the place of human beings within the world.	

Source: SCAA, 1996b.

There is the identity of being a European, for example. Morrell (1996) has recently analysed the European content of the National Curriculum foundation subject documents, and demonstrated that 'the European Dimension has been virtually excluded from the National Curriculum Orders' (p.1).

Regional identities are denied, either by ignoring them, by leaving them to an optional and self-determined 'local' element in the History and Geography Orders, or relegated to inferior status, as in the way in which the English Orders make regional dialects 'non standard forms … [only to be] used for effect or technical reasons' (DfE, 1995, p. 3). Class, gender and ethnic identities are also denied in the need to create a national identity.

All these possible alternatives are not, in themselves, incompatible with a national identity. But they are not permissible when the national identity is so weak and vulnerable that they threaten to engulf it. Roast beef was never the staple foodstuff of Britain or of England. It was the temporary fare of the more prosperous members of society. National identity has always been a confused and confusing fiction that only really exists in a fictional and nostalgic heritage. Our heritage is as safe, enduring and sustaining as is our roast beef: it is mutant and dangerous. The curriculum is a major tool in the construction of identity, and it must be used with care. All curricula are forged: they are socially constructed, they are at times malleable, and at other times more rigid. This book has attempted to distinguish some of the competing traditions in curriculum design and purpose, and to analyse some of the ideologies that drive its construction.

References

Ahier, J. (1988) *Industry, Children and the Nation*, London: Falmer.

Ahier, J. (1995) 'Hidden Controversies in Two Cross-Curricular Themes', in Ahier, J. and Ross, A. (eds) *The Social Subjects Within the Curriculum: Children's Social Learning in the National Curriculum*, London: Falmer, pp. 139–56.

Ahier, J. and Ross, A. (1995a) 'Introduction', in Ahier, J. And Ross, A. (eds) *The Social Subjects within the Curriculum: Children's Social Learning in the National Curriculum*, London: Falmer, pp. 1–8.

Ahier, J. and Ross, A. (eds) (1995b) *The Social Subjects within the Curriculum: Children's Social Learning in the National Curriculum*, London: Falmer.

Aitkin, M., Bennett, N. and Hresketh, J (1981) 'Teaching Styles and Pupil Progress: A Re-analysis', *British Journal of Educational Psychology*, 51, 2, pp. 170–86.

Aldrich, R. (1988) 'The National Curriculum: An Historical Perspective', in Lawton, D. and Chitty, C. (eds) *The National Curriculum*, Bedford Way Papers 33, London: Institute of Education.

Alexander, R. (1984) *Primary Teaching*, Eastbourne: Holt, Rinehart & Winston.

Alexander, R. (1988) 'Garden or Jungle? Teacher Development and Informal Primary Education', in Blyth, W.A.L. (ed.) *Informal Primary Education Today*, London: Falmer.

Alexander, R., Rose, J. and Woodhead, C. (1992) *Curriculum Organisation and Classroom Practice in Primary Schools: A Discussion Paper*, London: DES.

Amis, K. (1969) 'Pernicious Participation', in Cox, C. and Dyson, A. (eds) *Fight for Education: A Black Paper*, London: Critical Quarterly Society, pp. 9–10.

Anderson, B. (1991) *Imagined Communities* (2nd edn), London: Verso.

Anderson, D. (ed.) (1981) *The Pied Pipers of Education*, London: Social Affairs Unit.

Apple, M.W. (1990) *Ideology and Curriculum* (2nd edn), London: Routledge.

Aristotle (1962) *The Politics* (trans. T.A. Sinclair, revised and represented T.J. Saunders), Harmondsworth: Penguin.

Arnot, M. (ed.) (1985) *Race and Gender: Equal Opportunities Policies in Education*, Oxford: Pergammon/Open University Press.

Ascherson, N. (1995) 'It is not snobbish to say that leylines and astro-archaeology are inventions', *Independent on Sunday*, 19 February.

Baker, K. (1993) *The Turbulent Years: My Life in Politics*, London: Faber.

Ball, S. (1981) *Beachside Comprehensive*, Cambridge: Cambridge University Press.

Ball, S.J. (1982) 'Competition and Conflict in the Teaching of English: A Socio-Historical Analysis', *Journal of Curriculum Studies*, 14, 1, pp. 1–28.

Ball, S.J. (1990) *Politics and Policy Making in Education: Explorations in Policy Sociology*, London: Routledge.

Ball, S.J. (1994) *Education Reform*, Buckingham: Open University Press.

Banks, O. (1955) *Parity and Prestige in English Secondary Education*, London: Routledge.

Bantock, G.H. (1968) *Culture, Industrialisation and Education*, London: Routledge.

Bantock, G.H. (1986) 'The Attack on the Culture of Quality', in O'Keeffe, D. (ed.) *The Wayward Curriculum, A Cause for Parents' Concern?*, London: Social Affairs Unit.

Barcan, A. (1986) 'English: Two Decades of Attrition', in O'Keeffe, D. (ed.) *The Wayward Curriculum: A Cause for Parents' Concern?*, London: Social Affairs Unit.

Barnes, D., Sestini, E., Cooper, B. and Bliss, I. (1987) 'Language, Power and the Curriculum', in Richards, C. (ed.) *Power and the Curriculum: Issues in Curriculum Studies*, Driffield: Nafferton.

Barnett, C. (1986) *The Audit of War*, London: Macmillan.

Bates, I., Clarke, J., Cohen, P., Finn, D., Moore, R. and Willis, P. (1984) *Schooling for the Dole: The New Vocationalism*, London: Macmillan.

Bates, I., Bloomer, M., Hodkinson, P. and Yeomans, D. (1998) 'Progressivism and the GNVQ: Context, Ideology and Practice', *Journal of Education and Work* 11, 2, pp. 109–25.

Benn, C. and Simon, B. (1972) *Half Way There*, Harmondsworth: Penguin.

Bennett, N. (1976) *Teaching Styles and Pupil Progress*, London: Open Books.

Berger, P. and Luckmann, T. (1966) *The Social Construction of Reality*, Harmondsworth: Penguin.

Bernstein, B. (1962a) 'Linguistic Codes, Hesitation Phenomena and Intelligence', *Language and Speech* 5, pp. 31–46 (reprinted in Bernstein, 1971b, pp. 76–94).

Bernstein, B. (1962b) 'Social Class, Linguistic Codes and Grammatical Elements', *Language and Speech* 5, pp. 221–40 (reprinted in Bernstein, 1971b, pp. 95–117).

Bernstein, B. (1971a) 'On the Classification and Framing of Educational Knowledge', in Young, M.F.D. (ed.) *Knowledge and Control: New Directions for the Sociology of Education*, London: Collier-Macmillan.

Bernstein, B. (1971b) *Class, Codes and Control. Volume 1: Theoretical Studies Towards a Sociology of Language*, London: Routledge & Kegan Paul.

Bernstein, B. (1975) *Class, Codes and Control. Volume 3: Towards a Theory of Educational Transmissions* (2nd edn), London: Routledge & Kegan Paul.

Bernstein, B. (1990) *Class, Codes and Control. Volume 4: The Structuring of Pedagogic Discourse*, London: Routledge.

Bernstein, B. (1996) *Class, Codes and Control. Volume 5: Pedagogy, Symbolic Control and Identity: Theory, Research, Critique*, London: Falmer.

Black, P. (1993) 'The Shifting Scenery of the National Curriculum', in Chitty, C. and Simon, B. (eds) *Education Answers Back*, London: Lawrence & Wishart.

Blair, T. (1996) *New Britain: My Vision of a Young Country*, London, Fourth Estate.

Bloom, B.S. et al. (1956) *Taxonomy of Educational Objectives: 1, The Cognitive Domain*, London: Longman.

Bloomer, M. (1998) ' "They tell you what to do and then they leave you to get on with it": The Illusion of Progressivism in GNVQ', *Journal of Work and Education* 11, 2, pp. 167–86.

Blyth, W.A.L. (1967) *English Primary Education* (2 vols) (rev. edn), London: Routledge & Kegan Paul.

Blyth, W.A.L. (ed.) (1988a) *Informal Primary Education Today*, London: Falmer.

Blyth, W.A.L. (1988b) 'Five Aspects of Informality in Primary Education: A Historical Sketch', in Blyth, W.A.L. (ed.) *Informal Primary Education Today*, London: Falmer.

Blyth, W.A.L. (1988c) 'Bases for the Primary Curriculum', in Clarkson, M. (ed.) *Emerging Issues in Primary Education*, Lewes: Falmer.

Blyth, W.A.L. (1990) *Making the Grade for Primary Humanities*, Buckingham: Open University Press.

Blyth, W.A.L. (1992) 'Themes and Dimensions: Icing or Spicing?' in Hall, G. (ed.) *Themes and Dimensions of the National Curriculum*, London: Kogan Page, pp. 17–27.

Blyth, W.A.L. et al. (1976) *Place, Time and Society 8–13: Curriculum Planning in History, Geography and Social Science*, Bristol: Collins/ESL.

Blyth, W.A.L., Rudd, A., Derricott, R., Cooper, K. and Wenham, P. (1987) 'Aspects of Power in the Genesis and Development of One Curriculum Project', in Richards, C. (ed.) *Power and the Curriculum: Issues in Curriculum Studies*, Driffield: Nafferton.

Board of Education (1904) *The New Code: Regulations for Secondary Schools*, London: HMSO.

Board of Education (1905) *Handbook of Suggestions for the Consideration of Teachers and Others Concerned with the Work of Public Elementary Schools*, London: HMSO.

Board of Education (1926) *Report of the Consultative Committee on the Education of the Adolescent* [Hadow Report], London: HMSO.

Board of Education (1931) *Report of the Consultative Committee on the Primary School* [Hadow Report], London: HMSO.

Board of Education (1933) *Report of the Consultative Committee on Infant and Nursery Schools* [Hadow Report], London: HMSO.

Board of Education (1938) *Report of the Consultative Committee on Secondary Education with Special Reference to Grammar Schools and Technical High Schools* [Spens Report], London: HMSO.

Board of Education (1943) *Curriculum and Examinations in Secondary Schools: Report of the Committee of the Secondary School Examinations Council* [Norwood Report], London: HMSO.

Bourdieu, P. (1971) 'Intellectual Field and Creative Project', in Young, M.F.D. (ed.) *Knowledge and Control*, London: Collier-Macmillan, pp. 161–88.

Bourdieu, P. (1974) 'The School as a Conservative Force: Scholastic and Cultural Inequalities ['L'École conservatrice', in *Revue française de sociologie* 7, 1966, trans. J. Whitehouse], in Eggleston, J. (ed.) *Research in the Sociology of Education*, London: Methuen, pp. 32–46.

Bourdieu, P. and Passeron, J.-C. (1990) *Reproduction in Education, Society and Culture* (2nd edn), trans. R Nice, London: Sage.

Bowles, S. and Gintis, H. (1972) 'IQ and the Social Class System', *Social Policy* 3, 4.

Bowles, S. and Gintis, H. (1976) *Schooling in Capitalist America: Educational Reform and the Contradictions of Economic Life*, London: Routledge.

Bowles, S. and Gintis, H. (1981) 'Contradiction and Reproduction in Educational Theory', in Barton, L., Meighan, R. and Wallis, S. (eds) *Schooling, Ideology and the Curriculum*, London: Falmer, pp. 45–60.

Bowles, S. and Gintis, H. (1988) 'Schooling in Capitalist America: Reply to our Critics', in Cole, M. (ed.) *Bowles and Gintis Revisited: Correspondence and Contradiction in Educational Theory*, Lewes: Falmer.

Boyson, R. (1975a) 'Maps, Chaps and your Hundred Best Books', *Times Educational Supplement* 17 October 1975.

Boyson, R. (1975b) *The Crisis in Education*, London: Woburn Press.

Briault, E. (1985) 'The Other Paymaster: The View from the Local Authorities', in Plaskow, M. (ed.) *The Life and Death of the Schools Council*, London: Falmer.

Brown, A. (1990) 'From Notional to National Curriculum: The Search for a Mechanism', in Dowling, P. and Noss, R. (eds) *Mathematics versus the National Curriculum*, London: Falmer.

Brown, A. (1992) 'Mathematics: Rhetoric and Practice in Primary Teaching', in Riley, J. (ed.) *The National Curriculum and the Primary School: Springboard or Straightjacket?*, London: Kogan Page.

Browne, G. (1969) 'Notes from a Junior School Headmistress', in Cox, C. and Dyson, A. (eds) *Fight for Education: A Black Paper*, London: Critical Quarterly Society, p. 50.

Burgess, R. (1984) 'It's not a Proper Subject: It's Just Newsom', in I. Goodson and S. Ball (eds) *Defining the Curriculum: Histories and Ethnographies*, London: Falmer, pp. 181–200.

Byrne, W. (1974) *Planning and Educational Inequality*, Slough: NFER.

CACE (England) (1959) *15 to 18* [Chair: Sir Geoffrey Crowther], London: HMSO.

CACE (England) (1963) *Half our Future* [Chair: John Newsom], London: HMSO.

CACE (England) (1967) *Children and their Primary Schools* [Chair: Lady Plowden], London: HMSO.

Calder, A. (1969) *The People's War: Britain 1939–45*, London: Jonathan Cape.

Callaghan, J. (1976) Speech at Ruskin College, Oxford, 18 October, in the *Times Educational Supplement*, 22 October 1976.

Callaghan, J. (1987) *Time and Chance*, London: Collins.

Carr, E.H. (1964) *What is History?* Harmondsworth: Penguin.

Carr, W. and Hartnett, A. (1996) *Education and the Struggle for Democracy*, Buckingham: Open University Press.

Cha, Y.-K. (1991) 'Effect of the Global System on Language Instruction, 1850–1986', *Sociology of Education* 64, 1, pp. 19–32.

Chitty, C. (1988a) 'Central Control of the Curriculum', *History of Education* 17, 4, pp. 321–34.

Chitty, C. (1988b) 'Two Models of a National Curriculum: Origins and Interpretation', in Lawton, D. and Chitty, C. (eds) *The National Curriculum*, Bedford Way Papers 33, London: Institute of Education.

Chitty, C. (1989) *Towards a New Education: The Victory of the New Right?*, London: Falmer.

Chitty, C. (1991) *Post-16 Education*, London: Kogan Page.

Chitty, C. and Simon, B. (eds) (1993) *Education Answers Back*, London: Lawrence & Wishart.

Chorley, R. J. and Haggett, P. (1967) *Frontiers in Geographical Teaching*, London: Methuen.

Coleman, J. et al. (1966) *Equality of Educational Opportunity*, Washington, DC: US Government Printing Office.

Coleman, J. S., Hoffer, T. and Kilgore, S. (1981) *Public and Private Schools*, Chicago: National Opinion Research Centre.

Colley, L. (1992) *Britons: Forging the Nation 1707–1837*, London: Pimlico.

Connor, W. (1978) 'A Nation is a Nation, is a State, is an Ethnic Group, is a...', *Ethnic and Racial Studies* 1, 4, pp. 39–388.

Conquest, R. (1969) 'Undotheboys Hall', in Cox, C. and Dyson, A. (eds) *Fight for Education: A Black Paper*, London: Critical Quarterly Society, pp. 17–20.

Conservative Party (1987) *General Election Manifesto*, London: Conservative Central Office.

Cooper, B. (1984) 'On Explaining Change in School Subjects', in Goodson, I. and Ball, S. (eds) *Defining the Curriculum: Histories and Ethnographies*, London: Falmer, pp. 45–63.

Coulby, D. (1989) 'The National Curriculum', in Bash, L. and Coulby, D. *The Education Reform Act: Competition and Control*, London: Cassell Educational.

Cox, B. (1991) *Cox on Cox: An English Curriculum for the 1990s*, London: Hodder & Stoughton.

Cox, B. (1992) *Politicians and Professionals Made Tongue-tied by Authority: New Orders for English – A Response by the National Association for the Teaching of English*, London: NATE.

Cox, B. (1995) *Cox on the Battle for the English Curriculum*, London: Hodder & Stoughton.

Cox, B. and Dyson, A. (eds) (1969) *Fight for Education: A Black Paper*, London: Critical Quarterly Society.

Cox, B. and Dyson, A. (1970) *Black Paper Two: The Crisis in Education*, London: Critical Quarterly Society.

Craft, A. (1995) 'Indoctrination and Empowerment? The Case of Economic and Industrial Understanding', in Ahier, J. and Ross, A. (eds) *The Social Subjects within the Curriculum: Children's Social Learning in the National Curriculum*, London: Falmer, pp. 157–67.

Crawford, G. (1970) 'The Primary School: A balanced view', in Cox, B. and Dyson, A. (eds) *Black Paper Two: The Crisis in Education*, London: Critical Quarterly Society.

Crawford, K. (1999) 'The Social Construction of Curriculum: Economic and Industrial Under-standing as a Cross-Curricular Theme', PhD thesis, University of North London.

Crick, B. and Porter, A. (1981) 'Political Education', in White, J., Black, P., et al., *No Minister: A Critique of the DES Paper 'The School Curriculum'*, Bedford Way Papers, 4, London: Institute of Education, pp. 25–33.

Cunningham, P. (1988) *Curriculum Change in the Primary School since 1945: Dissemination of the Progressive Idea*, London: Falmer.

Dale, R. (1998) *Education, Training and Employment*, Buckingham: Open University Press.

Dale, R, Esland, G. and Macdonald, M. (eds) (1976) *Schooling and Capitalism: A Sociological Reader*, London: Routledge & Kegan Paul/Open University Press.

Darling, J. (1994) *Child-Centred Education and its Critics*, London: Paul Chapman.

David, T. (1973) 'Against Geography', in Bale, J., Graves, N. and Walford, R. (eds) *Perspectives in Geographical Education*, Edinburgh: Olive & Boyd.

Dean, D. (1992) 'Preservation or Renovation? The Dilemmas of Conservative Educational Policy 1955–1960', *20th Century British History* 3, 1, pp. 3–31.

Dearden, R. (1981) 'Balance and Coherence: Some Curricular Principles in Recent Reports', *Cambridge Journal of Education*, 11, 2.

DES (1972) *Report of the Committee of Inquiry into Teacher Education and Training* [Chair: Lord James], London: HMSO.

DES (1976a) *School Education in England: Problems and Initiatives* [The Yellow Book], London: HMSO.

DES (1976b) *Educating Our Children: Four Subjects for Debate*, London: HMSO.

DES (1977a) *Education in Schools: A Consultative Document*, Cmnd 6969, London: HMSO.

DES (1977b) *Curriculum 11–16* [The Red Book], London: HMSO.

DES (1977c) *Local Authority Arrangements for the School Curriculum: Circular 14/77*, London: HMSO.

DES (1978) *Primary Education in England: A Survey by HM Inspectors of Schools*, London: HMSO.

DES (1979a) *Local Authority Arrangements for the School Curriculum: Report on the Circular 14/77 review*, London: HMSO.

DES (1979b) *Aspects of Secondary Education in England: A Survey by HM Inspectors of Schools*, London: HMSO.

DES (1980a) *A Framework for the School Curriculum: Proposals for Consultation by the Secretaries of State for Education and Science and for Wales*, London: HMSO.

DES (1980b) *A View of the Curriculum (HMI Series: Matters for Discussion No. 11)*, London: HMSO.

DES (1980c) *Girls and Science (HMI Series: Matters for discussion No. 13)*, London: HMSO.

DES (1981a) *The School Curriculum*, London: HMSO.

DES (1981b) *Schools and Working Life*, London: HMSO.

DES (1981c) *The School Curriculum, Circular 6/81*, London: DES.

DES (1982a) *Education 5–9: An Illustrative Survey of 80 First Schools in England*, London: HMSO.

DES (1982b) *Mathematics Counts: Report of the Committee of Inquiry into the Teaching of Mathematics in Schools* [Chair: Dr W. Cockcroft], London: HMSO.

DES (1982c) *Science Education in Schools: A Consultative Paper*, London: DES.

DES (1983a) *Curriculum 11–16: Towards a Statement of Entitlement: Curricular Reappraisal in Action*, London: HMSO.

DES (1983b) *9–13 Middle Schools: An Illustrative Survey*, London: HMSO.

DES (1983c) *Teaching Quality*, London: HMSO.

DES (1983d) *The School Curriculum: Circular 8/83*, London: DES.

DES (1984a) *English from 5 to 16: Curriculum Matters 1* (An HMI Series), London: HMSO.

DES (1984b) *The Organisation and Content of the 5–16 Curriculum: A Note by the Department of Education and Science and the Welsh Office* [mimeo], London: DES.

DES (1985a) *The Curriculum from 5 to 16: Curriculum Matters 2* (An HMI Series), London: HMSO.

DES (1985b) *Mathematics from 5 to 16: Curriculum Matters 3* (An HMI Series), London: HMSO.

DES (1985c) *Music from 5 to 16: Curriculum Matters 4* (An HMI Series), London: HMSO.

DES (1985d) *Home Economics from 5 to 16: Curriculum Matters 5* (An HMI Series), London: HMSO.

DES (1985e) *Education 8–12 in Combined and Middle Schools*, London: HMSO.

DES (1985f) *History in the Primary and Secondary Years: An HMI view*, London: HMSO.

DES (1985g) *Science 5:16: A Statement of Policy*, London: HMSO.

DES (1985h) *Better Schools*, Cmnd 9469, London: HMSO.

DES (1985i) *Education for All: Report of the Committee of Inquiry into the Education of Children from Ethnic Minority Groups* [The Swann Report], Cmnd 9453, London: HMSO.

DES (1986a) *English from 5 to 16: Curriculum Matters 1* (An HMI Series) (2nd edn, incorporating responses), London: HMSO.

DES (1986b) *Health Education from 5 to 16: Curriculum Matters 6* (An HMI Series), London: HMSO.

DES (1986c) *Geography from 5 to 16: Curriculum Matters 7* (An HMI Series), London: HMSO.

DES (1986d) *Draft Statement on the Principles of Teaching Politically Controversial Issues in Schools and Colleges*, London: DES.

DES (1987a) *Mathematics from 5 to 16: Curriculum Matters 3* (An HMI Series), (2nd edn, incorporating responses) London: HMSO.

DES (1987b) *Modern Languages to 16: Curriculum Matters 8* (An HMI Series), London: HMSO.

DES (1987c) *Craft, Design and Technology from 5 to 16: Curriculum Matters 9* (An HMI Series), London: HMSO.

DES (1987d) *Primary Schools: Some Aspects of Good Practice*, London: HMSO.

DES (1987e) *Press Release 11/87: Kenneth Baker's Speech to the North of England Education Conference*, 9 January, London: DES.

DES (1987f) *Press Release 22/87: Kenneth Baker's Speech to the Conference of the Society of Chief Education Officers* 23 January, London: DES.

DES (1987g) *National Curriculum Subject Working Groups: Terms of Reference* [sent to Chairs of the Mathematics and Science Working Groups, April 1987], quoted in DES 1987h, pp. 35–8.

DES (1987h) *The National Curriculum 5–16: A Consultation Document*, July, London: DES.

DES (1987i) *National Curriculum: Interim Report of the Working Group on Mathematics*, London: DES.

DES (1988a) *Careers Education and Guidance from 5 to 16: Curriculum Matters 10* (An HMI Series), London: HMSO.

DES (1988b) *History from 5 to 16: Curriculum Matters 11* (An HMI Series), London: HMSO.

DES (1988c) *Classics from 5 to 16: Curriculum Matters 12* (An HMI Series), London: HMSO.

DES (1988d) *A Survey of Personal and Social Education Courses in some Secondary Schools: A Report by HM Inspectors*, London: HMSO.

DES (1988e) *Report of the Committee of Inquiry into the Teaching of the English Language* [The Kingman Report], London: HMSO.

DES (1988f) *National Curriculum: Task Group on Assessment and Testing: A Report*, London: DES.

DES (1988g) *National Curriculum: Three Supplementary Reports: Task Group on Assessment and Testing*, London: DES.

DES (1988h) *National Curriculum: First Report of the Working Group on English: Primary Stage*, London : DES.

DES (1989a) *Environmental Education from 5 to 16: Curriculum Matters 13* (An HMI Series), London: HMSO.

DES (1989b) *Personal and Social Education from 5 to 16: Curriculum Matters 14* (An HMI Series), London: HMSO.

DES (1989c) *Information Technology from 5 to 16: Curriculum Matters 15* (An HMI Series), London: HMSO.

DES (1989d) *Physical Education from 5 to 16: Curriculum Matters 16* (An HMI Series), London: HMSO.

DES (1989e) *Drama from 5 to 16: Curriculum Matters 17* (An HMI Series), London: HMSO.

DES (1989f) *Her Majesty's Inspectorate – Aspects of Primary Education: The Teaching and Learning of Children under Five*, London: HMSO.

DES (1989g) *Her Majesty's Inspectorate – Aspects of Primary Education: The Teaching and Learning of Science*, London: HMSO.

DES (1989h) *Her Majesty's Inspectorate – Aspects of Primary Education: The Teaching and Learning of Mathematics*, London: HMSO.

DES (1989i) *Her Majesty's Inspectorate – Aspects of Primary Education: The Teaching and Learning of History and Geography*, London: HMSO.

DES (1989j) *National Curriculum: History Working Group: Interim Report*, August, London: DES.

DES (1990a) *Her Majesty's Inspectorate, An Inspection Review – Aspects of Primary Education: The Teaching and Learning of Drama*, London: HMSO.

DES (1990b) *Her Majesty's Inspectorate – Aspects of Primary Education: The Teaching and Learning of Language and Literacy*, London: HMSO.

DES (1990c) *National Curriculum: History Working Group: Final Report*, April, London: DES.

DES (1990d) *National Curriculum: History for Ages 5 to 16: Proposals of the Secretary of State*, July, London: DES.

DES (1991a) *Her Majesty's Inspectorate – Aspects of Primary Education: The Teaching and Learning of Music*, London: HMSO.

DES (1991b) *Her Majesty's Inspectorate, An Inspection Review – Aspects of Primary Education: The Teaching and Learning of Physical Education*, London: HMSO.

DES (1991c) *Press Release 2/91: Speech of the Secretary of State Kenneth Clarke to the North of England Education Conference, 4 January 1991*, London: DES.

DES (1992a) *Curriculum Organisation and Classroom Practice in Primary Schools: A Discussion Paper* [Alexander, R., Rose, J. and Woodhead, C.], London: HMSO.

DES (1992b) *Choice and Diversity*, London: HMSO.

Dewey, J. (1900) *The School and Society*, Chicago: University of Chicago Press.

Dewey, J. (1916) *Democracy and Education*, New York: Macmillan.

Dfe (1995) *English in the National Curriculum*, London: HMSO.

Donoghue, B. (1987) *Prime Minister: The Conduct of Policy under Harold Wilson and James Callaghan*, London: Cape.

Durkheim, E. (1897) (1970) *Suicide: A study in Sociology*, London: Routledge & Kegan Paul.

Durkheim, E. (1938) *L'Evolution pédagogique en France*, Paris: Acan. [Trans P. Collins, *The Evolution of Educational Thought: Lectures on the Formation and Development of Secondary Education in France*, London: Routledge (1977).]

Durkheim, E. (1956) *Education and Sociology*, New York: The Free Press.

Eggleston, J. (1978) *The Sociology of the School Curriculum*, London: Routledge.

Elton, G. R. (1967) *The Practice of History*, Sydney.

Emerson, R., (1960) *From Empire to Nation*, Cambridge, MA: Harvard University Press.

Flew, A. (1986) 'Education against Racism', in O'Keeffe, D. (ed.) *The Wayward Curriculum*, London: Social Affairs Unit.

Froebel, F. (1826) (1893) *The Education of Man*, New York: Appleton.

Froebel, F. (1840) (1896) *Pedagogics of the Kindergarten*, New York: Appleton.

Froome, S. (1970) 'The Mystique of Modern Maths', in Cox, B. and Dyson, A. (eds) *Black Paper Two: The Crisis in Education*, London: Critical Quarterly Society.

Galton, M., Simon, B. and Croll, P. (1980) *Inside the Primary Classroom*, London: Routledge & Kegan Paul.

Garnett, A. (1969) 'Teaching Geography: Some Reflections', *Geography* 54 (November).

Gellner, E. (1964) 'Nationalism', in *Thought and Change*, London: Weidenfeld & Nicolson, pp. 158–69.

Gellner, E. (1983) *Nations and Nationalism*, Oxford: Blackwell.

Gilbert, R. (1995) 'Education for Citizenship and the Problems of Identity in Post-modern Political Culture', in Ahier, J. and Ross, A. (eds) *The Social Subjects within the Curriculum: Children's Social Learning in the National Curriculum*, London: Falmer, pp. 11–30.

Gipps, C. and Stobart, G. (1993) *Assessment: A Teacher's Guide to the Issues*, London: Hodder & Stoughton.

Gleeson, D. and Hodkinson, P. (1995) 'Ideology and Curriculum Policy: GNVQ and Mass Post-Compulsory Education in England and Wales', *British Journal of Education and Work* 8, 3, pp. 5–19.

Golby, M. (1988) 'Traditions in Primary Education', in Clarkson, M. (ed.), *Emerging Issues in Primary Education*, Lewes: Falmer.

Golby, M. (1989) 'Curriculum Traditions', in Moon, B., Murphy, P. and Raynor, J. (eds) *Policies for the Curriculum*, London: Hodder & Stoughton.

Goldsmiths College, University of London (1965) *The Raising of the School Leaving Age: Second Pilot Course for Experienced Teachers*, London: Goldsmiths College.

Goodson, I. (1984a) 'Subjects for Study: Towards a Social History of Curriculum', in Goodson, I. and Ball, S. (eds) *Defining the Curriculum: Histories and Ethnographies*, London: Falmer, pp. 25–44.

Goodson, I. (1984b) *Defining the Curriculum: Histories and Ethnographies*, London: Falmer.

Goodson. I. (1987) *School Subjects and Curriculum Change: Studies in Curriculum History* (rev. edn), London: Falmer.

Goodson, I. (1988) *The Making of Curriculum: Collected Essays*, Lewes: Falmer.

Goodson, I. (ed.) (1994) *Studying Curriculum: Cases and Methods*, Buckingham: Open University Press.

Goodson, I. and Dowbiggin, I. (1994) 'Curriculum History, Professionalisation and the Social Organisation of Knowledge', in Goodson, I (ed.) *Studying Curriculum: Cases and Methods*, Buckingham: Open University Press.

Gordon, P. (1978) 'Tradition and Change in the Curriculum', in Lawton, D., Gordon, P. et al., *Theory and Practice of Curriculum Studies*, London: Routledge, pp. 121–7.

Gordon, P., Aldrich, R. and Dean, D. (1991) *Education and Policy in England in the Twentieth Century*, London: Woburn Press.

Graham, D. (1993) *A Lesson for Us All: The Making of the National Curriculum*, London: Routledge.

Gramsci, A. (1971) *Selections from the Prison Notebooks*, trans. Q. Hoare and G. Nowell Smith, London: Lawrence & Wishart.

Gregory, D. (1978) *Ideology, Science and Human Geography*, London: Hutchinson.

Grundy, S. (1987) *Curriculum: Product or Praxis?*, Lewes: Falmer.

Hall, G. (ed.) (1992) *Themes and Dimensions of the National Curriculum: Implications for Policy and Practice*, London: Kogan Page.

Halsey, A., Heath, A. and Ridge, J. (1980) *Origins and Destinations*, Oxford: Oxford University Press.

Hamilton, J. (1976) Speech to the Association of Education Committees, reported in *The Teacher*, 2 July.

Hammersley, M. (1984) 'Making a Vice of our Virtues: Some Notes on Theory in Ethnography and History', in Goodson, I. and Ball, S. (eds) *Defining the Curriculum: Histories and Ethnographies*, London: Falmer, pp. 15–24.

Hargreaves, A. (1994) 'Critical Introduction', in Goodson, I. (ed.) *Studying Curriculum: Cases and Methods*, London: Falmer.

Haviland, J. (ed.) (1988) *Take Care, Mr Baker*, London: Fourth Estate.

Heal, C. (1992) 'Humanities: Round the World and Through the Ages', in Riley, J. (ed.) *The National Curriculum and the Primary School: Springboard or Straightjacket?*, London: Kogan Page.

Hewitson, J.N. (1969) *The Grammar School Tradition in a Comprehensive World*, London: Routledge & Kegan Paul.

Hill, D. (1986) 'Urban Studies: Closing Minds?' in O'Keefe, D. (ed.) *The Wayward Curriculum*, London: Social Affairs Unit.

Hillgate Group (1986) *Whose Schools? A Radical Manifesto*, London: Hillgate Group.

Hirst, P.H. (1965) 'Liberal Education and the Nature of Knowledge', in R D Archanbauld (ed.) *Philosophical Analysis and Education*, London: Routledge.

Hirst, P. (1967) 'The Logical and Psychological Aspects of Teaching a Subject', in Peters, R.S. (ed.) *The Concept of Education*, London: Routledge.

Hirst, P.M. and Peters, R.S. (1970) *The Logic of Education*, London: Routledge & Kegan Paul.

Hobsbawm, E. and Ranger, T. (eds) (1983) *The Invention of Tradition*, Cambridge: Cambridge University Press.

Hodkinson, P. (1991) 'Liberal Education and the New Vocationalism: A Progressive Partnership', *Oxford Review of Education*, 17, 1, pp. 73–88.

Hodkinson, P. (1998) 'Choosing GNVQ', *Journal of Work and Education*, 11, 2, pp. 151–65.

Hodson, D. (1988) 'Towards a Kuhnian Approach to Curriculum', *School Organisation*, 8.

Honeybone, R. (1954) 'Balance in Geography and Education', *Geography*, 34.

House of Commons (1976) *10th Report: House of Commons Expenditure Committee*, London: HMSO.

Hoyle, E. (1976) *Innovation and the School*, Milton Keynes: Open University Press.

Hunt, A. (1970) 'The Tyranny of Subjects', in Rubinstein, D. and Stoneman, C. (eds) *Education for Democracy*, Harmondsworth: Penguin.

Illich, I.D. (1973) *Deschooling Society*. Harmondsworth: Penguin.

Inhelder, B. and Piaget, J. (1958) *The Growth of Logical Thinking from Childhood to Adolescence*, London: Routledge & Kegan Paul.

Jackson, P.W. (1968) *Life in Classrooms*, New York: Holt Rinehart & Winston.

Jamieson, I. (1984) *We Make Kettles*, London: Longmans/Schools Council.

Jamieson, I. (1985) 'Corporate Hegemony or Pedagogic Liberation: the Schools–Industry Movement in England and Wales', in Dale, R. (ed.) *Education, Training and Employment: Towards a New Vocationalism*, Oxford: Pergamon.

Jamieson, I. and Lightfoot, M. (1982) *Schools and Industry*, Schools Council Working Paper 73, London: Methuen.

Jamieson. I. and Watts, A (1987) 'Squeezing out Enterprise', *Times Educational Supplement*, 18 December.

Jencks, C. (1972) *Inequality: A Reassessment of the Effects of Family and Schooling in America*, New York: Basic Books.

Jenkins, E. (1979) *From Armstrong to Nuffield: Studies in Twentieth Century Science Education*, London: John Murray.

Jennings, A. (1985) 'Out of the Secret Garden', in Plaskow, M. (ed.) *The Life and Death of the Schools Council*, London: Falmer.

Johnson, C. (1969) 'Freedom in Junior Schools', in Cox, B. and Dyson, A. (eds) *Fight for Education: A Black Paper*, London: Critical Quarterly Society.

Johnson, R. (1992) 'Radical Education and the New Right', in Rattansi, A. and Reeder, D. (eds) *Rethinking Radical Education: Essays in Honour of Brian Simon*, London: Lawrence & Wishart.

Jones, K. (1989) *Right Turn: The Conservative Revolution in Education*, London: Hutchinson Radius.

Jones, K. (1991) 'Conservative Modernisation', in Moore, R. and Ozga, J. (eds) *Curriculum Policy*, Oxford: Pergammon.

Joseph, K. (1984) Speech at the North of England Education Conference, press release, London: DES.

Kamens, D. and Benavot, A. (1991) 'Elite Knowledge for the Masses: The Origins and Spread of Mathematics and Science Education in National Curricula', *American Journal of Education*, 99, 2, pp. 137–80.

Kamin, L.J. (1977) *The Science and Politics of IQ*, Harmondsworth: Penguin.

Kelly, A. (1985) 'Changing Schools and Changing Society: Some Reflections on the Girls into Science and Technology Project', in Arnot, M. (ed.) *Race and Gender: Equal Opportunities Policies in Education*, Oxford: Pergammon/Open University.

Kennedy, P. (1988) *The Rise and Fall of the Great Powers*, London: Unwin Hyman.

Kennett, J. (1973) 'The Sociology of Pierre Bourdieu', *Educational Review*, 25, 3, pp. 237–49.

King, A.R. and Brownell, J.R. (1966) *The Curriculum and the Disciplines of Knowledge*, New York: Wiley.

Kirk, G. (1986) *The Core Curriculum*, Sevenoaks: Hodder & Stoughton.

Knight, C. (1990) *The Making of Tory Education Policy in Post-War Britain, 1945–1986*, London: Falmer.

Kogan, M. (1978) *The Politics of Educational Change*, Manchester: Manchester University Press.

Kuhn, T. (1970) *The Structure of Scientific Revolutions* (2nd edn), Chicago: University of Chicago Press.

Labov, W. (1978) *Sociolinguistic Patterns*, Oxford: Basil Blackwell.

Lawson, D., Plummeridge, C. and Swanwick, K. (1993) *The National Curriculum in Music at Key Stages 1 and 2: A Research Report*, London: Institute of Education, University of London.

Lawson, N. (1992) *The View from Number 11: Memoirs of a Tory Radical*, London: Corgi.

Lawton, D. (1975) *Class, Culture and the Curriculum*, London: Routledge & Kegan Paul.

Lawton, D. (1981) 'Shall We Try Again, Minister?', in White, J., Black, P., et al., *No Minister: A Critique of the DES Paper 'The School Curriculum'*, Bedford Way Papers, 4, London: Institute of Education, pp. 52–5.

Lawton, D. (1984) *The Tightening Grip: Growth of Central Control of the School Curriculum*, Bedford Way Papers, 21, London: Institute of Education.

Lawton, D. (1989) *Education, Culture and the National Curriculum*, Sevenoaks: Hodder & Stoughton.

Lawton, D. (1994) *The Tory Mind on Education, 1979–94*, London: Falmer.

Lawton, D., Campbell, J. and Burkitt, V. (1971) *Social Studies 8–13* (Schools Council Working Paper 39), London: Evans/Methuen.

Lawton, D., Gordon, P., Ing, M., Gibby, B., Pring, R. and Moore, T. (1978) *Theory and Practice of Curriculum Studies*, London: Routledge & Kegan Paul.

Lawton, D. and Gordon, P. (1996) *Dictionary of Education* (2nd edn), London: Hodder & Stoughton.

Layton, D. (1972) 'Science as General Education', *Trends in Education*, January.

Layton, D. (1973) *Science for the People*, London: Allen & Unwin.

Letwin, O. (1988) *Grounding Comes First*, London: Centre for Policy Studies .

Lilley, I. (ed.) (1967) *Freidrich Froebel: A Selection from his Writings*, Cambridge: Cambridge University Press.

MacDonald, M. (1977) *The Curriculum and Cultural Reproduction*, Buckingham: Open University Press.

MacKinder, H.J. (1887) 'On the Scope and Methods of Geography', *Proceedings of the Royal Geographical Society*, 9.

Maclure, S. (1986) *Educational Documents: England and Wales, 1816 to the Present Day* (5th edn), London: Methuen.

Mann, J. (1985) 'Who Killed Schools Council?', in Plaskow, M. (ed.) *The Life and Death of the Schools Council*, London: Falmer.

Mannheim, K. (1936) *Ideology and Utopia*, New York: Harcourt, Brace & World.

Marcuse, H. (1964) *One-Dimensional Man*, London: Routledge & Kegan Paul.

Marquand, D. (1988) 'The Paradoxes of Thatcherism', in Skidelsky, R. (ed.) *Thatcherism*, London: Chatto & Windus.

Measor, L. (1983) 'Gender and the Sciences', in Hammersley, M. and Hargreaves, A. (eds) *Curriculum Practice: Some Sociological Case Studies*, Lewes: Falmer.

Measor, L. (1984) 'Pupil Perceptions of Subject Statuses', in I. Goodson and S. Ball (eds) *Defining the Curriculum: Histories and Ethnographies*, London: Falmer, pp. 201–18.

Mehlinger, H. (ed.) (1981) 'Social Studies around the World', in *UNESCO Handbook for the Teaching of Social Studies*, Beckenham: Croom Helm.

Merson, M. (1992) 'The Four Ages of TVEI: A Review of Policy', *British Journal of Education and Work*, 5, 2.

Meyer, J. (1977) 'The Effects of Education as an Institution', *American Journal of Sociology*, 83.

Meyer, J., Kamens, D. and Benavot, A. (1992) *School Knowledge for the Masses: World Models and National Primary Curricular Categories in the Twentieth Century*, London: Falmer.

Millar, (1985) 'Taming the Mind: Continuity and Change in the Rhetoric of School Science', *Journal of Curriculum Studies*, 17, 4.

Ministry of Education (1960) *Secondary School Examinations other than the GCE* [The Beloe Report], London: HMSO.

Ministry of Education (1964) *Report of the Working Party on the Schools' Curricula and Examinations* [The Lockwood Report], London: HMSO.

Moon, B., Murphy, P. and Raynor, J. (eds) (1989) *Policies for the Curriculum*. London: Hodder & Stoughton.

Morrell, F. (1996) *Continent Isolated: A Study of the European Dimension in the National Curriculum in England*, London: Federal Trust.

Mortimore, P., Salmon, O., Stoll, L., Lewis, D. and Ecob, R. (1988) *School Matters: The Primary Years*, London: Open Books.

Musgrove, F. (1971) *Patterns of Power and Authority in English Education*, London: Methuen.

Nairn, T. (1977) *The Break-up of Britain: Crisis and Neo-Nationalism* (2nd edn), London: New Left Books.

Namier, L. (1952) 'History', *Avenues of History*, London: Hamish Hamilton, pp. 1–10.

National Curriculum Council (1990a) *Curriculum Guidance 3: The Whole Curriculum*, York: NCC.

National Curriculum Council (1990b) *Curriculum Guidance 4: Education for Economic and Industrial Understanding*, York: NCC.

National Curriculum Council (1990c) *Curriculum Guidance 5: Health Education*, York: NCC.

National Curriculum Council (1990d) *Curriculum Guidance 6: Careers Education and Guidance*, York: NCC.

National Curriculum Council (1990e) *Curriculum Guidance 7: Environmental Education*, York: NCC.

National Curriculum Council (1990f) *Curriculum Guidance 8: Education for Citizenship*, York: NCC.

National Curriculum Council (1990g) *National Curriculum Council Consultation Report: History*, York: NCC (December).

NCC/SEAC (1993a) *The National Curriculum and its Assessment (Interim Report)* (The 'Dearing Review'), London/York: SEAC/NCC.

NCC/SEAC (1993b) *The National Curriculum and its Assessment* (The 'Dearing Review'), London/York: SEAC/NCC.

Nyerere, J. (1968) 'The Intellectual Needs Society', in Nyerere, J. *Freedom and Development: Uhuru na Maendeleo*, Dar es Salaam: Oxford University Press (1973), pp. 23–9.

Nyerere, J. (1970) 'Relevance and Dar es Salaam University', in Nyerere, J. *Freedom and Development: Uhuru na Maendeleo*, Dar es Salaam: Oxford University Press (1973), pp. 192–203.

Oakeshott, M. (1974) *Rationalism in Politics and Other Essays*, London: Methuen.

Oakeshott, M. (1989) *The Voice of Liberal Learning: Michael Oakeshott on Education*, ed. Fuller, J., Newhaven, CT: Yale University Press.

OECD (1975) *Educational Development Strategy in England and Wales*, New York: OECD.

O'Hear, A. (1996) 'Culture and the Curriculum', outline paper distributed at SCAA Conference on *Culture Curriculum and Society*, London, February.

O'Keeffe, D. (1979) 'Capitalism and Correspondence: A Critique of Marxist Analyses of Education', *Journal of Higher Education*.

O'Keeffe, D. (1981) 'Labour in Vain: Truancy, Industry and the School Curriculum', in Anderson, D. et al. (eds) *The Pied Pipers of Education*, London: Social Affairs Unit.

O'Keeffe, D. (ed.) (1986) *The Wayward Curriculum: A Cause for Parents' Concerns?*, London: Social Affairs Unit.

Ozolins, U. (1979) 'Lawton's "Refutation" of a Working-Class Curriculum', in Johnson, L. and Ozolins, U. (eds) *Melbourne Working Papers*, Melbourne: University of Melbourne.

Parsons, T. (1966) *Societies: Evolutionary and Comparative Perspectives*, Englewood Cliffs, NJ: Prentice-Hall.

Pearce, I./EEA (1987) Letter from Pearce (SCDC Officer responsible for Education for Economic Awareness Programme) to 'All initiatives and projects economic awareness/understanding field', 28 July, London: EEA.

Pestalozzi, J. (1802) (1894) *How Gertrude Teaches her Children*, London: Swan Sonnenschein.

Peters, R.S. (1965) 'Education as Initiation', in Archambault, R.D. (ed.) *Philosophical Analysis and Education*, London: Routledge & Kegan Paul.

Peters, R.S. (ed.) (1969) *Perspectives on Plowden*, London: Routledge & Kegan Paul.

Phenix, P., (1964) *Realms of Meaning: A Philosophy of the Curriculum for General Education*, New York: McGraw-Hill.

Plaskow, M. (ed.) (1985) *The Life and Death of the Schools Council*, London: Falmer.

Pring, R. (1972) 'Focus of Knowledge and General Education', *General Education*, 19.

Pring, R. (1976) *Knowledge and Schooling*, London: Open Books.

Pring, R. (1978) 'Curriculum Content: Principles of Selection', in Lawton, D., Gordon, P. et al., *Theory and Practice of Curriculum Studies*, London: Routledge, pp. 137–43.

Pring, R. (1995) *Closing the Gap: Liberal Education and Vocational Preparation*, London: Hodder & Stoughton.

Proctor, N. (1990) *The Aims of Primary Education and the National Curriculum*, Lewes: Falmer.

Quicke, J. (1988) 'The "New Right" and Education', *The British Journal of Educational Studies*, 26, 1.

Ranke, L. Von (1885) 'Vorrede zur ersten Ausgabe', *Geschiten der romanischen und germanischen Völker von 1494 bis 1514* (3rd edn), Leipzig (trans. F. Stern, in Stern, F. (ed.) *Varieties of History*, 1956, Cleveland: Meridian Books).

Rawling, L. (1990) 'The Right Attack on Sociology', *Social Science Teacher*, 19, 3, pp. 74–5.

Rawls, J. (1971) *A Theory of Justice*, Oxford: Oxford University Press.

Raynor, J. (1989) 'A National or a Nationalist Curriculum?', in Moon, B., Murphy, P. and Raynor, J. (eds) *Policies for the Curriculum*, London: Hodder & Stoughton.

Regan, D. (1986) 'Sociology and Politics: Unsuitable Subjects for Schools', in O'Keeffe, D. (ed.) *The Wayward Curriculum*, London: Social Affairs Unit.

Reid, W. A. (1984) 'Curricular Topics as Institutional Categories: Implications for Theory and Research in the History and Sociology of School Subjects', in Goodson, I. and Ball, S. (eds) *Defining the Curriculum: Histories and Ethnographies*, London: Falmer, pp. 67–75.

Ribbins, P. and Sherrat, B. (1997) *Radical Education Policies and Conservative Secretaries of State*, London: Cassell.

Richards, C. (1988) 'The Curriculum from 5 to 16: Background, Content and Some Implications for Primary Education', in Clarkson, M. (ed.), *Emerging Issues in Primary Education*, Lewes: Falmer.

Richards, C. (1998) 'Changing Primary/Elementary School Curricula', in Moyles, J. and Hargreaves, L. (eds) *The Primary Curriculum: Learning from International Perspectives*, London: Routledge.

Riley, J. (ed.) (1992) *The National Curriculum and the Primary School: Springboard or Straightjacket?*, London: Kogan Page.

Robbins, D. (1990) *The Work of Pierre Bourdieu: Recognising Society*, Buckingham: Open University Press.

Ross, A. (1992) 'Promoting the Enterprise Culture or Developing a Critique of the Political Economy? Directions for Economic and Industrial Understanding', in Hutchings, M. and Wade, W. (eds) *Developing Economic and Industrial Understanding in the Primary School*, London: PNL Press, pp. 48–60.

Ross, A. (1993) 'The Subjects that Dare not Speak their Name', in Campbell, J. (ed.) *Breadth and Balance in the Primary Curriculum*, London: Falmer.

Ross, A. (1995a) 'Nationalism and International Trends in the Social Studies Curriculum', *Proceedings of the First Conference of the International Association for Children's Social and Economics Education*, June, Glasgow.

Ross, A. (1995b) 'The Rise and Fall of the Social Subjects in the Curriculum', in Ahier, J. and Ross, A. (eds) *The Social Subjects within the Curriculum: Children's Social Learning in the National Curriculum*, London: Falmer.

Ross, A. (1995c) 'The Whole Curriculum, the National Curriculum and Social Studies', in Ahier, J. and Ross, A. (eds) *The Social Subjects within the Curriculum: Children's Social Learning in the National Curriculum*, London: Falmer.

Ross, A. (1996) 'Curriculum, Nationalism, Identity and Individualism: The Roast Beef of England', in Shah, S. (ed.), *National Initiatives and Equality Issues: Papers Presented at the Inaugural Conference of the Centre for Equality Issues in Education, November 1966*, Aldenham: Centre for Equality Issues in Education, University of Hertfordshire.

Rousseau, J.-J. (1964 [1762]) *Emile*, in *Oeuvres Complètes*, ed. B. Gagnebin and M. Roaymond, Vol. 3, Paris.

Rowland, S. (1987) 'Where is Primary Education Going?', *Journal of Curriculum Studies*, 19, 1.

Rubinstein, D. and Simon, B. (1972) *The Evolution of the Comprehensive School 1926–1972*, London: Routledge & Kegan Paul.

Rutter, M., Maughan, B., Morimoe, P., and Outson, J. (1979) *Fifteen Thousand Hours*, London: Open Books.

Salter, B. and Tapper, T. (1981) *Education, Politics and the State*, London: Grant McIntyre.

Samuel, R. (1995) *Theatres of Memory*, London: Verso.

Samuel, R. (1996) ' "Heritage" and the School Curriculum', paper given at SCAA Conference on *Culture Curriculum and Society*, London, February.

SCAA (Schools Curriculum and Assessment Authority) (1996a) *Curriculum, Culture and Society: Papers for a Conference on 7–9 February*, London: SCCA.

SCAA (1996b) *National Forum for Values in Education and the Community: Conference Report, 30 October*, London: SCAA.

SCDC/EEA (1987) *Planning Conference on Economic Awareness, 21/22 July 1986*, Mimeo, London: SCDC (Schools Curriculum Development Committee/Educating for Economic Awareness).

Schools Council (1968) *Young School Leavers* (Schools Council Enquiry 1), London: HMSO.

Schools Council (1969) *The Middle Years of Schooling from 8 to 13* (Schools Council Working Paper 22), London: HMSO.

Schools Council (1975a) *The Whole Curriculum 13–16* (Schools Council Working Paper 53), London: Methuen Education.

Schools Council (1975b) *The Curriculum in the Middle Years* (Schools Council Working Paper 55), London: Methuen Education.

Schools Council (1981) *The Practical Curriculum* (Schools Council Working Paper 70), London: Methuen Education.

Schools Council (1983) *Primary Practice: A Sequel to 'The Practical Curriculum'* (Schools Council Working Paper 75), London: Methuen Education.

Schools Council/ Nuffield Foundation (1972) *The Humanities Curriculum Project: An Introduction*, London: Heinemann.

Schools Inquiry Commission (1868) *Report of the Commissioners* [the Taunton Commission], London: HMSO.

Scruton, R. (1991) 'The Myth of Cultural Relativism', in Moore, R. and Ozga, J. (eds) *Curriculum Policy*, Oxford: Pergamon.

SED (1965) (Scottish Education Department) *Primary Education in Scotland* (The Primary memorandum), Edinburgh: HMSO .

Seeley, J. (1966) 'The "Making" and "Taking" of Problems', *Social Problems*, 14.

Selbourne, D. (1994) *The Principle of Duty*, London: Sinclair-Stevenson.

Shipman, M. (1971) 'Curriculum for Inequality', in Hooper, R. (ed.) *The Curriculum: Context, Design and Development*, Edinburgh: Oliver & Boyd.

Simon, B. (1953) 'Intelligence Testing and the Comprehensive School', reprinted 1978 in Simon, B. *Intelligence, Psychology, Education*, London: Lawrence & Wishart.

Skilbeck, M. (1975) 'School-based Curriculum Development', in Lee, V. and Zeldin, D. (eds) *Planning in the Curriculum*, London: Hodder & Stoughton, pp. 18–34.

Skilbeck, M. (1976) 'Three Educational Ideologies', *Curriculum Design and Development: Ideologies and Values*, Buckingham: Open University Press.

Spours, K. and Young, M. (1988) 'Beyond Vocationalism: A New Perspective on the Relationship between Work and Education', *British Journal of Education and Work*, 2, 2, pp. 5–14.

Steadman, D.E. et al. (1978) *Schools Council Impact and Take-up Project: First Interim Report*, London: Schools Council.

Steadman, D.E. et al. (1980) *Schools Council Impact and Take-up Project: Second Interim Report*, London: Schools Council.

Stenhouse, L. (1975) *An Introduction to Curriculum Research and Development*, Oxford: Heinemann Educational.

Stones, E. (1971) *Readings in Educational Psychology*, London: Methuen.

Stronach, I. (1989) 'Education, Vocationalism and Economic Recovery: The Case Against Witchcraft', *British Journal of Education and Work*, 3, 1, pp. 5–31.

Tate, N. (1994) 'Off the Fence on Common Culture', *Times Educational Supplement*, July 29, p. 11.

Tate, N. (1996) 'Curriculum, Culture and Society', keynote paper distributed at SCAA Conference on *Culture Curriculum and Society*, London, February.

Thacker, C. (1979) *The History of Gardens*, London: Croom Helm.

Thatcher, M. (1987) Speech to Conservative Party Conference, October, reported in the *Times Educational Supplement*.

Thatcher, M. (1993) *The Thatcher Years*, London: HarperCollins.

Thomas, N. (1990) *Primary Education from Plowden to the 1990s*, London: Falmer.

Thornton, M. (1992) 'The Role of Government in Education', address given at de Montford University, Leicester, 3 December, reprinted in Chitty, C. and Simon, B. (eds) *Education Answers Back: Critical Responses to Government Policy*, London: Lawrence & Wishart, pp. 160–75.

Tizzard, B. and Hughes, M. (1984) *Young Children Learning: Talking and Thinking at Home and at School*, London: Fontana.

Tomlinson, J. (1985) 'From Projects to Programmes: The View from the Top', in Plaskow, M. (ed.) *Life and Death of the Schools Council*, London: Falmer, pp. 123–32.

Tomlinson, J. (1993) *The Control of Education*, London: Cassell.

Torrance, H. (1981) 'The Origins and Development of Mental Testing in England and Wales', *Journal of Sociology of Education*, 2, 1.

Tosh, J. (1989) *The Pursuit of History*, London.

Tough, J. (1976) *Listening to Children Talking*, London: Ward Lock Educational.

Tracey, C. W. (1962) 'Biology: Its Struggle for Recognition in English Schools during the Period 1900–60', *School Science Review*, 43, 150.

Trenaman, N. (1981) *Review of the Schools Council: A Report from Mrs Nancy Trenaman to the Secretaries of State for England and Wales and to the LEA Associations*, October, London: DES.

Tyler, R. (1949) *Basic Principles of Curriculum and Instruction*, Chicago: Chicago University Press (reprinted as 'The Form of Objectives', in Lee, V. and Zeldin, D. (eds) *Planning in the Curriculum*, Sevenoaks: Hodder & Stoughton.)

United Kingdom (1943) *Educational Reconstruction*, Cmd 6458, London: HMSO.

United Kingdom (1964) *Committee on Higher Education: Report* [Chair Lionel Robbins], Cmnd 2154–5, London: HMSO.

United Kingdom (1968) *First Report of the Public Schools Commission, Vol. 1* [Chair: John Newsom], London: HMSO.

United Kingdom (1975) *A Language for Life: Report of the Committee of Inquiry* [Chair: Lord Bullock], London: HMSO.

Vallance, E. (1974) 'Hiding the Hidden Curriculum: An Interpretation of the Language of Justification in Nineteenth-Century Educational Reform', *Curriculum Theory Network*, 4, 1, pp. 5–21.

Vernon, P. (ed.) (1957) *Secondary School Selection*, London: Methuen.

'Voltaire' (F.-M. Arouet) (1758) *Candide* (trans. J. Butt, 1949), Harmondsworth: Penguin.

Watts, A.F., Pidgeon, D.A. and Yates, A. (1952) *Secondary School Entrance Examinations*, London: Newnes.

Watts, A.G., Jamieson, I., and Miller, A. (1989) 'School-based Work Experience: Some International Comparisons', *British Journal of Education and Work*, 3, 1, pp. 33–47.

Weber, E. (1979) *Peasants into Frenchmen: The Modernisation of France, 1870–1914*, London: Chatto & Windus.

Weinstock, A. (1976) *Times Educational Supplement*, 23 January.

White, J. (1969) 'The Curriculum Mongers: Education in Reverse', *New Society*, 336, 6 March.

White, J. (1981) 'Enigmatic Guidelines', in White, J., Black, P. et al. *No Minister: A Critique of the DES Paper 'The School Curriculum'*, Bedford Way Papers 4, London: Institute of Education, pp. 9–17.

Whitehead, D. (1980) *The Dissemination of Educational Innovation in Britain*, London: Hodder & Stoughton.

Whitty, G. (1974) 'Sociology and the Problem of Radical Educational Change', in Flude, M. and Ahier, J. (eds) *Educability, Schools and Ideology*, London: Halstead Press.

Whitty, G. (1985) *Sociology and School Knowledge: Curriculum Theory, Research and Politics*, London: Methuen.

Whitty, G. (1988) 'The New Right and the National Curriculum: State Control or Market Forces?', *Journal of Educational Policy*, 4, 4, pp. 329–41.

Whitty, G. (1992) 'Lessons from Radical Curriculum Initiatives: Integrated Humanities and World Studies', in Rattansi, A. and Reeder, D. (eds) *Rethinking Radical Education: Essays in Honour of Brian Simon*, London: Lawrence & Wishart.

Wiener, M. (1981) *English Culture and the Decline of the Industrial Spirit, 1850–1980*, Cambridge: Cambridge University Press.

Williams, R. (1961) *The Long Revolution*, London: Chatto & Windus.

Willis, P. (1977) *Learning to Labour: How Working Class Kids get Working Class Jobs*, London: Saxon House.

Wolf, A. (1995) *Competence Based Assessment*, Buckingham: Open University Press.

Wong, S.-Y. (1991) 'The Evolution of Social Science Instruction, 1900–86', *Sociology of Education*, 64, 1, pp. 33–47.

Wong, S.-Y. (1992) 'The Evolution and Organisation of the Social Science Curriculum', in Meyer, J., Kamens, D. and Benavot, A. *School Knowledge for the Masses: World Models and National Primary Curricular Categories in the Twentieth Century*, London: Falmer, pp. 124–38.

Woodrow, M. (1998) *From Elitism to Inclusion: Good Practice in Widening Participation*, London: CVCP.

Wrigley, J. (1983) 'Confessions of a Curriculum Man', *Curriculum*, 4, 2, p. 35.

Yates, A. and Pidgeon, D.A. (1957) *Admission to Grammar Schools*, London: Newnes.

Yeomans, D. (1998) 'Constructing Vocational Education: from TVEI to GNVQ', *Journal of Education and Work*, 11, 2, pp. 127–49.

Young, M. (1971) *Knowledge and Control*, London: Collier-Macmillan.

Young, M. (1977) 'Taking Sides against the Probable', in Jenks, C. (ed.) *Rationality, Education and the Social Organisation of Knowledge*, London: Routledge.

Young, M. (1993) 'A Curriculum for the 21st Century? Towards a New Basis for Overcoming Academic/Vocational Divisions', *British Journal of Educational Studies*, 41, 3, pp. 203–22.

Index